Nations Matter

Craig Calhoun, one of the most respected social scientists in the world, re-examines nationalism in light of post-1989 enthusiasm for globalization and the new anxieties of the twenty-first century. *Nations Matter* argues that pursuing a purely postnational politics is premature at best and possibly dangerous.

Despite all the evils perpetrated in its name, nationalism is not a mere moral mistake. It is crucial to most existing democracy. It provides solidarity vital to projects of social inclusion and distributive justice. It offers potential for integration across lines of ethnic and other differences. It supports investment in public institutions rather than privatization. Nations are also bases for contesting neo-liberal versions of globalization that threaten social institutions built through generations of struggle.

Rather than wishing nationalism away, it is important to transform it. One key is to distinguish the ideology of nationalism as fixed and inherited identity from the development of public projects that continually remake the terms of national integration. Standard concepts like "civic" vs. "ethnic" nationalism can get in the way unless they are critically re-examined – as an important chapter in this book does.

This book is essential reading for undergraduate and postgraduate students of sociology, history, political theory and all subjects concerned with nationalism, globalization, and cosmopolitanism.

Craig Calhoun is University Professor of the Social Sciences at New York University and President of the Social Science Research Council.

Nations Matter
Culture, History, and the Cosmopolitan Dream

Craig Calhoun

Routledge
Taylor & Francis Group

LONDON AND NEW YORK

First published 2007
by Routledge
2 Park Square, Milton Park, Abingdon, Oxon OX14 4RN

Simultaneously published in the USA and Canada
by Routledge
270 Madison Ave, New York, NY 10016

Routledge is an imprint of the Taylor & Francis Group, an informa business

© 2007 Craig Calhoun

Typeset in Sabon and Frutiger by
RefineCatch Limited, Bungay, Suffolk
Printed and bound in Great Britain by
TJ International Ltd, Padstow, Cornwall

British Library Cataloguing in Publication Data
A catalogue record for this book is available from the British Library

Library of Congress Cataloging in Publication Data
A catalog record for this book has been requested

ISBN10: 0–415–41186–6 (hbk)
ISBN10: 0–415–41187–4 (pbk)
ISBN10: 0–203–96089–0 (ebk)

ISBN13: 978–0–415–41186–8 (hbk)
ISBN13: 978–0–415–41187–5 (pbk)
ISBN13: 978–0–203–96089–9 (ebk)

Contents

Acknowledgments   vii

Introduction   1

1   Is it time to be postnational?   11

2   Nationalism matters   27

3   Nationalism and ethnicity   51

4   Nationalism and civil society   77
    Democracy, diversity, and self-determination

5   Nationalism, political community, and the
    representation of society   103
    Or, why feeling at home is not a substitute for public space

6   Inventing the opposition of ethnic and civic nationalism   117
    Hans Kohn and The Idea of Nationalism

7   Nationalism and the cultures of democracy   147

    Conclusion   169

    Notes   173
    Bibliography   211
    Index   231

Contents

Acknowledgments

Nationalism commonly represses the debts each cultural community owes to others. Pajamas seem American now, not Indian. Innumerable imported ideas and habits and even the English language have come to seem essentially and naturally American. And the English are naturally tea drinkers. It is hard to recall that the French didn't invent wine.

It is much the same with books. Each author weaves his own story or argument, drawing on the creations of innumerable others, often unsure where ideas originated, often wrongly confident it is with himself. I have been writing on nationalism since the early 1990s and reading about it much longer. My work has been deeply informed by the writings of others. It has also been informed by a wide range of conversations with people struggling to work out – or sure they had already worked out – just how the national related to the international and the local in their lives. Conversations in Eritrea, Ethiopia, and Sudan; India, Japan, and China; Russia, Poland, and Hungary; Canada, the US, and Mexico; Turkey, Lebanon, and Israel; France, Britain, and Germany; Australia, Singapore, and Malaysia all have informed my thinking. The conversations have taken place in bars and coffee shops and railroad cars I won't try to cite, but also in universities and academic symposiums. The latter debts demand more formal if still inevitably incomplete acknowledgment.

Arguments in this book were developed in the course of speeches at the universities of Amsterdam, British Columbia, California (Berkeley and Los Angeles), Copenhagen, Ghana, Hawaii, Khartoum, Manchester, North Carolina, Oslo, Saskatchewan, Southern California, Stockholm, Toronto, Warwick, and Washington; at Bristol, Candido Mendes, Columbia, Harvard, Istanbul Bilgi, La Trobe, McGill, New York, Princeton, Vanderbilt, Yale, and York universities; at the City University of New York, the National University of Singapore, the Universidad Andina Simón Bolívar, and the New School for Social Research (which was briefly called the New School University but happily reconsidered and is now simply the New School). They were developed in conferences of the Academy of Latinity, American Anthropological Association, American Political Science Association, American Sociological Association, Indian Council for Social Science Research, International Sociological Association, International Studies Association, and Norwegian Sociological Association. At every one of those venues, at least one person (and very often many more) challenged my arguments and made me think harder. So did my students at North Carolina, NYU, and Columbia. Michael Kennedy, Alexandra Kowalski, Steven Pfaff, Olga Sezneva, Guobin Yang, and Michael Young deserve special mention for their dissertations on related topics which were important learning experiences for me.

I won't attempt to thank all the individuals who helped me with this work. I must thank Rogers Brubaker who convinced me to publish the slightly ungainly collection of essays without waiting for time to turn the whole into a better integrated book. I am grateful to Alan Sica and Irving Louis Horowitz for convincing me to write an introduction to a new edition of Hans Kohn's *The Idea of Nationalism* and thus causing me to learn a great deal. My students have likewise pushed me to keep learning as well as teaching. Several chapters show the mark of my learning as Benjamin Meaker Visiting Professor at the University of Bristol. My understanding of both nationalism and struggles to transcend it has been informed by my years as President of the Social Science Research Council. The SSRC works in impressively international ways – which always reveal that the international is not the non-national and that the cosmopolitan is not the seamlessly universal. I am indebted to my colleagues both among the staff and in the far-flung networks the SSRC sustains. As always, my dept to other members of the Center for Transcultural Studies is large, especially in this case Dilip Gaonkar, Charles Taylor, and Michael Warner. Larger still, and less limited to intellectual matters, is my debt to my wife, Pamela DeLargy, without whom I would have missed much.

Most chapters of this book are revised versions of earlier publications. I am happy to acknowledge the publications which have granted permission:

"Is It Time to Be Postnational?" pp. 231–56 in Stephen May, Tariq Modood, and Judith Squires (eds.), *Ethnicity, Nationalism, and Minority Rights*. Cambridge: Cambridge University Press, 2004.

"Nationalism Matters," pp. 16–39 in Don Doyle and Marco

Pamplona (eds.), *Nationalism in the New World*. Athens, GA: University Press of Georgia, 2006.

"Nationalism and Ethnicity," *Annual Review of Sociology*, Vol. 19 (1993), pp. 211–39.

"Nationalism and Civil Society: Democracy, Diversity and Self-Determination," *International Sociology*, Vol. 8, No. 4 (1993), pp. 387–411.

"Nationalism, Political Community, and the Representation of Society: Or, Why Feeling at Home Is Not a Substitute for Public Space," *European Journal of Social Theory*, Vol. 2, No. 2 (1999), pp. 217–31.

"Foreword" to Hans Kohn, *The Idea of Nationalism*. New Brunswick, NJ: Transaction Publishers, 2005.

"Nationalism and the Cultures of Democracy," *Public Culture*, Vol. 19, No. 1 (2007), pp. 151–73.

In preparing this book, I have benefited from the editorial assistance of Leah Kazanjian Florence – superb as always and lovingly provided. Leah is an American of Armenian roots; very much a New Yorker (from Queens) though a long-time North Carolinian; a follower of Meher Baba who has lived in India and traveled the world in a circuit of fellow Baba-lovers; and a specialist in making better English prose of words of non-native writers, including as managing editor of the Latin American Research Review; and my former assistant and long-time friend. Leah's life is testimony to the reality of transnational circuits and solidarities. Yet, even as she and her husband John contemplate whether to retire abroad or how – legally – to avoid US taxes, I don't think she for a moment doubts that nations matter. She simply knows that nationalists do not control the whole story of how they matter. And that more personal bonds matter more.

Introduction

Nationalism is not a moral mistake. Certainly it is too often implicated in atrocities, and in more banal but still unjust prejudices and discriminatory practices. It too often makes people think arbitrary boundaries are natural and contemporary global divisions ancient and inevitable. But it is also a form of social solidarity and one of the background conditions on which modern democracy has been based. It has helped secure domestic inclusion and redistributive policies even while it has inhibited cosmopolitan attention to the needs of non-nationals. Nationalism helps locate an experience of belonging in a world of global flows and fears. Sometimes it underwrites struggle against the fantastically unequal and exploitative terms on which global integration is being achieved.

We should approach nationalism with critical attention to its limits, illusions, and potential for abuse, but we should not dismiss it. Even where we are deeply critical of the nationalism we see, we should recognize the continued importance of national solidarities. Even if we wish for a more cosmopolitan world order, we should be realistic enough not to act on mere wishes.

The term "nation" has roots in ancient Rome. Part of what we mean by both nation and nationalism is even older. Greeks had loyalty to city-states with distinctive ways of life and to Hellas vs. its enemies (however much they also fought among themselves). Egyptians and Assyrians had the memories of vanquished golden ages.

The ancient Jews were a still stronger prototype. The Hebrew Bible is among other things the story of the formation of the Jewish nation. There is continuity between the Hebrew term translated as "nation" and the Roman usage. Both refer to a people organized as such on the basis of descent. For the Romans, however, this distinguished subject and barbarian peoples from the Roman polity itself, for that was organized as a state in which citizenship (and other forms of participation) were not essentially matters of family and lineage. Rome never saw itself primarily as a nation; to be Roman was to be a member not merely of a people but a polity, and (to play on terms from the nineteenth century), to be part of a civilization not only a culture. This was particularly true as the Roman Empire worked out structures of inclusion for people who were not "ethnic" Romans (and less true to the extent ethnic prejudices limited such inclusion).

Rome did have culture, of course. It had language and historical accounts of itself; it promoted both a civic religion and family piety. The religion of the Jews was arguably a more basic feature of their collective identity but Jewish "faith" and ethnonational identity were closely bound with each other. Christianity would momentously join the mix before the Roman Empire entered its decline. Like Rome itself, it would claim to transcend particularities of ethnocultural and national belonging. It was available in principle to all. Its Western variant remained explicitly supra-national but Eastern Christianity came eventually to be organized more clearly on national lines, differentiated by language as well as patriarchal authority.

Many features of modern nations were thus in play well before the modern era. The subject peoples and barbarian challengers of the Roman Empire had collective identities, ways of life and ways of belonging organized more or less on bases of kinship and descent. The different "nations" into which the scholars at medieval universities were organized reflected territorial origins and linguistic differences Latin had to bridge. Byzantium too was a meeting place of different cultures and more than in Western Europe their self-organization was complemented by imperial rule. Islamic rulers would develop this pattern further in the Ottoman Empire with its millet system. Islam was as supra-ethnic and universalistic as Christianity but the Ottoman rulers tolerated diverse *ethnie*, granting them autonomy in religious life and much of everyday life as well as demanding military service.

But in neither the Ottoman Empire nor the West were nations basic units of political organization before the rise of the modern state. In neither were they understood as formal equivalents, or sovereign – basic units for recognition of self and other at the same time. In neither was the collective organization of "the people" basic to political legitimacy in the way that descent, divine authority, and sometimes simply military success were. In neither was the development and integration of national culture an active project nor the relationship of culture to territory marked by sharp boundaries.

All these were new features. They did not develop overnight. They were shaped by both the religion and the wars of the Protestant Reformation. They were influenced by both the internal organization of early modern empires and rebellions against them. The Peace of Westphalia codified interstate relations as international. Through the whole early modern period increasingly effective state administration was crucial. So eventually were modern empires in which the relations between "home" nations and colonies were basic.

Nations were understood in largely "ethnic" terms, but ethnicity was thereby transformed (see Chapter 3). While the rhetoric of descent, familial relations, and blood ties were widespread, language and common culture transcending kinship ties became more influential. In cities, market relations, and military service, ethnicity worked more as a cultural category and less as a network of kin relations. Ethnicity was sometimes sustained and given sharper boundaries by differential incorporation into states – not least where other dimensions of cultural difference coincided with religious distinction. But while nation-builders frequently discriminated against minorities they were typically more respectful of majorities than earlier elites had been. Where lords and serfs had often spoken different languages, sharing demotic tongues became basic to official affairs as well as daily life. National culture became increasingly a literature culture (though it did not cease being culture and in important ways culturally particular, thereby; it did not leap into simple universalism). Commoners enjoyed increasing opportunities in state service as well as in business. Social mobility, often accompanied by geographic mobility to cities, underwrote a sense of belonging to the nation. The rise of individualism and modern nationalism informed each other as persons came to be understood as more or less sovereign, and – if not equals in all senses – equivalently members of the nation. Increasingly, nations became structures of integration at the level of states (or aspirations to autonomous states).

Not least of all, nationalism was transformed by its new role in a discursive formation which treated nations as the prepolitical bases for political legitimacy. If the authority of rulers derived not from descent, or God, or from might itself but from the well-being of "the people" over whom they ruled, the constitution of such peoples mattered in a new way. In this context, whatever was ancient about "nations" was transformed by nationalism.

The idea of a nation-state is arguably pernicious. The hyphen ties the notion of a historically or naturally unified people who intrinsically belong together to that of a modern polity with unprecedented military power and capacity for effective internal administration. It has been a recipe for conflicts both internal and external. Populations straddle borders or move long distances to new states while retaining allegiances to old nations. Dominant groups demand that governments enforce cultural conformity, challenging both the individual freedom and the vitality that comes from cultural creativity.

And yet, the nation-state neither can be nor should be wished away. Source of so many evils, it is also the framework in which the modern era produced history's most enduring and successful experiments in large-scale democracy. It continues to shape not just the fact of democracy but diversity in its forms (as Chapter 7 suggests). It is basic to the rule of law, not only because most law remains a domestic matter of nation-states but because most international law is literally that: structured by agreements among nation-states. Not least of all, while globalization has produced innumerable paths across state borders, it has opened these very unevenly and disproportionately to the benefit of those with access to high levels of fluid capital. Conversely, it has made belonging to a nation-state and having clear rights within a nation-state more, not less, important. The fact that Hannah Arendt observed more than half a century ago remains true: human rights are secured mainly when they are institutionalized as civil rights.[1]

In the 1990s, optimistic after the end of the Cold War, a number of enthusiasts for globalization suggested that sovereign states were obsolete. Money, media, and human migrations all flowed across borders; Why should military and political power maintain borders? States bolstered by nationalist passions – and nationalists eager to gain state power – were behind many of the twentieth century's bloody wars. Surely there was – and remains – a good prima facie case for hoping nation-states might organize less of human loyalty, power, and conflict. And of course new reasons for hating abuses of state authority merged with ancient resentments of state power. But it is one thing to seek limits on the exercise of state power and another to contemplate transcending it. It is one thing to encourage a cosmopolitan pluralism of perspectives and another to regard nationalism as merely a fading inheritance and not a recurrently renewed source of solidarity. It is one thing to seek to advance global civil society and another to imagine democracy can thrive without effective states.

The many evils of the late twentieth and early twenty-first centuries called forth a widespread indignation and, among many, a determination to act. The idea of human rights moved to the forefront not only of discussion but of court cases and treaties. Humanitarian interventions were proposed and implemented in a widening range of circumstances. Ethnic cleansing and genocidal nationalism made the notion that sovereignty should be a barrier to international efforts to do good ring hollow. An international criminal court was created (if not universally recognized). Indeed for a time there seemed no occupation more virtuous than that of a human rights activist or humanitarian aid worker.

Almost imperceptibly these shifted from volunteer pursuits and accidental careers for physicians and pacifists to new professional roles, complete with academic courses and credentials, funding from major foundations and national governments, and increasing bureaucracy. And humanitarian action became increasingly intertwined with military interventions, whether for peacekeeping or regime change.

At the same time, protesters challenged the dominance of capitalist corporations over the course of globalization. This was misleadingly termed the anti-globalization movement. Though there were some campaigners truly bent on enhancing the autonomy of local populations, most were actually proponents of a different sort of globalization. They objected to environmental depredation, sweatshops, and high prices for necessary drugs but they worked on a global scale and imagined the world in terms of global connections – albeit connections among ordinary people without the powerful mediation of corporations and states.

The movement contesting capitalist globalization has not been theory-driven, but its protagonists have shared a general account of the problems of the world in which the twin centers of power – capitalist corporations and nation-states – pursue a logic of self-aggrandizement that neither the natural world nor its human inhabitants can afford. Many have found the language of Michael Hardt and Antonio Negri sympathetic: they represent the heterogeneous "multitude" of the world who struggled to be free of a seamless and destructive but nearly exhausted "empire."[2]

Something of the same quasi-theory – that states and corporations are both bad and unnecessary – has been widespread among human rights activists and humanitarian aid workers. Both groups, of course, saw first hand the vicious ways in which state elites pursued or held on to power and firms sought or sustained profits. The Sudan is one of the largest scale and longest-lasting examples. Its central government has seldom cared much for the people of Darfur in its west, the non-Arabs of its south, or for that matter most ordinary Sudanese. But the central government has cared about holding the country together and defeating any secessionist movements. It cared all the more when oil was discovered in the south – as did global corporations seeking to extract that oil in "peace." And it cared all the more when it took on a more pronounced Islamic identity and mission. Despite religious commitment (and partly because of intra-Islamist struggles), it became a peculiarly bad government, but also one too weak to establish peace or prosperity in the Sudan; it unleashed brutal war and civil violence against and among its own people. So there were refugees and internally displaced people, rape as a tactic of war, robber militias, and spreading diseases left untreated. The state did not look very good.

Yet by the beginning of the twenty-first century, there were not many left for whom the fantasy of overcoming the state was not tinged with anxiety. Yes, state power was often overweaning, often corrupt, and often mobilized in evil ways. But weak states typically failed their citizens and crises in strong states often unleashed violence and disrupted both lives and livelihoods. Pandemic diseases, global crime, human rights abuses, and forced migration all revealed the dark side to globalization – yet all seemed to call at least in part for better states, not an end to states. Could outsiders make peace in Sudan or would that depend on a more representative, honest, and competent Sudanese government? Or in a range of other African countries, could outside interventions contain the spread of AIDS unless states joined the struggle? And yet, partly because of structural adjustment programs pushed with fiscal good intentions and disastrous human consequences by the World Bank and others, most African states had neither money nor personnel nor health care systems to address AIDS – or for that matter malaria and other diseases. The "failed state" seemed as problematic as the abusive state. And this was not only an issue in Africa but in different local configurations around the world.

A great buzzword of the 1990s was "civil society" (see Chapter 4). And indeed, strengthening civil society – loose institutions part neither of the state nor of large-scale projects of capital accumulation – has been an important trend in many places. Both local and transnational voluntary organizations have grown and played crucial roles. Many are religiously inspired and some denominationally organized. Others are secular. All reflect efforts to create social organization on the basis of voluntary relations among people rather than the coercion of either political authority or capital. And yet, civil society organizations depend on money as well as personal connections. And except where states are able to regulate such organizations they are largely unaccountable and non-transparent. Civil society without a public sphere is not necessarily democratic. Civil society is a hugely valuable complement and sometimes corrective to states and markets, but not a substitute for either.[3] It is no accident that "global governance" has become almost as ubiquitous a concern in the current decade as global civil society was in the last. But the issues are not only global; they are also national and local. Intermediate powers and solidarities still matter.

Individual sovereign states confront a variety of global flows and processes against which they are weak and which in turn weaken some of their other capacities. Global currency and equity markets make it hard for individual countries to operate autonomous fiscal or industrial policies. Global crime is hard to fight with the tools of national legal systems (and especially their domestic criminal law). Global diseases challenge domestic health care systems. Yet these challenges faced by contemporary states no more make them irrelevant than the history of abuses of state power makes the stability and public services states can deliver unimportant. And crucially, most actually existing democracy has been achieved in and through states.

Nationalism figured significantly in the rise of democracy. It developed as a reflection of growing popular political participation – and demands for recognition by ordinary people – and as a source of solidarity among citizens. Of course nationalism was also promoted from above and used to mobilize ordinary people for war. It reflected the development of the state system but it also informed it. Today, however, nationalism is considered most often – at least in cosmopolitan global circles – as at best the basis for a morally illegitimate (and perhaps ill-educated, even tasteless) preference for one's countrymen or culture over those of the rest of the world. More basically, it is identified with its role in coupling ethnic differences to state projects and resulting horrors from Bosnia and Kosovo to Rwanda and Burundi. Or in its American form it is identified with an overeager resort to force internationally and an overzealous domestic patriotism used to justify erosion in civil liberties.

This has left liberal political theory at something of an impasse. It is grounded implicitly but deeply in the presumption of states and nationalist ideas of how these relate to peoples. Yet it is also deeply committed to ideas of liberty and rights framed largely in individualistic terms. On the one hand there is a long tradition of work on "getting governance right." On the other hand there is a long tradition of debunking nationalism as the source of either state legitimacy or citizen solidarity. The two traditions came together in visions of cosmopolitan democracy, or at least global politics organized in terms of a hierarchy of identities and organizations, none conceived as exclusively virtuous, or important, or sovereign.[4] These are largely attractive visions, but they have two important limits which I attempt to address in this book.

First, they tend to underestimate the work done by nationalism and national identities in organizing human life as well as politics in the contemporary world. They often treat nationalism as a sort of error smart people will readily move beyond – or an evil good people must reject – and so as theories they grasp less well than they should the reality of the contemporary world. They generalize largely from the "bad nationalism" of fascism, ethnic cleansing, and war and neglect the many other dimensions of national solidarity. And what goes for nationalism goes also to a considerable extent for ethnicity and religion and other forms of solidarity, identity, and cultural valuation that seem merely sectional from some cosmopolitan vantage points.

Second, in failing to attend well enough to nationalism, ethnicity, and related claims to solidarity, the otherwise attractive cosmopolitan visions have also underestimated how central nationalist categories are to political and social theory – and to practical reasoning about democracy, political legitimacy, and the nature of society itself. I don't mean that we should prefer nationalist accounts, but rather that we should take them seriously and see how deeply imbricated they are in our conceptual frameworks rather than trying to wish them away. As Chapter 2 asserts, nationalism matters.

Nationalism matters not least because it has offered such a deeply influential and compelling account of large-scale identities and structures in the world – helping people to imagine the world as composed of sovereign nation-states. The world has never matched this imagining, but that does not deprive the nationalist imaginary of influence. Even the most emphatically anti-nationalist political philosophers reveal this influence, for example when they uncritically distinguish domestic from international affairs. Historians organize not only their individual studies but most of the very profession of history in terms of national categories. Sociologists draw more of their concept of society from the nationalist imaginary than they realize (see Chapter 5).

Discussion of political and legal citizenship requires attention to social solidarity. Current approaches to citizenship, however, tend to proceed on abstract bases, neglecting this sociological dimension. This is partly because a tacit understanding of what constitutes "a society" has been developed through implicit reliance on the idea of "nation." Issues of social belonging are addressed more directly in communitarian and multiculturalist discourses. Too often, however, different modes of solidarity and participation are confused. Scale is often neglected. The model of "nation" again prefigures the ways in which membership and difference are constructed. The present volume suggests the value of maintaining a distinction among relational networks, cultural or legal categories, and discursive publics. The first constitute community in a sense quite different from either of the latter two. Categories, however, are increasingly prominent in large-scale social life. But the idea of public is crucial to conceptualizing democratic participation.

My effort here is not to offer a comprehensive account of nationalism or national identity and still less of ethnicity or all the problems of belonging in an increasingly global world. More modestly, I try to lay out some of the character and influence of nationalism, to make clear something of why and how it matters, and to situate nationalism and ethnicity in relation to the idea of a cosmopolitan global order. This last involves recognizing the tensions between two different ways of imagining the world. These social imaginaries are powerful enough, moreover, that they shape the world, making it what it is, not just making pictures that match it more or less well. Most cosmopolitan visions oppose themselves to nationalism, but it has also figured in their conceptual heritage. The very formative opposition of ethnic and civic nationalism, discussed in detail in Chapter 6, is itself part of a framing of cosmopolitanism within the nationalist imaginary.

The present book is not a history of nationalism, but it is informed by insistence on seeing nationalism as a historical phenomenon. Nationalism is neither simply an inheritance always already there before modernity nor is it simply a set of values or beliefs which might become obsolete or be corrected and therefore vanish without trace. Rather, nationalism – as a conceptual framework, a discursive formation, a rhetoric, a structure of loyalties and sentiments – takes shape within history and informs history. There are specific histories within the era of nationalism's influence, histories shaped by the availability and pervasiveness of nationalism. But there is also a history of nationalism.[5] And both sorts of history involve changes that come as people think with old concepts in new circumstances and make innovations that have influences beyond their intentions. Most historical change is a matter of greater or lesser transformations in what exists, not abandonment of the existing for a new ideal.

If we are to limit, or reform, or move beyond nationalism we need to take it seriously, not dismiss it. We need to ask for whom it is easy and for whom it is hard to make such moves and why. We need to consider the changing meanings of nationalism and the innovations people make in nationalist rhetoric and practice. We need to respect the importance of belonging to nations and other groupings of human beings smaller than humanity as a whole. We need to understand that such belonging does different sorts of work for different people – inspires some, protects some, consoles some, as well as makes political opportunities for some.

Not only is nationalism not a moral mistake, it is not vanishing. National identities and loyalties and structures of integration are among the many complications of the actual historical world in which moral decisions must be made. Globalization challenges nation-states and intensifies flows across their borders, but it doesn't automatically make them matter less. Because nations matter in varied ways for different actors, it is important to think carefully about how they are produced and reproduced, how they work and how they can be changed. It matters whether nationalist appeals mobilize citizens for ethnic cleansing, external war, or internal loyalty to regrettable regimes. It matters whether nationalist appeals mobilize citizens for democratic projects, mutual care, or redistribution of wealth. Prior histories of nation-making may predispose people towards one sort of project or another, but the projects themselves also make and remake nations. Whatever is made of them, nations matter.

1

Is it time to be postnational?

In the wake of 1989, talk of globalization was often celebratory. It seemed a fulfillment of modernity's hopes, perhaps even a transcendence of modernity's flaws. This was true not only among anti-communist ideologues, corporate elites, and followers of Francis Fukuyama's Hegelian announcement of the end of history. Enthusiasm for globalization was also prominent on the left. Even while an anti-corporate movement gathered strength, many were eager to proclaim the rise of international civil society as a transcendence of the nation-state. Very few listened to reminders that national struggles in much of the world were among the few viable forms of resistance to capitalist globalization.[1]

Many embraced an ideal of cosmopolitan democracy. That is, they embraced not just cosmopolitan tastes for cultural diversity (which too often rendered culture an object of external consumption rather than internal meaning); not just the notion of hybridity with its emphasis on porous boundaries and capacious, complex identities; and not just cosmopolitan ethics emphasizing the obligations of each to all around the world. They embraced also the notion that the globe could readily be a polis, and humanity at large organized in democratic citizenship.[2] This is an attractive but very elusive ideal.

The discourse of globalization is gloomier in the first decade of the twenty-first century than it was in the 1990s. Stock market bubbles burst, and even recovery has felt insecure; reviving equity prices have not been matched by creation of jobs. The world's one superpower has announced and implemented a doctrine of pre-emptive invasion of those it sees as threatening. Awareness of the global vitality of religion is growing, but intolerant fundamentalists seem to thrive disproportionately. Despite new doctrines of active intervention a host of humanitarian emergencies and local or regional conflicts kill by the tens of thousands and impoverish by the millions. And the dark side of globalization includes diseases from SARS to AIDS and trafficking in women, drugs, and guns.

If 1989 symbolized (but only partly caused) the pro-global enthusiasms of the 1990s, 9/11 symbolizes (and also only partly caused) the reversal in mood. Some ask why we didn't see it coming. Focusing on 9/11 encourages the sense that simply a new event or malign movement defines the issue – as though, for example, terrorism were the fundamental underlying issue rather than a tactic made newly attractive by a combination of global organization and communications media on the one hand and local grievances and vulnerabilities on the other. We would do better to ask why we didn't see "it" – the dark side of globalization, or at least its Janus-faced duplicity – already there.

As globalization proceeded after 1989, shocks and enthusiasms alternated. The relative peacefulness of most post-communist transitions – despite the dispossession and disruption they entailed – brought enthusiasm; fighting among national groups in the former Soviet Union and Yugoslavia was a shock. There was an enthusiasm for global economic integration and the rapid development of Asian "tigers," and a shock with the currency crisis of 1997. There was an enthusiasm for information technology as the harbinger and vehicle of freer communication and new wealth, and a series of shocks with the extent to which the Internet brought pornography and spam, then the dot.com bust, then a range of new surveillance regimes. There was enthusiasm for European integration, and repeated shocks when wars erupted in Europe and the European Union could not achieve an effective common defense or foreign policy, and when immigration was linked to resurgent racism and nationalism. There was enthusiasm for global democracy, and shock and disillusionment as war came even to highly touted new democracies like Ethiopia and Eritrea and intertwined political and economic meltdown in Argentina. There was enthusiasm for both human rights and humanitarian intervention, and shock when the two came into conflict as the world failed to find an adequate way to address genocide and ethnic war in Central Africa.

Indeed, an explicit attack not only on nationalism but on the state was important to many of the enthusiasts. This was fueled not only by a growing confidence in global civil society (and potential supports for it, like the Internet). It was also driven by the tragic civil wars and ethnic slaughters of the era. Not only did these offer extreme examples of the evils associated with ethnicity and nationalism, they provided spectacles of possibly avertable tragedies in the face of which self-interested governments refused to act, sometimes citing notions of state sovereignty as rationale. So support grew for "humanitarian" interventions into crises, and also the belief that the crises were evidence of failed states and sovereignty only a distraction.[3]

For most of the 1990s, shocks failed to hold back enthusiasm. This was nowhere more evident than in the proliferation of cosmopolitan visions of globalization. These were (and are) internally heterogeneous. All, however, participated in a common contrast to overly strong politics of identity or claims to group solidarity. They extolled human rights and humanitarian interventions by "global society" into local messes. They praised hybridity and multiple, overlapping political memberships. Mostly produced from the political center and soft left, they shared with neoliberalism from the harder right a contempt for states which they understood mainly as authoritarian and dangerous. In this they reflected the libertarian side of 1960s conflicts, New Left disappointments in the welfare state, and a general anti-authoritarianism.[4] They focused not only on multilateral institutions but on the possibility that individuals might emancipate themselves from the sectionalism and restrictions of groups. Whether mainly ethical, political, socio-psychological, or cultural in their orientation, advocates of a more cosmopolitan world rejected nationalism, at least fundamentalism if not all religion, and most strong claims on behalf of ethnic groups. And so, the cosmopolitans suffered September 11 as an especially severe shock, and the continuing prominence of national security agendas and both religious and ethnic identities as a gloomy regression from what had seemed a clear progress.

To some extent this continues – in speeded up form – a pattern common to the whole modern era. Enthusiasms for transcending old forms of political power have alternated since the Enlightenment – perhaps since the seventeenth century – with appeals for solidarity in the face of insecurity and state action to build better societies. And with wars. "In a pattern of maniacal relapses and recoveries throughout European history, globalism keeps promising to arrive, always seems, in fact, to be just around the corner if not already here, but which continues to find its reality only in an unfulfilled desire against a backdrop of preparations for future war."[5]

There is much to feel gloomy about in the contemporary world, including the crisis of multilateral institutions, the prominence of reactionary political groups including but not limited to nationalists, and the assertion of military power as the solution to many of the problems of global inequality and instability. But this chapter is not about the dark side of globalization, nor is it a challenge to the cosmopolitan ideal. Rather, it is an attempt to ask whether nationalism can be left behind so easily as cosmopolitans sometimes imagine. I shall suggest cosmopolitanism and nationalism are mutually constitutive and to oppose them too sharply is misleading.[6] To conceptualize cosmopolitanism as the opposite to nationalism (and ethnicity and other solidarities) is not only a sociological confusion but an obstacle to achieving both greater democracy and better transnational institutions.[7] And I shall suggest there are good reasons why nationalism survives – even though nationalist projects are certainly not all good – and good reasons to doubt whether we are entering a postnational era.

Beyond the nation-state?

Advocates for a cosmopolitan global order frequently present this as moving beyond the nation-state. Jürgen Habermas, for example, writes of a "post-national constellation."[8] Martin Köhler sees movement from "the national to the cosmopolitan public sphere," with "a world developing as a single whole thanks to the social activity and the deliberate will of a population sharing common values and interests, such as human rights, democratic participation, the rule of law and the preservation of the world's ecological heritage."[9] Köhler certainly recognizes that adequate structures of authority are not yet in place on a global scale; he is a moderate cosmopolitan who still sees a role for states. Ulrich Beck is more extreme. He describes a "politics of post-nationalism" in which "the cosmopolitan project contradicts and replaces the nation-state project."[10]

Many other writers discuss the end of the Westphalian state system – by which they mean mostly an idea about sovereignty and the mutual recognition of states introduced at the close the Thirty Years War.[11] The Treaty of Westphalia is perhaps a convenient marker for the transition to a global order of nation-states, and the development of an international approach to national sovereignty, but the image of Westphalia is usually evoked in a way that exaggerates the extent to which nation-states were already effective and discrete power-containers in 1648, and the basic units of international politics for the next three and a half centuries. In the first place, empires thrived for the next 300 years, though more as European projects abroad than on the continent of Europe itself. Second, the nation-state order was hardly put in place in 1648, even in Europe. It would be more accurate to say that after 1648 nation-state *projects* increasingly shaped history, both domestically in efforts to bring nation and state into closer relationship and internationally in the organization of conflict and peace-making. Indeed, the very distinction of domestic from international is a product of these projects; it was minimally conceptualized in 1648 and for a very long time the interplay of nationalism and cosmopolitanism was not at all a simple opposition.[12]

The nation-state became relatively clearly formulated and increasingly dominant in Europe and the Americas during the nineteenth century. In much of the rest of the world, nationalism flourished in the twentieth century. In both cases, post-imperial projects were prominent. The project of trying to make states and nations line up remains very active in the twenty-first century, with colonialism receding as the relevant background. Indeed, conflicts in Central Asia, the Balkans, Central Africa, and South Asia reveal the extent to which nationalism and the nation-state project are current and not merely historical concerns. Moreover, these are not conflicts of a radically different sort from those that beset Europe in the era when modern states were first being consolidated there. Religion, culture, language, kin relations, demagogues, and economic opportunists mixed with the pursuit of political power, defensible borders, and state sovereignty in Europe as well. And Europeans complicated the matter further by pursuing overseas empires even while they consolidated national states at home. France – the paradigmatic nation of most theories of nationalism – was not only forged out of local wars and impositions of state power that unified the hexagon, even in its most revolutionary and nationalist moments it was also imperial. The first French republic tried to repress Haitian independence just as the Fourth and Fifth republics tried to repress Algerian independence.

The image of a Westphalian order thus marginalizes empire inappropriately, and deflects attention from the disorder and conflict wrought by attempts to make nation-states the dominant organizational units of sovereignty and monopolies of force. It flattens into legal abstraction an era that saw the world's most destructive wars and the development and recurrence of modern genocide, as well as the creation of a rich range of interstate institutions and agreements. The Peace of Westphalia certainly did not usher in a 350-year reign of peace, though arguably it inaugurated the cycle of philosophical and political declarations of plans for perpetual peace and wars to end all wars.[13]

And so it is unclear just what a "post-Westphalian" order signifies. For some, especially those for whom the European continent is the primary referent, it is more or less synonymous with "post-national constellation." And here too there are both domestic and international implications. The first is that cultural commonalities organized and mobilized in nationalism underwrote the necessary solidarities of citizens with states through most of the modern era, though now it is in some combination necessary and desirable to move beyond this. What lies beyond may be either solidarities based on the loyalties of citizens to specific political institutions, such as what Habermas has called "constitutional patriotism," or a move beyond particularistic solidarities altogether to some sort of ethical cosmopolitanism in which obligations to humanity as such supersede citizenship, community, and other more local bonds.[14] Second, internationally, the implication is simply that states cannot organize global politics or even the affairs once ostensibly contained in their own boundaries well enough to be considered the primary units of global order.

One of the problems with this discussion is that its empirical referents are unclear. Assertions are made like "in the second age of modernity the relationship between the state, business, and a society of citizens must be redefined."[15] Which state (and for that matter what organization of business and society of citizens)? Discussion of whether the state is growing stronger, declining, or merely remaining effective in international relations or for securing domestic welfare is quite frequently carried on without specification as to whether the state in question is, say, the United States of America or Chad. There is also an elision between discussions of a possible global "post-national constellation" or cosmopolitan democracy and debates over the integration of the European Union. The latter may be a model for what a postnational order might look like. Without going into that in any depth, however, it needs to be said (a) that it is not clear how well this is proceeding, and (b) that while European integration might be "post" the specific nation-state projects dominant for the last 300 years, it is not at all clear that it does not involve a new project of much the same kind, rather than fundamentally different.[16]

The last is an important point. The European Union is clearly an important innovation in many ways, and it clearly goes beyond anything imagined by the signatories of the Treaty of Westphalia. But one could focus on continuity rather than novelty. One could see the European Union as potentially a further centralization of political power and integration of both state administration and civil society of much the same sort as that which made modern France or Germany out of once less unified and often warring smaller polities. Indeed, Habermas's idea of "constitutional patriotism" – the loyalty of citizens to their political institutions rather than to any pre-existing ethnic nation – is itself a reworking of the idea of civic nationalism.[17]

Many discussions of globalization and cosmopolitan governance proceed as though it were obvious that the specific states that have claimed sovereignty in the language of Westphalia define a determinate scale of social organization, as though "nation" must refer to the cultural solidarities and identities organized at the level of those states. But what we see all over the world is that the scale of national projects varies and is hotly contested – precisely because there are no "natural" nations and there is no naturally best scale for a state. It was an illusion of Romantic nationalism and the "Springtime of Peoples" in the first half of the nineteenth century that there could somehow be an autonomous state for every nation.

A post-Westphalian Europe does not in itself invalidate the projects of sovereignty and self-determination in countries of Asia or Africa. Nor does it necessarily mean in all senses a postnational Europe (though it may mean transcending the limits of existing European nation-states). As David Held says, "globalization is best understood as a spatial phenomenon, lying on a continuum with 'the local' at one end and 'the global' at the other. It denotes a shift in the spatial form of human organization and activity to transcontinental or interregional patterns of activity, interaction and the exercise of power."[18] But this "shift" is not neutral. It advantages some and disadvantages others. And that is in fact a crucial reason for the continuing reproduction of nationalism, and a reason why caution is warranted before suggesting that nationalist projects are inherently regressive and cosmopolitan projects progressive. And it is especially problematic to suggest that from a standpoint of apparent academic neutrality that in fact coincides with the centers of current global political and economic power or former colonial power. The liberal state is not neutral. Cosmopolitan civil society is not neutral. Even the English language is not neutral. This doesn't mean that any of the three is bad, only that they are not equally accessible to everyone and do not equally express the interests of everyone.

Transformations in scale and struggles for equity

Globalization doesn't just happen. It is to a large extent imposed. This is misrecognized, though, when globalization is presented as simply the course of history, the mandate of necessity to which individuals and states must adapt or perish. Fortunately, as Kymlicka has noted, "globalization, far from encouraging political apathy, is itself one of the things which seems to mobilize otherwise apathetic people."[19]

Capitalism is perhaps the single most important driver of globalization, but hardly the only one. Capitalist globalization itself was never simply a matter of "the economy" separate from states or culture projects. From the East India Company to overseas missions to Hollywood, globalization has revealed the distinctions among economy, polity, and culture to be at most analytical and sometimes ideological but never simply factual.

One of the dominant patterns in modern history is the organization of power and capital on ever larger scales, and with new intensity. This precipitates a race in which popular forces and solidarities are always running behind. It is a race to achieve social integration, to structure the connections among people, and to organize the world. Capital and political power are out in front – sometimes in collusion and sometimes in contention with each other. Workers and ordinary citizens are always in the position of trying to catch up. As they get organized on local levels, capital and power integrate on larger scales.

The formation of modern states was both a matter of expansion, as smaller states gave way in the process of establishing centralized rule over large, contiguous territories, and of intensification, as administrative capacity was increased and intermediate powers weakened. Likewise, the growth of capitalism involved increases in both long distance and local trade, the development of both larger and more effectively adminis-tered enterprises, the extension of trade into financial markets and pro-duction relations, and the subjection of more and more dimensions of social life to market relations. State formation and capitalism coincided in empires and sometimes imperialism without formal empire. Postcolonies, even where they did constitute more or less integrated nation-states, could seldom achieve the autonomy promised by nationalist ideology precisely because they confronted global capitalist markets and unequal terms of trade.

Certainly there have long been and still are outright rejections of capitalist globalization, including communitarian efforts to defend small islands of self-sufficiency and larger-scale socialist projects of autochthonous development. And there are certainly rejections of gov-ernmental power, whether articulately anarchist or simply resistant. But for the most part, popular struggles have demanded neither an end to economic expansion nor the elimination of political power but a much greater fairness in the structure of economy and polity. They have sought, in other words, that integration come with equity and opportun-ity (the latter commonly problematically identified with growth). This is the primary concern of trade unions in advanced capitalist countries. It is the primary concern of minority groups in multicultural polities (and nearly all polities are multicultural). And it is the primary con-cern of people in the world's poorer and less powerful states – if not necessarily of those running the states. Indeed, an important dimen-sion of nationalism is rooted in popular demands for equity. Though cosmopolitan thought often rejects nationalism as some combination of manipulation by the central state, ancient ethnic loyalty, or desire to benefit at the expense of others – all phenomena that are real – it commonly misses the extent to which nationalism not only expresses solidarity or belonging but provides a rhetoric for demanding equity and growth. Nationalism – not cosmopolitanism – has underwritten most successful projects of economic redistribution – including especially those within European countries.

The demand that states operate for the benefit of nations comes in part from "below" as ordinary people insist on some level of participa-tion and commonwealth as a condition of treating rulers as legitimate.

But the integration of nation-states is an ambivalent step. On the one hand, state power is a force in its own right – not least in colonialism but also domestically – and represents a flow of organizing capacity away from local communities. On the other hand, democracy at a national level constitutes the greatest success that ordinary people have had in catching up to capital and power.

Ordinary people in many countries have achieved a modicum of democracy, and a number of other gains, but they did not choose the "race" in which electoral democracy is one of their partial victories. This was for the most part imposed by the development of more centralized states and the integration of capitalist markets. Most ordinary people experienced a loss of collective self-determination before the eventual gains of nineteenth- and twentieth-century democratization. They experienced this loss as the communities and institutions they had created were overrun and undermined by state and market forces. This doesn't mean that workers two generations later were not in many ways materially better off, or that life chances in the advanced industrial countries were not generally better than in those that did not go through similar transformations. It does not mean that many workers would not have preferred the chance to be owners. It does mean that many of those who lived through the transformations lost – and bitterly resented losing – both what has recently been called "social capital" and the chance to choose ways of life based on their own values and manner of understanding the world. And there are threats of similar loss today if neoliberal ideology leads to both the "extensification" and the "intensification" of market economies and capitalist production without provision of greater equity.

Struggles against colonial rule have often reflected similar issues and paradoxes. Dominated peoples have simultaneously sought to resist foreign rule and to forge nations by drawing disparate "traditional" groups together.[20] A claim to common "traditional" culture underwrites both nationalism and sectional or "communal" resistance to it (each of which is a project of groups placed differently in a larger field, not simply a reflection of pre-existing identity – though never unrelated to ongoing cultural reproduction). Nations appear simultaneously as always already there cultural commonalities, as new projects occasioned by colonialism and independence struggles, and as impositions of certain constructions of the national culture over other identities and cultural projects within the ostensible nation. The situation of struggle against external colonial power makes larger categories of "indigenous" solidarity useful, but the achievement of these is always a redistribution of power and resources – usually away from more or less autonomous local communities, subordinated cultures, and other groups. The sociologist Pierre Bourdieu describes one version of this, as true he argues for early twenty-first century neoliberal globalization as it was for the French colonization of Algeria:

> As I was able to observe in Algeria, the unification of the economic field tends, especially through monetary unification and the generalization of monetary exchanges that follows, to hurl all social agents into an economic game for which they are not equally prepared and equipped, culturally and economically. It tends by the same token to submit them to standards objectively imposed by competition from more efficient productive forces and modes of production, as can readily be seen with small rural producers who are more and more completely torn away from self-sufficiency. In short, *unification benefits the dominant.*[21]

Those who resist such market incursions or the similar centralizations of state power are commonly described as "traditional" by contrast to modern. Their defense of community, craft, religion, and kinship is seen as somehow irrational. It is indeed often backward-looking, though not always, and not for this reason incapable of generating social innovation and sometimes truly radical visions of a better society. But to look backward is not inherently irrational, especially when there is no guarantee that the future amounts to progress – or that what some deem progress will advance the values ordinary people hold dearest.

Moreover, the communities and institutions that are defended by those who resist the incursions of expanding and intensifying capitalist markets and state administrations are not simply dead forms inherited from the past. They are social achievements, collectively created often in the face of considerable opposition. They provide some level of capacity for ordinary people to organize their own lives – imperfectly, no doubt, but with potential for improvement and some level of autonomy from outside forces. As Bourdieu remarks, their defense is rendered all the more rational by the extent to which unification benefits the dominant. And as I shall argue here, extremely rapid changes in social organization may especially benefit the dominant, disrupt life more, and reduce chances for social struggle to win compromises and create alternative paths of development.

The same is true, at least potentially, for the project of unifying the working class in order to fight better against more centralized capitalism. The Marxist notion of a progress from local struggles through trade union consciousness to class struggle is an account of "modern" unification in the pursuit of more effective struggle (based, according to the theory, on recognition of true underlying interests in solidarity). But even if unification is necessary to contest impositions of power from "outside" it is not necessarily egalitarian in its "internal" organization. Class unification can only come about if non-class goals and identities are subordinate. Marxists often discuss nationalist or ethnic struggles as though these are merely diversions from the "correct" solidarity necessarily based on class.[22] But all such unifying solidarities – class and nation alike – are achieved in struggle and at the expense of others. This makes them neither artificial nor erroneous, but products of history.

Products of history may nonetheless be constitutive for personal identity, social relationships, and a sense of location in the world. In other words, it is a mistake to leap from the historical character of national and other solidarities to an account of "the invention of tradition" which implies that national traditions are mere artifice and readily swept away. Among other things, this misrepresents what is at stake in discussion of "tradition." Too often, to be sure, scholars take at face value (and perhaps have their own investments in) traditionalists' accounts of respect for ancient ways of life. But it is equally erroneous to imagine that demonstrating a point of origin sometime more recent that the primordial mists of ancient history debunks national culture. It is not antiquity that defines tradition. Rather, tradition is better grasped as a mode of reproduction of culture and social practices that depends on understandings produced and reproduced in practical experience and embedded in interpersonal relations, rather than rendered entirely abstractly, as a set of rules or more formal textual communication. So tradition is not simply a set of contents, but a mode of reproduction of such contents. It works for people when it successfully organizes projects in their lives.

As a kind of ubiquitous involvement in culture, often incorporated prereflectively as *habitus*, tradition works best where change is gradual so that there can be continual adaptation embedded in the ordinary processes of reproduction. But it is misleading to approach "tradition" as the opposite of progress, as referring to simple continuity of the past, or as simple backwardness. Tradition is partly backward-looking, a project of preserving and passing on wisdom and right action. But as a project, it is also forward-looking. Traditions must be reconstructed – sometimes purified and sometimes enhanced – whether this is explicitly announced or not. Moderns have tended to look on changes to a story or a statement of values as necessarily falling into three categories: deceptions, errors, or clearly announced revisions. But in fact the constant revision of living traditions works differently. It is not as though there is simply a "true" or authoritative version at time one, against which the "changes" are to be judged. Rather, the tradition is always in the process of production and reproduction simultaneously. Usually reproduction predominates enormously over production – and thus there is continuity from the past. But this is achieved not merely by reverence but by action. People put the culture they have absorbed (or that has been inculcated into them) to work every time they take an action. But they also adapt it, mobilize the parts of it that fit the occasion and indeed their strategy. They do this commonly without any conscious decision and certainly without the intent of acting on the tradition. Put another way, tradition is medium and condition of their action, not its object, even though their actions will (collectively and cumulatively) have implications for tradition. Language is a good example, as people use it to accomplish innumerable ends, and shape it through the ways in which they use it, but only very exceptionally through an intention to do so.

It is misleading, thus, to equate tradition simply with antiquity of cultural contents. Max Weber is often cited for such a view, but this is an incomplete reading. Like most thinkers since the Enlightenment, Weber opposed mere unconscious reflex or unexamined inheritance to rationality as conscious and sensible action. He saw traditional action as "determined by ingrained habituation," and thought that it lay very close to the borderline of what could be called meaningfully oriented action.[23] His account was a forerunner – albeit problematic and limited – of Bourdieu's deeper development of the idea of *habitus*. Habitus reaches beyond mere habituation and is less deterministic. Above all, it situates action in a field of social relations, not as the decontextualized expression or choice or even interaction of individuals.[24] Bourdieu reveals habitus to matter more in modern societies than Weber thought traditional action did; indeed, in important ways Bourdieu deconstructs the opposition of traditional to modern, showing for example how much reproduction there is within ostensibly progressive modernity. The crucial point, however, is that Weber approached tradition through its medium of reproduction – ingrained habituation. He may have grasped that too narrowly, but the approach was sound.

What Weber defined by its backward-looking character was not so much tradition as traditional*ism*. This was what Weber described as "piety for what actually, allegedly, or presumably has always existed."[25] Here too there is an echo in Bourdieu, who in his studies of colonial Algeria made much of the difference between "traditional" Berber society, which he was as much obliged to reconstruct as he was able to observe it in his fieldwork in Kabylia, and the traditionalism that was deployed by various indigenous interpreters of Berber culture in the context of rapid social change and destabilization of old ways of life. Both in the countryside and among labor-migrants to Algerian cities, Bourdieu observed self-declared cultural leaders who proffered their accounts of true and ancient traditions. But these accounts were already codifications – whether formally written down or not – at least one step removed from the ubiquitous reproduction of social life and culture in constant interaction.[26] We could think of traditionalism as the mobilization of specific contents of older culture as valuable in themselves, even if now disconnected from their previous modes of reproduction and ways of life.

This excursus on tradition is important, not least because twenty-first-century cosmopolitans could easily repeat the errors of their fore-bears who thought religion was clearly vanishing in a secularizing world. Cosmopolitans are apt to see traditional culture as a set of contents, possibly erroneous, rather than a basic underpinning for many people's practical orientation to the world. They are apt to approach it with an eye to sorting its good from its bad elements – keep that folk art perhaps but lose that patriarchy. I do not mean that normative evalu-ation is illegitimate. It may even be inevitable. But the various specific contents of living cultural tradition do not present themselves as discrete, disconnected artifacts to be selected or discarded. While they are not necessarily tightly woven into a functional system, they are joined, not simply in an abstract cultural system but in the concrete dispositions to action.[27] Tradition is not a kind of possession, a good to which people have a right so long as it doesn't conflict with other more basic goods. To think of it thus misses the extent to which culture is constitutive, and also misses the extent to which rapid social change is not merely disorienting but disempowering. It misses the extent to which roots in traditional culture and communal social relations are basic to the capacity for col-lective resistance to inequitable social change – like that brought by global capitalism and perhaps exacerbated by some of the ways in which the United States uses its state power. Last but not least, absorbing the typical modern orientation to tradition as simply backward-looking leads many cosmopolitans to miss the extent to which new forward-looking projects are built – perhaps "grown" would be a better word – on traditional roots. I refer both to the extent to which self-conscious pro-jects for a better society draw on themes in traditional culture – seeking not simply to resist change but to achieve in new ways things traditionally thought good – and to the extent to which even without self-conscious projects tradition offers a medium for bringing diverse people together in common culture. Indeed, much of the actually existing cosmopolitan bridging of ethnic boundaries depends not on abstract universalism but on the commingling of older traditions and the production of new ones in informal relationships and local contexts.

Both roots and the need for roots are asymmetrically distributed. It is often precisely those lacking wealth, elite connections, and ease of movement who find their membership in solidaristic social groups most important as an asset. This is so whether the groups are communities, crafts, ethnicities, nations, or religions. Different groups of people struggle both to maintain some realms of autonomy and to gain some voice in (if not control over) the processes of larger-scale integration. The idea that there are clearly progressive and clearly reactionary positions in these struggles is misleading. So is the idea that there is a neutral position offering a cosmopolitan view that is not itself produced in part through tradition.

Philosophers have long proposed both ideal social orders and ethical precepts for individual action based on the assumption that individuals could helpfully be abstracted from their concrete social contexts, at least for the purposes of theory. The motivations for such arguments have been honorable: that existing social contexts endow much that is both evil and mutable with the force and justification of apparent necessity, and that any starting point for understanding persons other than their radical equality in essential humanness and freedom opens the door to treating people as fundamentally unequal. Such theories, grounded in the abstract universality of individual human persons, may provide insights. They are, however, fundamentally unsound as guides to the world in which human beings must take actions. They lead not only to a tyranny of the abstract ought over real moral possibilities, and to deep misunderstandings of both human life and social inequality, but also to political programs which, however benign and egalitarian their intentions, tend to reproduce problematic power relations.

Among the instances of these problems is the overeager expectation that the world could happily be remade through ethical, political, sociopsychological, and cultural orientations in which individual freedom and appropriations of the larger world would require no strong commitment to intervening solidarities. This reveals a certain blindness in cosmopolitan theory, blindness toward the sociological conditions for cosmopolitanism itself and toward the reasons why national, ethnic, and other groups remain important to most of the world's people. It is about the ways in which cosmopolitanism – however attractive in some ways – is compromised by its formulation in liberal individualist terms that block appreciation of the importance of social solidarity. Nussbaum, for example, discerns two opposing traditions in thinking about political community and the good citizen: "One is based upon the emotions; the other urges their removal."[28] While each in its own way pursues freedom and equality, the first relies too much on compassion for her taste. "The former aims at equal support for basic needs and hopes through this to promote equal opportunities for free choice and self-realization; the other starts from the fact of internal freedom – a fact that no misfortune can remove – and finds in this fact a source of political equality." But surely this is a false opposition. Instead of adjudicating between the two sides in this debate, we should ask how to escape from it.

Conclusion

I have argued that there are good reasons to think we are not entering very abruptly into a postnational era. These reasons go beyond mere temporary assertions of state power, especially in the "security" policies of the US and other wealthy countries. It is not at all clear, for example, that the European Union is a "postnational" project rather than a continuation of the same trend that produced national unification in France and Germany and subordinated Scottish, Irish, Welsh and indeed English identities in the British state. Nor is it clear that the projects of broadening and deepening national solidarities and trying to join them to popular states are without value for people in most of the world's developing – or *un*developing – countries.

Fairness in global integration is not just a matter of achieving the "best" abstract design of global institutions. It necessarily also includes allowing people inhabiting diverse locations in the world, diverse traditions, and diverse social relationships opportunities to choose the institutions in and through which they will integrate.

I have suggested that most cosmopolitan theories are individualistic in ways that obscure the basic importance of social relationships and culture. I have defended tradition, thus, and urged thinking of it as a mode of reproduction of culture and practical orientations to action, not as a bundle of contents. On this basis I have suggested that when globalization causes abrupt social transformations it is typically disempowering, but that tradition importantly underpins popular resistance to asymmetrical globalization. Projects grounded in tradition can be forward-looking; they are not always captured by demagogic traditionalists extolling stasis or a return to some idealized past.

No one lives outside particularistic solidarities. Some cosmopolitan theorists may believe they do, but this is an illusion made possible by positions of relative privilege and the dominant place of some cultural orientations in the world at large. The illusion is not a simple mistake, but a misrecognition tied to what Pierre Bourdieu called the "*illusio*" of all social games, the commitment to their structure that shapes the engagement of every player and makes possible effective play.[29] In other words, cosmopolitans do not simply fail to see the cultural particularity and social supports of their cosmopolitanism, but cannot fully and accurately recognize these without introducing a tension between themselves and their social world. And here I would include myself and probably all of us. Whether we theorize cosmopolitanism or not, we are embedded in social fields and practical projects in which we have little choice but to make use of some of the notions basic to cosmopolitanism and thereby reproduce it. We have the option of being self-critical as we do so, but not of entirely abandoning cosmopolitanism because we cannot act effectively without it. Nor should we want to abandon it, since it enshrines many important ideas like the equal worth of all human beings and – at least potentially – the value of cultural and social diversity. But we should want to transform it, not least because as usually constructed, especially in its most individualistic forms, it systematically inhibits attention to the range of solidarities on which people depend, and to the special role of such solidarities in the struggles of the less privileged and those displaced or challenged by capitalist globalization.

2

Nationalism matters

Nationalism is easily underestimated. To start with, in its most pervasive forms it is often not noticed. Analysts focus on eruptions of violence, waves of racial or ethnic discrimination, and mass social movements. They fail to see the everyday nationalism that organizes people's sense of belonging in the world and to particular states, and the methodological nationalism that leads historians to organize history as stories in or of nations and social scientists to approach comparative research with data sets in which the units are almost always nations. It is important not to start inquiries into nationalism by selecting only its most extreme or problematic forms for attention. Equally, it is important not to imagine it as exceptional, about to vanish, a holdover from an earlier era lacking in contemporary basis; it is hardly good scholarship to wish nationalism away.

On the contrary, nationalism is a discursive formation that gives shape to the modern world.[1] It is a way of talking, writing, and thinking about the basic units of culture, politics, and belonging that helps to constitute nations as real and powerful dimensions of social life. Nations do not exist "objectively": before they exist discursively. Equally, however, nations conjured out of talk and sentiment are also "real" material structures of solidarity and recognition. To say that nationalism is part of a social imaginary is not to say that nations are mere figments of the imagination to be dispensed with in more hard-headed analyses. As a discursive formation, nationalism (like, say, individualism) generates ever more discussion because it raises as many problems, aporias, and questions as it resolves.

There have been long, and I think generally fruitless, debates about the antiquity and origins of nationalism. Attempts to resolve them turn in large part on definitions, each of which is tendentious. Is nationalism essentially political, and linked to the emergence of the modern state? Elie Kedourie writes that

> Nationalism is a doctrine invented in Europe at the beginning of the
> nineteenth century. It pretends to supply a criterion for the
> determination of the unit of population proper to enjoy a government
> exclusively its own, for the legitimate exercise of power in the state,
> and for the right organization of a society of states. Briefly, the
> doctrine holds that humanity is naturally divided into nations, that
> nations are known by certain characteristics which can be ascertained,
> and that the only legitimate type of government is national
> self-government.[2]

But one might as well argue that nationalism is essentially cultural, and
as old as fellow-feeling among members of linguistic and ethnic communities. Or, more moderately, one might suggest that modern nationalism is a transformation wrought on such ancient ethnic identities by the
new circumstances of modernity, including not only states but popular
literacy, and with it newspapers and novels, mass educational systems,
museums and histories. Though their arguments are in other important
ways opposed, two of the most prominent contemporary analysts of
nationalism, Anthony Smith and Benedict Anderson, seem to agree on
this, with the former stressing continuity with the past and the "reality"
of ethnic traditions and the latter stressing imaginary construction, the
novelty of mass media, and the role of the state.[3]

In this context, it is perhaps instructive to note that we draw the
word "nation" from ancient Roman usage, in which nations were pre-
eminently subject peoples and Barbarians. Romans understood these to
be organized in terms of common descent and ways of life, rather than
properly political institutions. Romans themselves, thus, were not in an
important sense a nation, at least not from the mature Republic on. Nor
was nationality as such the basis for political community – though it was
a basis for exclusion. One might then locate the origins of nationalism –
or at least of Europe's characteristic nations – in the dissolution of the
Roman Empire and the development of a variety of different politico-
cultural groupings in medieval Europe.[4] This has the advantage of
reminding us that there is nothing "natural" about the link between
political community and cultural commonality and the development of
nationalism or the nation-state, either as actual (in varying extent) or as
idealized in doctrine. As a way of organizing political life and cultural or
ethnic claims (themselves commonly political), nationalism grows
neither in primordial mists nor in the abstract. It grows in relationship
to other political, cultural, and ethnic projects.

Nationalism is pervasive in the modern world because it is widely
used, not merely found. But it is used in different projects – claiming or
contesting the legitimacy of governments, demanding reorganization of

educational curricula, promoting the elimination of ethnic minorities in the pursuit of cultural or racial purity. Its meaning lies in the interconnections among these various uses, not in any one of them. There is no common denominator which precisely defines the set of "true" nationalisms or "true" nations by virtue of being shared by all and by no other political or cultural projects or formations. Yet nationalism is real, and powerful. Nationalism matters because it is a vital part of collective projects that give shape to the modern world, transform the very units of social solidarity, identity, and legal recognition within it, and organize deadly conflicts.

Nationalism flourishes in the wake of empires but also in active relationship to empires, including Austro-Hungarian, Spanish, Portuguese, British, French, and German but also, if distinctly, non-European empires. It flourishes also in competition among ostensible nations. It organizes both domestic and international struggles and indeed the very distinction of domestic from international. It matters more because it matters in so many different contexts. This gives added resonance and life to the rhetoric of nationalism even while it renders definitions problematic.

Theoretical and historiographical arguments about nationalism are heavily reliant on European examples – but also European political projects and debates and European misunderstandings. Better recognition of both the ways in which nationalism matters and the mutability of the ways in which the category of nation is deployed would likely come with more attention to the Americas, Asia, and Africa. In particular, it may help overcome not only a Eurocentric selection of examples, but biases and blind spots built into theory by thinking in terms of certain prototypical European arguments and categories. These are deeply integrated into theory and historiography as they have developed throughout European modernity. This is not to say that there are not comparable confusions in studies of the Americas or in the use of "nation" as a category in American political projects or academic research, and indeed many of these come in large part from importing European analytic perspectives too uncritically. Merely fitting the New World examples into an Old World framework won't help – and indeed may add confusion by reproducing the opposition of old to new and with it the implication that nationalism emerges as a process of maturation, the collective *bildung* of peoples as they gain the capacity for sovereignty, and with it the overcoming of older political forms like empire (or, relatedly, that further "maturation" overcomes nationalism itself in the production of cosmopolitan politics and identities).

European nationalism has from early on been deeply invested in three misrecognitions, which different constructions of European history and politics helped to embed in more general theories of nationalism. The first of these is that nations are relative equals. The second is that nation and empire are sharply opposed and incompatible political formations. The third is that nations are always already available only to be called forth in new mobilizations for action or discourses of legitimacy. Some analysts of Europe have recognized how each of these assertions misleads. Nonetheless, they have been important themes in the discursive formation by which nationalism is reproduced in and among European countries – and indeed elsewhere.

The New World has lessons to teach on each of the themes about which European self-understanding has been misleading. Let me evoke these briefly, with reference mainly to Europe, leaving the development of or contestation over the New World cases to specialist researchers.[5] I shall then turn to a review of general themes and debates structuring theories of nationalism. It is important, I think, for studies of nationalism in the New World to engage these debates well, grasping the overall range of arguments and positions and not simply happening on an interesting book here or there and putting its ideas to use in a new empirical context. But it is important too for scholars to be skeptical of the ways in which many issues and debates are posed in the dominant literature on nationalism. Among other things, for a scholarly literature it has been unusually caught up with praising or – recently much more often – debunking the objects of its study.

Three misrecognitions

European nationalism developed simultaneously as an account of internal integration and legitimacy of rule, and external differentiation and sovereignty. It had ancient roots but took its dominant forms in a modern era shaped by inconclusive wars and economic competition. It is important to see the shaping influence of a Europe in which many different states had long existed without any attaining domination over the whole. That Germany's Third Reich came closer than any previous project of continental integration since the dissolution of the Roman Empire only reveals the primary historical fact of a plurality of powerful states. But more on empire in a moment. Here what we should note is the relatively unusual character of Europe and its major influence on thinking about nationalism.

In few other regions of the world, if any, were several comparably powerful states forced to coexist with each other in relative equality without the peacekeeping and integrating influence of an overarching or at least central empire. Where empire was absent, either state-making was modest or state projects collided in wars, conquests, and expansion.

The latter was indeed Europe's pattern, and who is to say that it is not still; that the peace produced after World War II in part by projects of European union will not ultimately result in a supraEuropean state – whether imperial or national, or in some sense more novel.

European nationalism reflected, however, the relative stalemate in which a variety of different states could achieve substantial independence and pursue distinctive policies. This was not simply an inheritance from feudalism, which did indeed produce diverse polities but not the boundaries or domestic integration of modern states. On the contrary, it was only in the early modern period that this mode of political and social organization took shape. As late as the nineteenth century, patterns of procreation and family life varied more within states than among them.[6] As late as the middle of the nineteenth century the majority of French citizens spoke regional languages, not the standard French that first the royal Court and then the revolutionary Republic was concerned to perfect.[7] In other words, before the nineteenth century states organized less of social life and coincided less with cultural integration than the developing national ideal would suggest. As important, the Peace of Westphalia that ended the Thirty Years War in 1648 established a principle of independent sovereignty and mutual recognition which became basic to the flourishing of nationalism. The wars the peace brought to an end had their roots in large part in religion, and the peace sought to remove religion from international politics by in effect declaring it private and domestic. It did succeed in banishing religion from the academic study of international relations, but not of course from real-world politics. What it did do was break the disruptive influence of transitional religious movements and solidarities – for a time.

A variety of relatively small countries gained recognition in the peace, or later in the terms it outlined – most prominent initially were the Netherlands and the Swiss Confederation. The Swiss Confederation reminds us that the principle established at Westphalia was not yet that of the nation-state, but of the autonomous or sovereign state – for which nationalism could grow in importance as a discourse of domestic legitimacy and external recognition. The principle, moreover, was hardly the empirical actuality. And of course borders could be made more and more salient – not just by making them harder to cross but by building infrastructure and institutions that offered people benefits but stopped sharply at their edges.

The idea of nationalism, and indeed theories of nationalism, have been enormously shaped by the extent to which the big European states reached a balance of power, and through alliances and wars managed almost despite themselves to sustain it. The importance of Spain faded after the Thirty Years War, and the long process of constructing countries out of the Holy Roman Empire and eventually the other Hapsburg dominions began.[8] France was especially strong at first, and it is arguably at the moment of the French Revolution of 1789 that all the most frequently evoked elements of nationalism are first fully and clearly in play on the European Continent.[9] But France was never strong enough to dominate, Napoleon notwithstanding. Germany was long locked into a struggle to catch up in political integration and military might, but with increasing clarity became the continental counterweight to France. If Germany was initially the negative example in ideas of nationalism, because it lacked France's central state, its very projects of integration and their philosophical articulations – notably, for example, by Fichte – became extremely influential. The contrasts between France and Germany loomed extremely large in the development of nationalism in theory and practice, and to this day structure basic conceptual divides such as the contrast of civic and ethnic nationalism (which is, I think, overblown).[10] And England (still in the early stages of integration or transformation into Britain) became a third exemplar of a powerful nation-state.

Of course there were a number of smaller European states, and the number grew as various former Hapsburg dominions gained or struggled for independence. For at least 300 years, though, the crucial fact was the absence of an integrating continental power. The issue for smaller states then, was not so much to gain shelter under one or another empire as to gain recognition as a sovereign state. While there was always a lot of *realpolitik* to this, it was always bound up with the capacity to project identity as a nation. It is worth noting that this has remained a powerful factor in the politics of international recognition. When Slovenia and Croatia announced their independence from the former Yugoslavia, the United States (and Germany, leading the European powers) immediately recognized their sovereignty. When Bosnia-Herzegovina did the same, recognition was withheld – apparently on the grounds that it did not represent a "real nation," despite a longer history of territorial integrity and civic life, including 500 years of peace. Why not? Because it was explicitly multiethnic and multireligious.

So, to summarize and move on, lest I become too enmeshed in my European story, doctrines of nationalism long included the notion of the equivalence of each nation – at least each "real" or "historical" nation (and debates over what to do about "nationalities" that fell short of that constitute another story). This doctrine was influenced by and paired with that of individualism. The nation was conceptualized in part as a person, including a legal person on the model of kings as sovereigns. And as domestic law came increasingly to recognize human persons as equals so international law recognized national persons as equals. But of course they weren't. East Timor and the People's Republic of China,

Luxembourg and the United States are all recognized members of the United Nations and sovereign equals before international law. Yet it takes a rather grand leap of imagination to consider them equal in other senses. And this act of imagination was, I think, made possible significantly by a specific phase of European history. It was extended widely by the processes of decolonization that ended European overseas empires through the production of putative nation-states conceived on the model of such equivalence.[11]

The second misrecognition to which I pointed was the sharp contrast of nation to empire. We have already seen one source of this in the Peace of Westphalia. Though there was no clear-cut military triumph in the Thirty Years War, to a considerable extent it was the defeat of empire – represented by Spain and the Holy Roman Empire – by powers that would increasingly style themselves and organize themselves as nations, notably France and Sweden. During more or less the same period, European social theorists wrote extensively about foreign empires and the instructive lessons they offered to European countries. Montesquieu's *Persian Letters* is only one of the most famous such treatises to mark out the alleged contrast between the tyranny of empire and the liberties of European political arrangements. Of course many of these works, including Montesquieu's, were written at least as much to point out bits of tyranny at home as to criticize those abroad. But the fact that empire became so basic a foil was influential. It was in this discourse, for example, that the Ottoman Empire became (in European eyes) paradigmatically non-European and non-Western (with implications to the present day). To an important extent the same is true of Russia, and certainly China, Japan, and others were not merely exoticized but analyzed specifically as empires (and it is a somewhat tendentious question whether this was the right category to use in all cases).

The most important misrecognition in all of this was that it helped underwrite 200 years of European discourse in which discussions of national identity and citizenship were constructed by a contrast to the bad empires of others, without being much troubled by the fact that the emerging national states were themselves imperial powers. Even France, and even France in its most republican phases, was also an empire. Think only of the repression of Haiti's Revolution or note that though Republican France set up nominally republican institutions in Egypt it was still a conqueror. One of the challenges for current analysis of European history is coming to terms with the extent to which the forging of European national states was never purely a domestic affair, nor even simply a combination of domestic affairs with European international relations. It was importantly tied up with the development of colonial empires. If this is true for France, Britain, and Germany – as it certainly is

– it applies with equal force in the different cases of Spain and Portugal. The case of Britain is complicated also by the extent to which British empire began with English rule over the Celtic countries of Scotland, Ireland, and Wales. These were formally treated as imperial dominions before they were integrated into any project of British nationalism. But let me simply stop with putting on the table the extent to which national-ism should be recognized as almost always interwoven with empire. This may seem self-evident in some parts of the New World and if so this is a good thing for it will help produce a necessary corrective. But it is not always self-evident everywhere, as the very image of the United States as a republic suggests. It is hard for US citizens to grasp either westward expansion or overseas conquests like the Philippines as part of an imperial history. And in the context of contemporary US projections of global power pundits commonly describe as something new the notion that the United States might act like an empire.

The third misrecognition is perhaps most easily stated, though it is hard to deal with theoretically. This is the notion that nations are always already available to political projects as their prepolitical grounds. Put another way, the idea of "nation" is basic to the idea of "the people" as the source of political legitimacy. Far from being clearly opposed to democracy, thus, it is in many ways one of its conditions. The idea of nation does work for democratic political theory (and practice) but it is hard for most democrats to acknowledge this openly. For example, it answers the question of why particular people in a particular place bene-fit from the putatively universal rights identified by democratic theorists. Let me take just a moment to explicate the significance of this for liberal theory – partly because it matters not just theoretically but through the extent to which liberal theory suffuses modern state practices and the construction of international relations.

Relying at least tacitly on the idea of "nation" to give an account of why particular people belong together as the "people" of a particular state has historically done the double work of explaining the primary loyalty of each to all within the state, and the legitimacy of ignoring or discriminating against those outside. Liberal discussions of citizenship and political obligation relied on the background presumption of com-mon nationality to minimize troubling questions about ethnic or other intermediate solidarities (or relegate these to treatment as special cases). Moreover, liberal theory allowed the differentiation of domestic from international affairs on the basis of the same background assumptions. So long as the fiction of a perfect match between nations and states was plausible, thus, liberalism faced relatively few problems of political identity or the constitution and significance of groups, though it meant liberal theory was sociologically impoverished.

Most reasoning about justice, political obligation, and other problems thus assumed the context of "a society," while reasoning about
international relations addressed relations among such societies. It is
instructive to see how John Rawls, the most important liberal theorist of
the current era, addressed these issues. Rawls's (1971) classic theory of
justice presumed an individual state as the necessary context of analysis.[12]
A well-ordered society, Rawls insisted, was precisely not a community or
an association:

> we have assumed that a democratic society, like any political society,
> is to be viewed as a complete and closed social system. It is complete
> in that it is self-sufficient and has a place for all the main purposes of
> human life. It is also closed, in that entry into it is only by birth and
> exit from it is only by death.[13]

Rawls knew, of course, that this was a fiction, but he initially thought it
plausible, since his major focus was on what made "a" society just.
Accordingly, he postponed analysis of relations among states and transnational phenomena to a later step in analysis. Social changes of the
1990s – commonly summed up under the notion of intensified globalization – pressed the further step on him. Rawls's own approach was to
retain the notion of "peoples" or discrete societies, and then to propose a
"law of peoples" regulating relations among these.[14]

Jürgen Habermas also responded to the same social changes that
were making it hard to presume nation-states as the automatic contexts
for democracy, rights, or political order. His reflections were informed
not only by German and global affairs, but by the project of European
integration. Debates over whether Europe needed a constitution focused
many of his analyses.[15] Taking up Sternberger's concept of "constitutional patriotism," he stressed the idea of political loyalty to a constitutional arrangement as such – important both as a commitment to
procedures that would limit loyalties to substantive social groups
(nations or ethnicities) and as a referent for public discourse in which the
public itself assumes some of the legitimating function otherwise
assigned to nations.[16] Habermas insists that within all modern societies,
and even more in international amalgamations such as the European
Union, there will necessarily be multiple different substantive conceptions of the good life, and these will often be associated with different
social groups (though he does not stress the latter point). Constitutional
patriotism does not underwrite any of these in their specificity, but rather
a general commitment to justification of collective decisions in terms of
fairness. It thus allows for debate over how to balance direct reference to
universal rights and procedural norms with more specific political culture. But, insisting on a more "comprehensive" rights-based theory of

justice, Habermas is unwilling to accept the extent of variation among quasi-autonomous political cultures that Rawls's theory allowed.[17] Habermas's approach is more "cosmopolitan" in clearly favoring a global institutionalization of the sort of system of rights that has so far been institutionalized mainly (and often still incompletely and problematically) within individual states. Accordingly, Habermas approaches relations beyond nation-states in the same way as he approaches domestic affairs within states – as a matter of achieving a comprehensive, universalistic set of procedures and motivating political loyalties to them that transcend all substantive identities or groupings without prejudice for or against any.

Rawls and Habermas are only two among a wave of different liberal theoreticians to propose solutions to the problems of identity, belonging, and sovereignty in the context of the growing globalization of the post-1989 era. Many of these have assumed the label "cosmopolitan." To a considerable extent, this has involved trying to apply what had been basically "domestic" liberal theory to tackle more global questions. To their credit, the various theorists of a new cosmopolitan liberalism have recognized that it is no longer tenable to rely so uncritically on the idea of nation. Many have realized that their presumption of the internal integration and external singularity of "societies" does not match reality well. This is, of course, not just a result of social change. Nations were never as sharply bounded as nationalism suggested. And nationalism itself was always produced in international affairs. In the Americas, nationalism was a product of interAmerican relations and relations with Europe, never entirely "domestic."

One of the problems with the proposed cosmopolitan solutions is that they do not give adequate weight to the work done by notions of nationalism (and other projects of collective identity) in enabling people who are not well empowered to participate in global affairs as individuals to participate through collectivities. I have argued this point elsewhere, criticizing in particular the extent to which cosmopolitan thought exemplifies the "class consciousness of frequent travelers."[18] But here what I would stress most is the extent to which such cosmopolitan thinking, and liberal theory in general, approaches nations as inheritances rather than creations. If nationalism is approached as a new product it is generally debunked as an "invented tradition," or denigrated as a manipulation by opportunistic political entrepreneurs. But this underestimates the extent to which national identities have always and everywhere been created through a variety of historical projects. Nationalism has been implicated in the structure of the discipline of history, organized as so many national histories, thus generally implying the prior existence of the object studied. But of course the writing of national history has also been part of the creation of nations. Nationalism as a project has been seen under the problematic heading of "late nationalism," especially the ethnonationalisms of Europe's East. And the idea of founding nations rather than discovering them, has been left to other parts of the world, and is poorly integrated in the theoretical self-understanding of European theory.

Nationalism and social theory

Social theory has approached nationalism first as a political ideology structuring relations of power and conflict. It has focused on nationalism's relationship to ethnic violence and war, on the production of beliefs that one's own country is the best, and on the invocation of national unity to override internal differences. It has seen nationalism first through bellicose international relations and second through projects by which elites attempt to mobilize mass support. This has been an influential view both among scholars of nationalism[19] and among general social theorists who have tended to see nationalism largely as a problem to be overcome.[20]

A second strain of social theory, associated with modernization theory and anticipated by both Weber and Durkheim has seen nation-building as a crucial component of developing an effective modern society, one capable of political stability and economic development. Nationalism, as the ideology associated with such nation-building, is thus important to a phase in the process of becoming modern, and also a normal reflection of industrialization,[21] and state formation.[22] But however normal to a phase, it is also deeply implicated in power relations and conflicts and is prone to problematic manipulation by state elites.[23] And accounts of non-European nation-building have generally assumed a "natural" European model.

These first two lines of theory both emphasize politics and the state and treat nationalism mainly as a feature of the modern era. A third strain of social theory recognizes the role of nationalism in politics and conflict, but stresses also its more positive contributions to the production of culture, the preservation of historical memory, and the formation of group solidarity. Many of the most influential theorists in this group also place much greater stress on the sources of nationalism in ancient ethnicities that provide the basis for identities prior to any specific political mobilization.[24] A related point is that nationalism ought not to be approached only through its most extreme manifestations, but also grasped in its more banal forms – in a variety of ceremonial events, for example, and the organization of athletic competitions.[25] These contribute not only to specific group loyalties but to the reproduction of the general view that the world is organized in terms of nations and national identities.

Here the study of nationalism as a topic of social theory intersects with the more reflexive question of how nationalism has shaped a crucial unit of analysis in social theory, that of society. While "sociality" may be universal to human life, the idea of discrete, bounded, and integrally unitary "societies" is more historically specific. It appears in strong form as one of the characteristic, even definitive, features of the modern era.

This reflects political features – as for example both state control over borders and intensification of state administration internally help to produce the idea of bounded and unified societies,[26] and as arguments for political legitimacy increasingly claim ascent from the people rather than descent from God or inherited office. It also reflects cultural features, though many of these are not ancient inheritances but rather modern inventions or reforms, such as linguistic standardization, common educational systems, museums as vehicles of representation, and the introduction of national media. In one of the most influential studies of nationalism, Benedict Anderson has described it as productive of "imagined communities." By this he means that nations are produced centrally by cultural practices which encourage members to situate their own identities and self-understandings within a nation. Reading the same news, for example, not only provides people with common information, and common images of "us" and "them," but helps to reproduce a collective narrative in which the manifold different events and activities reported fit together like narrative threads in a novel, and interweaves them all with the life of the reader. Practices and institutions of state administration are central to this production of nations as categories of understanding – imagining – but they are not exhaustive of it and those who wield state power do not entirely control it.

To simplify the field, then, we can see four main themes in theories of nationalism (which may be combined in different ways by different authors): (1) nationalism as a source or form of conflict, (2) nationalism as a source or form of political integration, (3) nationalism as a reform and appropriation of ethnic inheritance, (4) nationalism as a new cultural creation. These themes are deployed in debates over "civic" vs. "ethnic" nationalism and over the "modernity" or "primordiality" of nations. But before we turn to debates within the field, we should consider further the underlying problem of nationalism as a source and a shaper of the notion of society itself.

Nationalism and the production of "societies"

Human beings have always lived in groups. The nature of these groups has, however, varied considerably. They range from families and small bands through clans and other larger kin organizations, to villages, kingdoms, and empires; they include religions and cultures, occupational groups and castes, nations, and more recently even global society to the extent it knits all humanity into a single group. In most of these cases, the self-understanding of members is crucial to the existence of the group – a kingdom, a religion, or a caste is both an "objective" collection of people and pattern of social organization and a "subjective" way in which people understand how they belong together and should interact. This is clearly true of the idea of nation. Without the subjective component of self-understanding, nations could not exist. Moreover, once the idea of nation exists, it can be used to organize not just self-understanding but categorizations of others.

The most basic meaning of nationalism is the use of this way of categorizing human populations, both as a way of looking at the world as a whole and as a way of establishing group identity from within.[27] In addition, nationalism usually refers not just to using the category of nation to conceptualize social groups, but also to holding that national identities and groups are of basic importance (and often that loyalty to one's own nation should be a commanding value). Nationalism is thus simultaneously a way of constructing groups and a normative claim. The two sides come together in ideas about who properly belongs together in a society, and in arguments that members have moral obligations to the nation as a whole – perhaps even to kill on its behalf or die for it in a war.

Nationalism, then, is the use of the category "nation" to organize perceptions of basic human identities, grouping people together with fellow nationals and distinguishing them from members of other nations. It is influential as a way of helping to produce solidarity within national categories, as a way of determining how specific groups should be treated (for example, in terms of voting rights or visas and passports), and as a way of seeing the world as a whole. We see this representation in the different colored territories on globes and maps, and in the organization of the United Nations. At the same time, clearly the boundaries of nations are both less fixed and more permeable than nationalists commonly recognize.

Central to nationalist discourse is the idea that there should be a match between a nation and a sovereign state; indeed, the nation (usually understood as prepolitical and always already there in historical terms) constitutes the ground of the legitimacy of the state. This is Kedourie's point in the passage I quoted near the beginning of this chapter. Gellner likewise avers that nationalism is "a political principle, which holds that the political and the national unit should be congruent."[28] Yet, nationalism is not merely a "political principle"; its reproduction is a matter of banal practices (Olympic competitions and holidays, *pace* Billig) and imaginative construction (museums, censuses, and habits of reading, *pace* Anderson) as well as political ideology. Moreover, whether or not ethnicity explains nationalism (or the origins of nations, *pace* Smith), common language and culture facilitate national integration and identification. And whether nationalism was born first as doctrine or less-articulated practices, or indeed born in Europe rather than – say, Spain's American colonies – is also subject to dispute.

A variety of claims are made about what constitute "proper" nations. For example, they are held ideally to have common and distinct territories, common and distinct national cultures (including especially languages), and sovereign states of their own. It is very difficult to define nations in terms of these claims, however, since there are exceptions to almost all of them. To take language as an example, there are both nations whose members speak multiple languages (Switzerland) and languages spoken by members of different nations (Spanish, Portuguese, English). Likewise, nationalist ideologies may hold that all members share distinctive common descent, constituting in effect a large kin group, but this is not definitive of nations in general. Nations are organized at a scale and with an internal diversity of membership that transcends kinship. No definition of nation (or of its correlative terms such as nationalism and nationality) has ever gained general acceptance.[29]

This is why I have argued that nationalism is better understood as a "discursive formation." It is a way of speaking that shapes our consciousness, but also is problematic enough that it keeps generating more issues and questions. As a discursive formation, nationalism is implicated in the widespread if problematic treatment of societies as bounded, integral, wholes with distinctive identities, cultures, and institutions. Charles Tilly has referred to the "pernicious postulate" that societies are bounded and discrete; Brubaker has similarly criticized "groupism"; Brubaker and Cooper have called for a relational approach, by contrast to ideas about clear collective identities; and Mann has argued for seeing social life in terms of multiple and overlapping networks rather than discrete societies.[30] Their critiques have hardly ended the problematic usage, partly because it is so deeply embedded in the way we speak and think. This is not an unmotivated error by social scientists; it is a participation, perhaps unwitting, in the nationalist rhetoric that pervades public life and contemporary culture.

Moreover, something of the same problem has long been apparent in studies of nationalism. Author after author has slipped from showing the artificially constructed and sometimes false character of national self-understandings and histories into suggesting that nations are somehow not real. Traditions may be no less real for being invented, however, or even for incorporating falsehoods. The critique of these claimed histories – and especially claims that they justify contemporary violence

– is important. But it is a sociological misunderstanding to think that the reality of nations depends on the accuracy of their collective self-representations.[31]

Ethnic and civic nationalism

The category of nation has ancient roots. As we have seen, both the term and two of its distinctive modern meanings were in play in the Roman Empire.[32] For the Romans, the term referred to descent groups (usually understood to have common language and culture as well). But the Romans commonly used such ethnic categorizations to designate those who were not Roman citizens. National origins, in this sense, were what differentiated those conquered by or at war with Romans from those fully incorporated into the Roman state, not what Romans claimed as the source of their own unity. But in the very distinction we see two sides of the discourse of nations ever since: first, an attribution of common ethnicity (culture and/or biological descent) and an idea of common membership of a state (citizenship, and more generally respect for laws and standards of behavior, which can be adopted not only inherited).

These two sides to the idea of nation shape an enduring debate over the extent to which a legitimate people should or must be ethnically defined, or can or should be civically constituted and what the implications of each might be. Ethnic nationalist claims, based on race, kinship, language, or common culture, have been widespread throughout the modern era. They sometimes extend beyond the construction of identity to the reproduction of enmity, demands that members place the nation ahead of other loyalties, and attempts to purge territories of those defined as foreign. As a result, ethnic nationalism is often associated with ethnic violence and projects of ethnic cleansing or genocide. However, ethnic solidarity is also seen by many as basic to national identity as such, and thus to the notion of the nation-state. While this notion is as much contested as defended, it remains influential.

In such usage, ethnic nationalism is commonly opposed to civic nationalism. The latter is understood as the loyalty of individual citizens to a state based purely on political identity. The opposition between two "types" of nationalism was formulated most influentially by Hans Kohn.[33] In his and almost all subsequent usage the analytic distinction was embedded in a privileging of the more "liberal" civic variant. This was seen as original while the ethnic was copied; as "Western" while the ethnic was "Eastern"; and as rational while the ethnic was emotional or sentimental. More recently, Jürgen Habermas (among others) has re-theorized civic nationalism as constitutional patriotism. He stresses the extent to which political loyalty may embrace a set of institutional arrangements rather than a prepolitical culture or any other extrapolitical source of solidarity.[34] Ethnic nationalism, conversely, refers precisely to rooting political identity and obligation in the existence of a prepolitical collective unit – the nation – which achieves political subjectivity by virtue of the state. The legitimacy of the state, in turn, is judged by reference to the interests of the nation.

The contrast of ethnic to civic nationalism is heavily influenced by the contrast of Germany to France.[35] Such contrast has been enduring, and has resulted in different understandings of citizenship. France has been much more willing, for example, to use legal mechanisms to grant immigrants French citizenship, while Germany – equally open to immigration in numerical terms – has generally refused its immigrants German citizenship unless they are already ethnic Germans.[36] Other countries vary on the same dimension (and in Europe, the EU is developing a mainly civic, assimilationist legal framework), but it is important to recognize that the difference is one of proportion and ideological emphasis.[37] As Smith has remarked, "all nations bear the impress of both territorial and ethnic principles and components, and represent an uneasy confluence of a more recent 'civic' and a more ancient 'genealogical' model of social cultural organization."[38] Not all scholars accept the distinction or hold it to be sharp; those who do use it often attribute ethnic nationalism to countries that are "late modernizers."[39]

Central to the idea of civic nationalism is the possibility for citizens to adopt national identity by choice. This is most commonly discussed in terms of the assimilation of individual immigrants into nation-states; civic nations can in principle be open to anyone who agrees to follow their laws. Citizenship in the state is seen as primary, rather than prior membership in a descent group or cultural tradition. The distinction is fuzzy, though, as a rhetoric of civic nationalism and citizenship can mask underlying commitments to particularistic cultural or racial definitions of what counts as a "proper" or good citizen. Thus (in a recently prominent example) even law-abiding Muslims may not seem sufficiently French to many, and conversely the French state may pass laws ostensibly enforcing neutrality on religion but in fact expressing particular ethnocultural mores. It is particularly difficult to frame rationales for limits on immigration in civic nationalist terms without falling back on ethnic nationalism.

At the same time, the civic nationalist tradition contains another thread. This is the notion that the nation itself is made, is a product of collective action. This is symbolized by revolutions and the founding of new states (which may include more or less successful efforts to call forth national solidarities). The idea of choice here is not simply that of individual membership, but of collective determination of the form and content of the nation itself – the effort to take control of culture as a historical project rather than merely receiving it as inheritance. When the revolutionary French National Assembly reformed the calendar and systems of measurement, thus, it was engaged not merely in administration of the state but in an effort to make a certain sort of nation – one with a more modern, rational culture. And of course the tension between attempting to make new culture and preserve old has been played out in the educational system ever since.

While much nationalist ideology has claimed definitive ethnic roots, social scientists are divided on the question and most prominent twentieth-century analysts of nationalism have sought to challenge the explanation of nationalism by ethnicity. Kohn and Hugh Seton-Watson stress the crucial role of modern politics, especially the idea of sovereignty.[40] Hobsbawm treats nationalism as a kind of second-order political movement based on a false consciousness which ethnicity helps to produce but cannot explain because the deeper roots lie in political economy not culture.[41] The dominant approach in contemporary scholarship approaches nationalism largely as an ideological reflection of state formation.[42] Gellner emphasizes industrialization, and also stresses the number of cases of failed or absent nationalisms: ethnic groups which mounted either little or no attempt to become nations in the modern senses.[43] This suggests that even if ethnicity plays a role it cannot be a sufficient explanation (though one imagines the nineteenth-century German Romantics would simply reply that there are strong, historic nations and weak ones destined to fade from the historic stage). Hayes argues for seeing nationalism as a sort of religion.[44] Hechter analyzes it in terms of strategic individual action aimed at maximizing mostly economic and political benefits.[45] Kedourie approaches nationalism as an ideology, and attempts to debunk nationalism by showing the untenability of the German Romantic cultural-ethnic claims.[46] Indeed, in their different ways, all these thinkers have sought to debunk the common claims nationalists themselves make to long-established ethnic identities.

Against this backdrop, Smith acknowledges that nations cannot be seen as primordial or natural, but nonetheless argues that they are rooted in relatively ancient histories. Smith argues that the origins of modern nationalism lie in the successful bureaucratization of aristocratic ethnie, which were able to transform themselves into genuine nations only in the West. In the West, territorial centralization and consolidation went hand in hand with a growing cultural standardization. Nations, Smith thus suggests, are long-term processes, continually re-enacted and reconstructed; they require ethnic cores, homelands, heroes and golden ages if they are to survive. "Modern nations and nationalism have only extended and deepened the meanings and scope of older ethnic concepts and structures. Nationalism has certainly universalized these structures and ideals, but modern 'civic' nations have not in practice really transcended ethnicity or ethnic sentiments."[47]

The ethnic similarities and bonds that contribute to the formation of nations may indeed be important and long standing, but in themselves they do not fully constitute either particular nations or the modern idea of nation. While some critics of ethnic explanations of nationalism emphasize the influence of state formation or other "master variables," a number assert that nations are created by nationalism – by this particular form of discourse, political rhetoric, or ideology – not merely passively present and awaiting the contingent address of nationalists.[48]

An emphasis on pre-existing ethnicity – even where this is rightly identified – is unable to shed much light on why so many modern movements, policies, ideologies, and conflicts are constituted within the discourse of nationalism. Indeed, as Gellner has suggested, the very self-recognition of ethnicities or cultures as defining identities is distinctively modern.[49] Walker Connor uses a similar point (ironically reversing the Roman roots of the term) to distinguish ethnic groups as "potential nations" from real nations: "While an ethnic group may, therefore, be other-defined, the nation must be self-defined."[50]

Explanations of nationalism, thus, need to address the contemporary conditions that make it effective in people's lives, their attempts to orient themselves in the world, and their actions. Such conditions are of course subject to change and nationalist constructions are apt to change with them. Thus Indian nationalists from the nineteenth century through Nehru were able to make a meaningful (though hardly seamless or uncontested) unity of the welter of subcontinental identities as part of their struggle against the British.[51] The departure of the British from India changed the meaning of Congress nationalism, however, as this became the program of an Indian state, not of those outside official politics who resisted an alien regime. Among other effects of this, a rhetorical space was opened up for "communal" and other sectional claims that were less readily brought forward in the colonial period.[52] Similarly, the proliferation of nationalisms in Eastern Europe attendant on the collapse of communist rule involved a "reframing" of older national identities and nationalist projects; the nationalisms of the 1990s were neither altogether new nor simply resumptions of those that pre-dated communism.[53] The opposition between primordiality and "mere invention" leaves open a very wide range of historicities within which national and other traditions can exert real force. As Renan famously stressed, nationalist histories are matters of forgetting as well as remembering, including forgetting the "deeds of violence which took place at the origin of all political formations."[54] At the same time, not least because academics commonly devote a good deal of energy to debunking popular nationalism, it is important to recall not only the deeds of violence but the cultural productivity that goes into nationalism – the symphonies and tangos, films and poetry.

Nationalism is partly a matter of narrative construction, the production (and reproduction and revision) of narratives locating the nation's place in history.[55] As Anderson puts it, nations move through historical time as persons move through biographical time; each may figure in stories like characters in a novel.[56] This is one reason why the continuity of ethnic identities alone does not adequately explain nationalism: the narrative constructions in which it is cast change and potentially transform the meaning of whatever ethnic commonalties may exist. Ironically, the writing of linear historical narratives of national development and claims to primordial national identity often proceed hand in hand. Indeed, the writing of national historical narratives is so embedded in the discourse of nationalism that it almost always depends rhetorically on the presumption of some kind of pre-existing national identity in order to give the story a beginning. A claim to primordial national identity is, in fact, a version of nationalist historical narrative.

Modernity vs. primordiality

A long-running debate in the literature on nationalism pits arguments that it is an extension of ancient ethnicity[57] against those who argue that it is essentially modern.[58] Majority scholarly opinion tends toward the latter view, though explanations differ. "Modernists" variously see nationalism rooted in industrialization,[59] state formation,[60] the rise of new communications media and genres of collective imagination,[61] and the development of new rhetorics for collective identity and capacities for collective action.[62] While many favor specific factors as primary explanations, most recognize that several causes are interrelated.

Many nationalists but few scholars see nationalism as ubiquitous in history and simply the "normal" way of organizing large-scale collective identity. Most social scientists point rather to the variety of political and cultural forms common before the modern era – empires and great religions, for example – and the transformations wrought by the rise of a new kind of intensive state administration, cultural integration, popular political participation, and international relations. Many of these social scientists argue that nations and nationalism in their modern sense are both new. In particular, they would argue that ethnicity as a way of organizing collective identity underwent at the least a substantial reorganization when it began to be deployed as part of ethnonationalist rhetoric in the modern era. Others, however, including notably Anthony

Smith and John Armstrong argue that there is more continuity in the ethnic core of nations, though they too would agree that modernity transformed – if it did not outright create – nationalism.[63]

The attraction of a claimed ethnic foundation to nations lies largely in the implication that nationhood is in some sense primordial and natural. Nationalists typically claim that their nations are simply given and immutable rather than constructions of recent historical action or tendentious contemporary claims. Much early scholarly writing on nations and nationalism shared in this view and sought to discover which were the "true" ethnic foundations of nationhood.[64] It is no doubt ideologically effective to claim that a nation has existed since time immemorial or that its traditions have been passed down intact from heroic founders. In no case, however, does historical or social science research support such a claim. All nations are historically created.

Noting this, one line of research emphasizes the manipulation of popular sentiments by the more or less cynical production of national culture by intellectuals and state-building elites. Hobsbawm and Ranger, for example, have collected numerous examples of the ways in which apparently definitive cultural markers of national identity can in fact be traced to specific acts of creation embedded in political (or sometimes marketing) projects rather than reflecting pre-existing ethnicity.[65] The Scots tartan kilt is a famous example, dating not from the mists of primordial Highland history but from eighteenth-century resistance to Anglicization and early nineteenth-century Romantic celebrations of a no longer troubling ethnic Scottishness.[66] Likewise, nineteenth-century Serbian and Croatian intellectuals strove to divide their common Serbo-Croatian language into two distinct vernaculars with separate literary traditions. But as this example makes clear, it is not obvious that because the "traditions" of nationalism are "invented" they are somehow less real or valid. Anderson finds the same fault with Gellner: "Gellner is so anxious to show that nationalism masquerades under false pretences that he assimilates 'invention' to 'fabrication' and 'falsity', rather than to 'imagining' and 'creation'."[67]

Hobsbawm and Ranger imply that long-standing, "primordial" tradition would somehow count as legitimate, while by contrast various nationalist traditions are of recent and perhaps manipulative creation. Many ideologues do claim origins at the dawn of history, but few scholars have doubted that cultural traditions are constantly renewed. What so-called "primordialists" have argued is that certain identities and traditions – especially those of ethnicity – are experienced as primordial.[68] Sociologically, thus, what matters is less the antiquity of the contents of tradition, than the efficacy of the process by which certain beliefs and understandings are constituted as unquestioned, immediate knowledge. This has more to do with current bases for the reproduction of culture than with history as such. Tradition, thus, needs to be distinguished from the "traditionalism" of those who claim to be its authoritative representatives, and who – especially in contexts of literacy and record-keeping – often enforce an orthodoxy foreign to oral tradition.[69]

Ethnicity or cultural traditions are bases for nationalism because they effectively constitute historical memory, because they inculcate it as "prejudice," not because the historical origins they claim are accurate (prejudice means, following Gadamer, not just prior to judgment, but constituting the condition of judgment[70]). Moreover, all traditions are "invented" (or at least in a more diffuse sense, created); none is truly primordial. This was acknowledged, though rather weakly, even by some of the functionalists who emphasized the notion of primordiality and the "givenness" of cultural identities and traditions.[71] All such traditions also are potentially contested and subject to continual reshaping, whether explicit or hidden. Some claims about nationality may fail to persuade because they are too manifestly manipulated by creators, or because the myth that is being proffered does not speak to the circumstances and practical commitments of the people in question.

Notions of nations as acting subjects are distinctively modern, part of a new way of constructing collective identity.[72] The idea of nation became a fundamental building block of social life during the early modern period, especially the eighteenth and nineteenth centuries. This said, there is no scholarly agreement about when modern nationalism began. Greenfeld dates it from the English Civil War, Anderson from Latin American independence movements, Alter from the French Revolution, and Breuilly and Kedourie both from German Romanticism and reaction to the French Revolution.[73] I have suggested that rather than trying to identify a single point of origin, scholars should see nationalism as drawing together several different threads of historical change.[74] As a discursive formation, it took on increasingly clear form through the early modern period and was fully in play by the Napoleonic era. While it is fruitless to search for a precise origin point for modern nationalism, it is possible to identify some of the social changes and conditions that helped to make it important.

Conclusion

First, nationalism reflected a distinctive scale of social organization, larger than cities (which in their hinterlands had previously been primary units of belonging and common culture for elites), villages, or kin groups. This was made possible partly by improved communication that enabled larger populations to interact with greater density – a matter simultaneously of roads, the spread of literacy, and wars that brought large populations together in common military organization and movements.[75] It was also facilitated by increased integration of trade among different regions within contiguous territories, and by the mobilization of new kinds of military and state power.[76]

Second, nationalism constituted a new ideology about primary identities. In this it competed not only with localism and family, but with religion.[77] In fact, nationalism was often furthered by religious movements and wars – notably in the wake of the Reformation – and national self-understandings were frequently religiously inflected (as in the Catholicism of Poland or the Protestantism of England). But nationalism involved a kind of secular faith, and a primary loyalty to the nation that was and is distinct from any religion that may intertwine with it.

Third, nationalism grew hand in hand with modern states and was basic to a new way of claiming political legitimacy. States furthered social integration among their subjects by building roads, mobilizing militaries, sponsoring education, and standardizing languages.[78] But they also were shaped by a cultural change which introduced a new, stronger idea of "the people" who were both governed by and served by a state. Indeed, the idea of the state as providing necessary services for the "commonwealth" was basic, and with it came the notion that the legitimacy of the state depended on its serving its people effectively and/or being recognized by them. Political legitimacy was to "ascend" from the people rather than descend from God or proper dynastic ancestry. This placed a new stress on the question of who the people might be. The notions that they were those who happened to have been born into the domain of a monarch, or conquered in war, were clearly inadequate. The idea of nation came to the forefront. It represented the "people" of a country as an internally unified group with common interests and the capacity to act.

The last point is crucial. The idea of nation not only laid claim to history or common identity. It purported to describe (or construct) a collective actor. As Charles Taylor has put it, statements like "We the people," as articulated in the United States Constitution, are performative, they put in play a strong claim to cohesion and capacity to act in concert.[79] Similarly, the *levée en masse* of the French Revolution symbolized the capacity of the people not merely to act but to shape history.[80]

The constitution of nations – not only in dramatic revolutionary acts of founding, but in the formation of common culture and political identities – is one of the pivotal features of the modern era. It is part of the organization of political participation and loyalty, of culture and identity, of the way history is taught and the way wars are fought. It not only shapes practical political identity and ideology, it also shapes the very idea of society in which much social theory is rooted. If nations are obsolete, this will matter a lot. But however troubled and troubling the national organization of politics is, I don't think there is much evidence nations are fading from the global scene.

3

Nationalism and ethnicity

Neither nationalism nor ethnicity is vanishing as part of an obsolete traditional order. Both are part of a modern set of categorical identities invoked by elites and other participants in political and social struggles. These categorical identities also shape everyday life, offering both tools for grasping pre-existing homogeneity and difference and for construct- ing specific versions of such identities. While it is impossible to dissociate nationalism entirely from ethnicity, it is equally impossible to explain it simply as a continuation of ethnicity or a simple reflection of common history or language. Numerous dimensions of modern social and cul- tural change, notably state-building (along with war and colonialism), individualism, and the integration of large-scale webs of indirect rela- tionships also serve to make both nationalism and ethnicity salient. Nationalism, in particular, remains the preeminent rhetoric for attempts to demarcate political communities, claim rights of self-determination and legitimate rule by reference to "the people" of a country. Ethnic solidarities and identities are claimed most often where groups do not seek "national" autonomy but rather a recognition internal to or cross- cutting national or state boundaries. The possibility of a closer link to nationalism is seldom altogether absent from such ethnic claims, how- ever, and the two sorts of categorical identities are often invoked in similar ways.

Introduction

One of the uglier ways in which nationalism gained popular and aca- demic attention in the early 1990s was the Serbian program of "ethnic cleansing." Promulgated by a psychiatrist (Radovan Karadzic) and other academically trained representatives of modern science, this policy helped to demonstrate that the nationalist upheavals and ethnic vio- lence that followed the collapse of Soviet-style communism were not simply throwbacks to some premodern reign of passion, sentiment, and primordial identity. The policy of "ethnic cleansing," like all of national-ism and ethnic politics, depended on social constructions of identity, mobilized members of the chosen ethnic group only unevenly, and served the interests of some participants far more than others. It forced many Serbs who had previously allied themselves with the vision of a multiethnic, democratic Bosnia-Herzegovina to resort to ethnic soli-darities in the face of civil war. Claiming these ethnic solidarities and the identity of Serbs as both ancient and seemingly "natural," the new ideo-logical mobilization successfully demanded that its adherents be willing both to kill and to die for their nation.

If there were any doubt about the importance of the claimed link between ethnicity and national self-determination, the fighting in what was once Yugoslavia should have dispelled it. The Yugoslav conflicts, moreover, stemmed in part from the very nationalities policy employed by the country's former Communist government, which both recognized subordinate nationalities and ethnic groups and drew state lines that intentionally cross-cut ethnic and national residential patterns.[1] Neither ethnic conflicts, nor the discourse of national identity, nor the practical power of nationalist mobilizations has receded into the premodern past despite the confidence of many earlier social scientists (an embarrass-ment especially for Marxists[2]). At the same time, the idea of the nation remains central to most attempts to define legitimate political com-munities.[3] A central theme in this discourse is the question of the extent to which nationalism should be understood as a continuation of long-standing patterns of ethnicity, or as something distinctively new and modern. This is the focus of the present review.[4]

The modernity of nationalism

The discourse of nationalism is distinctively modern. It is variously argued to have originated in the seventeenth-century British rebellion against monarchy,[5] the eighteenth-century struggles of New World elites against Iberian colonialism,[6] the French Revolution of 1789,[7] and the German reaction to that revolution and to German disunity.[8] But as Best puts it:

> Historians of nationalism agree to differ in their estimates of how much of it (and what sorts of it) already existed in the Atlantic world of 1785. They are at one in recognizing that that world by 1815 was full of it, and that although each national variety had of course its strong characteristics, those varieties had enough in common for it to constitute the most momentous phenomenon of modern history.[9]

In the early modern era the idea of nation as an aggregate of people linked by co-residence or common sociocultural characteristics took political and cultural connotations in struggles with and between states and over state-building. This led to the distinctively modern invocation of nationalism as "a theory of political legitimacy, which requires that ethnic boundaries should not cut across political ones, and, in particular, that ethnic boundaries within a given state – a contingency already excluded by the principle in its general formulation – should not separate the power-holders from the rest."[10] As Kedourie summed up a generation before, the discourse of nationalism typically offers three propositions: "that humanity is naturally divided into nations, that nations are known by certain characteristics which can be ascertained, and that the only legitimate type of government is national self-government."[11]

Nationalism has become the preeminent discursive form for modern claims to political autonomy and self-determination. The term was apparently coined in German by the philosopher Herder and in French by the Abbé Barruel just less than 200 years ago.[12] It was linked to the concept of nation-state in the notorious formulations of Woodrow Wilson and the League of Nations.[13]

In the wake of communism's collapse, nationalism and ethnic conflict appeared as the primary issues in the realignment of Eastern European politics and identity.[14] Indeed, in many instances communist governments had been actively involved in nationalist mobilization themselves, in varying degrees cynically and idealistically.[15] Appeals to the idea of nation also organize movements of ethnic separatism from Quebec[16] to the postcolonial states of Africa.[17] Nationalism is equally prominent in movements to integrate disparate polities, as in twentieth-century Arab nationalism[18] and nineteenth-century German nationalism before it.[19] New nationalisms proliferate throughout the developed West,[20] and attempts are made to decolonize the discourse of nationalism in the Third World and claim it for indigenous movements and meanings.[21] In East Asia, nationalism has throughout the twentieth century been the rhetoric not only of anti-imperialist struggles but of calls for strengthening and democratizing states from within.[22] Nationalism is anything but a thing of the past, thus, and even the newest claims to nationalism are often rooted in a rhetoric of pre-existing ethnicity.

Nationalism as discourse

Yet, despite this agreement about the contemporary salience of the discourse of nationalism, Hobsbawm makes a sharply contentious assertion when he writes "the basic characteristic of the modern nation and everything connected with it is its modernity."[23] Even the repetition of the term modern in both subject and predicate of his sentence does not save it from controversy, for Hobsbawm is arguing against a widespread view of both academics and nationalists themselves. This is the view that modern nations are based on ethnic identities that are in some sense ancient, primordial, possibly even natural or at least prior to any particular political mobilization. A great deal is at stake in this argument. Most crucially, can "nationhood" be taken as the prior basis for nationalist claims? Is self-determination, for example, a political right to be accorded all "true" nations, as the apostles of nationalism asserted in the mid-nineteenth-century "Springtime of the Peoples"?[24] Are Serbs intrinsically a nation, to revert to our opening example, such that any claims of multiethnic Bosnia-Herzegovina to include large Serbian populations are infringements on the rights of the Serbian nation? Or, is "nation" at best a rhetorical mode of making political claims, and at worst a way for certain elites to manipulate mass sentiments in pursuit of power? In more academic terms, does the prior existence of ethnicity explain nationhood, and does nationhood explain nationalism? Or is the notion of membership in a common nation (and perhaps even in an ethnic group) a product of nationalist (or ethnic) mobilization? Is nationalism simply a derivative result of state formation and other "material" aspects of modernization, or is it one of the primary constituents of modernity?

This issue is hard to keep entirely clear in our minds because most variants of nationalist rhetoric claim the nation as an always already existing basis for action, whether as the continuation of ancient ethnicity or as the result of historically specific acts of foundation. As moderns we are all participants in the discourse of nations whether we like it or not. Many of the categories and presumptions of this discourse are so deeply ingrained in our everyday language and our academic theories that it is virtually impossible to shed them, and we can only remind ourselves continuously to take them into account. A simple example is the assumption that "society" is a noun referring to self-sufficient units with clear boundaries. Tilly makes this the first of his "eight Pernicious Postulates of twentieth-century social thought": "Society" is a thing apart; the world as a whole divides into distinct "societies, each having its more or less autonomous culture, government, economy, and solidarity."[25]

This is a usage produced by the discourse and political salience of the modern idea of nation (and specifically its hyphenated conjunction with "state"). As Halle put it, "perhaps the idea alone can give the community the singleness and integrity which we attribute to it when we think of it as a corporate person."[26] In fact, societies have not always been and are not everywhere equally bounded, nor is it clear that they are as bounded in the archetypal cases of modern nation-states – e.g. France – as ordinary language (including ordinary sociological language) implies.[27] Even island Britain manifests a complex history and present struggle over external as well as internal boundaries.[28]

Given the multiple and overlapping networks of our social relations,[29] and given the large-scale international flows of our ideas, language, and cultural productions,[30] it should perhaps be a matter of principle to avoid using terms like society as though they referred to unitary, clearly demarcated objects. But this would be an extremely difficult principle to live up to. However sincere our intention to speak only of more or less consolidated patterns of social organization, more or less overlapping and densely integrated networks of social relations, more or less homogeneous cultural forms and contents, etc., we should soon be driven to speak both in proper nouns of Indians and Germans, Koreans and Kenyans, and in common nouns of societies or peoples. We live in a world-system which is organized into states and which thematizes certain cultural differences as constituting "cultures," while others are suppressed as unimportant internal or cross-cutting variations. This world-system makes both nationalism and claims to ethnic identity as problematic as they are imperative, even while it makes it hard to escape enough from the power of received categories to understand why they are problematic.

This is one reason why "nationalism" and corollary terms like "nation" have proved notoriously hard concepts to define.[31] The notion of nation is so deeply imbricated in modern politics as to be "essentially contested" (in Gallie's phrase), because any definition will legitimate some claims and delegitimate others. It also reflects more general problems with essentialist definitions.[32] Nation and nationalism are among those terms used to refer not to any clearly definable set, the members of which all share some common features which nonmembers lack, but rather to a cluster of "family resemblances" (in Wittgenstein's term). All of the available essentialist definitions are unstable and inherently contestable, thus, not only because they bias usage for or against various political claims, but because they are based either (i) on qualities which putative nations or nationalist movements share with admitted non-nations (such as ethnicity), or (ii) on qualities which are not clearly shared among all recognized members of the set of nations (like control over or ambition to control a state).

Though nationalisms are extremely varied phenomena, they are joined by common involvement in the modern discourse of nationalism. They are common objects of reference in international law, political debate, and even economic development programs. As Anderson has stressed, once the idea of imagining political communities as nations was developed, it was "modular" and could be transplanted into a wide range of otherwise disparate settings.[33] This is what raises the issue of whether Third World or postcolonial nationalisms express "authentic" indigenous concerns or are in some sense derivative discourses.[34] The discourse of nationalism is inherently international. Claims to nationhood are not just internal claims to social solidarity, common descent, or any other basis for constituting a political community; they are also claims to distinctiveness vis-à-vis other nations, claims to at least some level of autonomy and self-sufficiency, and claims to certain rights within a world-system of states.[35] In other words, however varied the internal nature of nationalisms, they share a common external frame of reference. Thus, even if nationalist claims to primordial origins, ancient ethnic pedigrees, or hallowed founding histories were all true, thus, and even if every nation had premodern roots (something manifestly impossible in the case of such settler societies such as the United States, Australia, or South Africa – at least as defined by their European populations), nationalism would still be a modern phenomenon. This is true even of "extreme" forms such as National Socialism, despite the tendency of modernization theorists and others to treat Nazism as a throwback to the premodern[36] rather than a problem of modernity.[37] Indeed, this phenomenon of claiming state-centered political rights on the basis of nationhood is arguably one of the defining phenomena of modernity.

The centrality of states

Those who argue for the priority of nations over nationalism seldom dispute the distinctiveness or centrality of modern states.[38] They would follow Tilly's summary, for example, in distinguishing empires, city-states, and other early formations from "states governing multiple contiguous regions and their cities by means of centralized, differentiated, and autonomous structures."[39] Debate centers on whether nationalism is a by-product of the creation of these states – and accordingly likely to disappear as they are transformed in the present era.[40] As Tilly develops his argument about the distinctive character of modern states, he stresses the consolidation of centralized administrative power, the development of capacities to mobilize otherwise civilian populations (and material resources such as industry) for interstate warfare, and the partitioning of the world into comparable states. These tendencies tie the politics and social organization of such states firmly to the modern era. Ambiguity arises only with regard to the role of culture, and more generally the claim of such states to be "national," or of various "peoples" without states to deserve such "national" states as a matter of right. Tilly suggests that we simply distinguish "national state" from "nation-state," restricting the latter term to those states "whose people share a strong linguistic, religious, or symbolic identity."[41] National states (though Tilly does not define the term) appear to be those which attempt to extend direct rule to their entire populations and expand their capacity to organize the lives of the members of those populations, whether for purposes of warfare or economic development. They are "national" by virtue of their attempt to integrate large populations and territories, and by contrast mainly to city-states (that do not fully integrate their hinterlands) and empires (that do not attempt to integrate or closely monitor the everyday affairs of those they rule).

As direct rule expanded throughout Europe, the welfare, culture, and daily routines of ordinary Europeans came to depend as never before on which state they happened to reside in. Internally, states undertook to impose national languages, national educational systems, national military service, and much more. Externally, they began to control movement across frontiers, to use tariffs and customs as instruments of economic policy, and to treat foreigners as distinctive kinds of people deserving limited rights and close surveillance. As states invested not only in war and public services but also in economic infrastructure, their economies came to have distinctive characteristics, which once again differentiated the experiences of living in adjacent states. To that degree, life homogenized within states and heterogenized among states.[42]

State-building produced a basic discontinuity with earlier forms of social organization.[43] At the same time, capitalist economic development knit together large-scale markets and transformed the units of economic activity and interest.[44] Tilly shifts emphasis away from culture but does not break sharply with the developmental narrative of older moderniza-tion theory.[45] This older modernization theory operated with a tension between its assumption of nation-states as basic units of modern politi-cal economy and its treatment of all "undesirable" forms of nationalism as merely inherited from previous eras, a sort of survival that could be expected to wane or moderate into acceptable patriotism in the long run even if it contributed to short-term eruptions every now and again.[46] Modernization theory thus predicted that when outlying regions were incorporated into a social system they would gradually be "homogen-ized" into cultural similarity with the rest of the system, nationalism centered on the encompassing state would grow, and contrary ethnic mobilization would be transitory. Researchers emphasizing capitalist economics more than state development often broke more sharply with modernization theory.[47] Thus Hechter attempted to show how ethnic mobilizations in Britain's Celtic periphery were precisely the result of incorporation into British political economy, but incorporation in a dis-advantaged position.[48] Hechter's account focuses primarily on how economic factors provoked ethnic mobilization; it offered much less account of why ethnic identity was salient. This led Smith to accuse

Hechter of economic reductionism.[49] The account of nationalism as a peripheral response to core expansion at best helps to explain levels of resentment and mobilization. It does not address the constitution of national identity or the modern conditions of its reproduction.[50]

The more materialist and state-centered view, moreover, carries a strong tendency to see not only nationalism but nationhood as basically following from rather than shaping the rise of European modernity. Nations are, in this view, produced by the rise of states (and/or the capitalist world-system). As Giddens puts it:

> By a "nation" I refer to a collectivity existing within a clearly demarcated territory, which is subject to a unitary administration, reflexively monitored both by the internal state apparatus and those of other states. . . . A "nation", as I use the term here, only exists when a state has a unified administrative reach over the territory over which its sovereignty is claimed.[51]

In such a usage, the relationship between nationalism and ethnicity is more or less coincidental. It is the modern state that defines nationhood, and pre-existing ethnic relations are revised either to coincide more or less with its boundaries or to constitute the basis of counter-state movements for the formation of new states. Such movements are rooted in power relations, not ethnic solidarities and distinctions per se.

Giddens and especially Tilly associate cultural accounts of nationalism with explanations in terms of pre-existing ethnic solidarities and differences. Gellner, by contrast, analyzes nationalism as a cultural phenomenon dependent not only on state formation and industrial society, but also on certain transformations of culture, such as the creation of "high cultures" and their changing relations with popular or folk cultures, and the imbrication of all particular cultures within a putatively context-free space of cross-cultural communication.[52] At the same time, he is clear in arguing that nationalism is distinctively modern and that it is not strictly the result of prior ethnicity:

> nationalism is not the awakening and assertion of these mythical, supposedly natural and given units. It is, on the contrary, the crystallization of new units, suitable for the conditions now prevailing, though admittedly using as their raw material the cultural, historical and other inheritances from the pre-nationalist world.[53]

Gellner holds that "nationalism . . . engenders nations, and not the other way round."[54] Similarly, Hroch (1985) argues that nationalism arose from activities of cultural elites seeking histories and constituted the identities of nations without necessarily giving those identities any immediate political purpose; once established, such nationalist claims were available for politicization by cross-class groups.[55]

The state-centered approach, in sum, clarifies one dimension of nationalism but obscures others. In particular, it (i) makes it hard to understand why national identity can stir the passions it does, and (ii) encourages analysts either to ignore ethnic and other identities that do not coincide with states or to treat them as somehow naturally given.

Ethnicity and history

A good deal is left unaddressed by analyses that rely on states or markets as material "bases" to explain the cultural "superstructures" of nationalism. This is a thinner approach, for example, than stressing "the interaction of two orders of concrete experience, that of everyday life and that of relations with the state," each crucial to the construction of the contrasting figures of citizen and foreigner.[56] Similarly, many approaches to these issues emphasize the constitution of a social realm (or "civil society") separate enough from the state that state–society relationships might become the focus of attention and even of disputes over legitimacy.[57] Accounts that proceed in an exclusively state-centered way are also apt to underestimate the many changes in patterns of culture that preceded and paved the way for nationalism (prominent themes in the older historiography of Kohn, Hayes, Meinecke, and Kedourie[58]). The Protestant Reformation, for example, was crucial as it replaced the universalistic notion of Christendom with local and regional variants of the common faith, mobilized popular participation, promulgated vernacular discourse and printed texts, and invoked the theological (and in some Calvinist variants political) sovereignty of the people against Church and monarchs).[59]

Later depoliticization of religion was, in turn, both an important concomitant of state-building and an autonomously significant trend. In Switzerland, for example, long-standing religious divisions were replaced by linguistic ones in the wake of mid-nineteenth-century revolutionary upheavals and nationalism. As late as 1848, Catholic territories made Protestantism unlawful (and vice versa). In the older regime, language was a matter of voluntary personal choice with little political significance. After the mid-century, the pattern was reversed. Territories were divided on linguistic lines and religion was a matter of personal preference with markedly reduced political consequence.[60] At the very least, state-centered and economy-centered accounts need cultural complements to deal with variation in the forms of nationalism.

The older modernization theories generally saw nationalism as a functional substitute for local communities, religions, and other sources of identity and security that were necessarily disrupted by the larger-scale, greater individualism, and more rapid social change of modernity.[61] Identification of individuals with the nation (rather than tribe or other section) was a functional need to be achieved in the course of modernization.[62] Such treatments owe a great deal to binary models of social change like Durkheim's account of the transition from mechanical to organic solidarity.[63] Haas puts forward a similar argument drawing on Weber and Toennies:

> The nation is a synthetic *Gemeinschaft*. In the mass setting of modern times, it furnishes the vicarious satisfaction of needs that have previously been met by the warmth of small, traditional, face-to-face social relations. As social life has been transformed by industrialization and social mobilization into something resembling a *Gesellschaft* based on interest calculations, the nation and nationalism continue to provide the integrative cement that gives the appearance of community.[64]

Nationalism is of interest to Haas solely as part of a process of rationalization.[65]

The implicit message of such theories is that attempts to maintain ethnic autonomy vis-à-vis the state is reactionary and anti-modern; nationalism is bad when it is like ethnicity, but good when it is tied to a modernizing state. Indeed, for both state elites and modernization theorists, ethnic groups are defined in relation to the nation-state as subordinate internal and/or cross-cutting identities: Jews, Transylvanians, Tibetans, Ibo. The distinction between nation and mere ethnic group is precisely the attribution to the former of the right to an autonomous state, or at least an autonomy of some sort within the state. On such an account it doesn't matter whether the nation is an ethnic group that has proved its superiority in historical struggle (material or ideological), or a multiethnic population.

Origin myths

Nationalisms vary, thus, between claims to have superseded traditional identities such as ethnicity by the founding of a true and modern nation, and claims to national identity and sovereignty rooted precisely in ancient ethnicity. The paradigmatic contrast of these two forms in the literature on nationalism is that between France and Germany. In both cases, historical narratives are mobilized to underpin the nationalist myths. The French narrative traces the nation to a modern act of founding by its members, people who were not constituted properly as French (rather than Provencal or Bearnaise, Protestant or Catholic) until that radically novel founding. It emphasizes the nation-making political form of the republic and the idea of citizenship.[66] In Germany, nationalist history-writing pushes further back in pursuit of a "naturalizing" account of German ethnicity; Germany must be rooted in an "always already existing" ethnic identity. German nationalists from Herder and Fichte forward have emphasized ethnic rather than "political" or "civic" criteria for inclusion in the nation.[67] When Renan described the nation as a "daily plebiscite," thus, he was not making a universalizing statement or offering a definition;[68] he was distinguishing those nations (such as France) that are the result of the free choices of their members from those (such as Germany) whose identity and cohesion are given to their members independently of any voluntary will. Such differences in nationalist narratives have practical consequences. Since voluntary will is so crucial to the narrative of French nationalism, for example, France makes it easier than Germany does for immigrants to attain citizenship (even though immigration itself, and right of legal residency, is no easier).[69]

There are many rhetorical attractions for nationalists to claim that their nations are simply given and immutable (i.e. ethnic) rather than constructions of recent historical action or tendentious contemporary claims. First and foremost, this claim "naturalizes" nationhood, and seems to leave third parties with the choice between recognizing a "natural" human identity or denying it and possibly even condoning its "genocide" (a neologism that reveals the specifically modern nature of this problem[70]). Where it is recognized that a nation has a founding moment, it is still attractive to see this as a consequence not merely of choice, but of a long narrative of historical development that historically locates the proto-nation in primordial times. Much early scholarly writing on nations and nationalism worked within this rhetoric and sought to discover which were the "true" ethnic foundations of nationhood.[71]

The contrasting rhetoric is tied both to ideas of popular sovereignty and to modernist (or Enlightenment) opposition to tradition. The claim to voluntary historical foundation (e.g. in US and French nationalist narratives) is a claim to the liberation of individuals both from illegitimate domination and from unreasoning acceptance of mere tradition. This rhetoric of liberating rationality thus assumes (though with opposite evaluation) the same idea of tradition as ancient, unquestioned inheritance as does the narrative of naturalizing primordiality. This is a problematic understanding of tradition and hence of ethnicity.

As ideology, it is no doubt effective to claim that a nation has existed since time immemorial or that its traditions have been passed down intact from heroic founders. Sociologically, however, what matters is not the antiquity of the contents of tradition, but the efficacy of the process by which tradition constitutes certain beliefs and understandings as unquestioned, immediate knowledge, as the basis for disputing or questioning other claims.[72] The focus is not simply on continuity, but on the reproduction of culture, the process of passing on that is the literal meaning of tradition.[73] What is reproduced is not simply content, but a "habitus" or orientation to social action.[74] Ethnicity or cultural traditions are bases for nationalism when they effectively constitute historical memory, when they inculcate it as habitus, or as "prejudice" (in Gadamer's sense of a precondition to judgment[75]), not when (or because) the historical origins they claim are accurate.

Weber expressed this common view in defining a traditional orientation as respect for that which has always existed, thereby suggesting that such an orientation must vanish in the face of modernity with its incessant social change.[76] Such a view provides for easy inversion: whenever traditions can be shown to be created and/or recent, they must be false. This is the implication of Hobsbawm and Ranger's treatment of nationalism, in which they argue that because the "traditions" of nationalism are "invented" they are somehow less real and valid.[77] But it is not clear why this should be so. Hobsbawm and Ranger seem to accept the notion that long-standing, "primordial" tradition would somehow count as legitimate, and therefore that illegitimacy follows from their demonstration that various nationalist traditions are of recent and perhaps manipulative creation. This seems doubly fallacious.

First, all traditions are "created," none is truly primordial. This was acknowledged, though rather weakly, even by some of the functionalists who emphasized the notion of (constructed) primordiality and the "givenness" of cultural identities and traditions.[78] Second, all traditions are internally contested and subject to continual reshaping, whether explicit or hidden. Potential lineage headmen argue over their status in terms of different narratives of descent and ancestral authority.[79] Similarly, as Leach and Barth and his colleagues have argued, ethnic identity is constituted, maintained, and invoked in social processes that involve diverse intentions, constructions of meaning, and conflicts.[80] Not only are there claims from competing possible collective allegiances, there are competing claims as to just what any particular ethnic or other identity means. Dispute by no means always undermines traditional identities. Ethnicity is a rhetorical frame within which certain disputes are conducted; participation in the disputes can actually reproduce ethnic understandings (changed or unchanged). There is a difference, thus, between disputes that challenge particular constructions of ethnic identity (or other aspects of tradition) and those that challenge the meaningfulness of ethnic identity as such.

In this context, the difference between the claims of nationhood and subordinate ethnicity need not be great.[81] Thus "nationalism" is identified with the state in both India and Africa, while "communalism" and "tribalism" are seen as divisive "ethnic" identities. Generally speaking, Nehru (and Indian predecessors back to the early nineteenth century) was more successful at invoking, claiming and/or creating a common sense of national identity than were most of his African counterparts. This was in part because of differences in the integration of precolonial "India" and the various colonial African states. But India too was in part a colonial creation, and the claim of national unity was developed in relation to British colonization (indeed, the length and intensity of British colonization may be as important a factor as precolonial history). In writing his popular history, *The Discovery of India*, Nehru was giving historical depth to a nationalist narrative that had as its other crucial base the more "modern" struggle against the British.[82] Indian nationalists thus attempted to appropriate both the rationalist rhetoric of liberation and the claim of deep ethnic history, tradition almost to the point of primordiality. In this attempt, they shared much with many anti- and postcolonial nationalisms. So long as the British ruled in India, the project of nurturing a sense of ethnic nationhood was facilitated by the contrast with the obviously crucial colonial "other." The departure of the British from India changed the meaning of Congress nationalism, however, as this became the program of an Indian state, not of those outside official politics and resisting an alien regime. Among other effects of this, a rhetorical space was opened up for "communal" and other sectional claims that were less readily brought forward before.[83] The opposition between primordiality and "mere invention," thus, leaves open a very wide range of historicities within which national and other traditions can exert real force.

Language and history

The translation of ethnicity into nationalism is partly a matter of converting the cultural traditions of everyday life into more specific historical claims. As Gellner suggests, this transformation is made possible partly by the development of a literate "high culture" and is an extension of its relationship to the everyday culture of face-to-face relationships.[84] Anderson develops this point with more systematic attention to the role of the "print capitalism" of newspapers and novels, which not only engage in history-making but constitute the nation as a community of like readers in the imagination of each.[85] This is true not just of the contents of tradition, as folklore gives way simultaneously to "scientific history" and national myth, but of the very medium. Not only literacy but space-transcending communications technologies from print through broadcast can play a crucial role both in linking dispersed populations and in creating the possibility for producing a popular memory beyond the scope of immediate personal experience and oral traditions.[86] Nowhere, however, is the issue clearer than in the historicizing approach to language of the early modern era. This reconstituted an aspect of the everyday cultural means of social life as part of a historical/ethnic claim to nationhood.

Particularly in Germany, language was given a central status from Herder and Fichte on. In stressing the "originality" of the German language and the "truly primal" nature of the German character, Fichte, for example, claimed a supra-historical status for German nationality.[87] Historically formed national characters were inferior, he argued, to the true metaphysical national spirits that were based on something more primal than common historical experience. This does not mean that Fichte and others of similar orientation saw glory only in the past. On the contrary, they envisaged a dramatic break with many aspects of the past and a national self-realization in what Fichte called a new history. The old history was not one properly self-made, not the product of the self-conscious action of the nation as historical actor. Here echoes of the French Revolution appear in German nationalist historiography. The rhetoric of nationalism came characteristically to involve the metaphor of awakening. This involved political, not just ethnic, claims. Positioning their nation within history allowed nationalists who claimed ancient roots still to evoke the heroism of creation and the prestige that since the Enlightenment adhered in many quarters to the production of something new – as in the United States' claim to be "the first new nation."[88]

Nationalism has a complex relationship to history. On the one hand, the production of historical accounts of the nation can figure very prominently (and this is hardly distinctive of Germany or the West; see examples in Nehru and Gandhi, and discussion in Chatterjee[89]). Indeed, the modern discipline of history is very deeply shaped by the tradition of producing national histories designed to give readers and students a sense of their collective identity. At the same time, however, nationalists are prone, at the very least, to the production of Whig histories, favorable accounts of "how we came to be who we are." As Ernest Renan wrote famously in 1882:

> Forgetting, I would even go so far as to say historical error, is a crucial factor in the creation of a nation, which is why progress in historical studies often constitutes a danger for [the principle of] nationality. Indeed, historical enquiry brings to light deeds of violence which took

place at the origin of all political formations, even those whose consequences have been altogether beneficial. Unity is always effected by means of brutality.[90]

Not only is the definition of nation subject to contest and struggle, the fruits and even the violence of these contests and struggles become inescapably part of who we are. For all its civic rationalism, France has hardly been free from appeals to ethnic nationalism. An ethnic conception of *la patrie* stood behind much of the attack on Dreyfus; Maurras sought to define a true French nation free of Jews, Protestants, Freemasons, and other foreigners.[91] Aspects of this heritage remain important in contemporary debates over immigration.[92] Indeed, Greenfeld goes so far as to group French nationalism with those to the East as "collectivistic-authoritarian" and based on *ressentiment* (by contrast to the "individualistic-libertarian" English variant);[93] France's violent and irrational Anglophobia is part of her evidence.[94]

Nineteenth- and twentieth-century nationalisms have been particularly obsessed with history, as with ethnicity, perhaps because most involve claims to nationhood which are in important ways problematic or challenged by existing states. Thus Gandhi's Hindu nationalist opponent, Savarkar, felt compelled to argue that "verily the Hindus as a people differ most [*sic*] markedly from any other people in the world than they differ amongst themselves. All tests whatsoever of a common country, race, religion, and language that go to entitle a people to form a nation, entitle the Hindus with greater emphasis to that claim."[95] Many Indian nationalist historians took on a dual challenge in writing their histories.[96] First, they sought to show that India was one country, against the British suggestion that without the alien Raj, disunity and conflict would reign amongst its many contending peoples (or "communities"). Second, they sought to show that this one country was essentially Hindu, not Muslim (and thus among other things constituted "indigenously" rather than by previous imperial invasions). Indian intellectuals from the nineteenth century on were often as cosmopolitan as their European counterparts (and certainly at least as likely to be multilingual). But this could never appear as unproblematic in the context of colonial rule as it had for the European enlighteners. Many Indian nationalists (including Nehru) wrote in English and spoke it more comfortably than any "Indian" language; they helped, indeed, to make English an Indian language. But this involved a tension between English as the language of the colonizer and as the putative *lingua franca* that was to help constitute one nation by cutting across the linguistic divisions of the subcontinent. Moreover, at the same time that some nationalists appropriated English as an Indian language, others produced a renaissance of modern Indian languages like Bengali or Marathi. As in Catalonia, Hungary, China, and elsewhere, nationalism meant producing a new, modern literature in the vernacular language. One dimension of this was the attempt to forge a unity between the language of literature and intellectuals and that of ordinary people – since groups previously separated by language were now to be united by a national language.

For the German Romantics, language was a key test of the existence of a nation.[97] Language, moreover, was understood primarily in terms of continuity, since "few things seem as historically deep-rooted as languages, for which no dated origins can ever be given."[98] Language often plays a key role in ethnic (or "naturalizing") versions of nationalism, since an ancient language, shared as the parental tongue among the members of the nation, seems a guarantee of its true existence prior to and separate from any particular set of political arrangements (including fragmentation or alien rule). But the language of nationalist movements is often not the parental tongue of the putative nation's members, not the first language of each, but rather the second language that unites them. It may be an elite language, shared among aristocrats and/or a bourgeoisie; it may be the language of a colonial power. The shared language is not the "test" of nationhood, but the means of imagining – and thereby creating – the nation.[99]

Language figures in at least three different ways in accounts of nationalism. First, it is a central part of the claim that nationhood is rooted in ethnicity. This leads to attempts to show the historic depth and distinctiveness of languages. Second, shared language is a condition (or at least a facilitator) of claimed national community regardless of whether it is ancient or distinctive. As Anderson stresses, the pioneering nationalisms of the Americas were launched in the colonial languages of Spanish and English. Third, opposition to linguistic variation is a key way in which nationalists in power attempt to make the nation fit the state. Thus most citizens of France did not speak French until the late nineteenth century, and only after the imposition of often-resented educational uniformity.[100] Russification programs begun under the Czars were carried forward by communist rulers after only brief revolutionary interruption. In the last of these three we see clearly the impact of state-building, and the strong case for a state-centered theory like Tilly's (discussed above). But such a theory offers little help in making sense of the first two, or even in explaining why language should be an issue. Part of the answer to this question has to do with the relationship between claims to pre-existing ethnicity and claims to founding historical moments and political forms. Part of it also has to do, however, with the issue of how people imagine the nation, how this particular category of identity had come to figure so prominently in the modern world.

Ethnic continuities

Generally speaking, the most prominent twentieth-century analysts of nationalism have rejected the claim that nationalism can be explained by pre-existing ethnicity. Kohn and Seton-Watson have stressed the crucial role of modern politics, especially the idea of sovereignty.[101] Hayes has argued for seeing nationalism as a sort of religion.[102] Kedourie has debunked nationalism by showing the untenability of the German Romantic claims.[103] More recently, Gellner has placed emphasis on the number of cases of failed or absent nationalisms: ethnic groups which mounted either little or no attempt to become nations in the modern senses.[104] This suggests that even if ethnicity plays a role it cannot be a sufficient explanation (though one imagines the nineteenth-century German Romantics would simply reply that there are strong, historic nations and weak ones destined to fade from the historic stage). Hobsbawm has largely treated nationalism as a kind of second-order political movement based on a false consciousness which ethnicity helps to produce but cannot explain because the deeper roots lie in political economy not culture.[105]

Against this backdrop, Anthony Smith has tried to show that nationalism has stronger roots in premodern ethnicity than others have accepted.[106] He acknowledges that nations cannot be seen as primordial or natural, but nonetheless argues that they are rooted in relatively ancient histories and in perduring ethnic consciousnesses. Smith agrees that nationalism, as ideology and movement, dates only from the later eighteenth century, but argues that the "ethnic origins of nations" are much older. Smith focuses on *ethnie* – ethnic communities with their myths and symbols – and shows that these exist in both modern and premodern times, and with substantial continuity through history. Because, Smith argues,

> myths, symbols, memories and values are "carried" in and by forms
> and genres of artifacts and activities which change only very slowly, so
> *ethnie*, once formed, tend to be exceptionally durable under "normal"
> vicissitudes, and to persist over many generations, even centuries,
> forming "moulds" within which all kinds of social and cultural
> processes can unfold and upon which all kinds of circumstances and
> pressures can exert an impact.[107]

This is the foundation both of particular nations and of the idea of nation.

Smith argues that the origins of modern nationalism lie in the successful bureaucratization of aristocratic *ethnie*, which were able to transform themselves into genuine nations only in the West.[108] In the West, territorial centralization and consolidation went hand in hand with a growing cultural standardization. "The indivisibility of the state entailed the cultural uniformity and homogeneity of its citizens."[109] "It would indeed not exaggerate the matter to say that what distinguished nations from *ethnie* are in some sense, 'Western' features and qualities. Territoriality, citizenship rights, legal code and even political culture, are features of society that the West has made its own. So is the realization of social mobility in a unified division of labour."[110] Well beyond the West, however, the compulsion for *ethnie* to enter the political arena is seemingly universal to the modern era. "In order to survive, *ethnie* must take on some of the attributes of nationhood, and adopt a civic model." Cross-class inclusion and mobilization for common political purposes are essential.[111] Conversely, rooted in ethnicity, nations are long-term processes, continually reenacted and reconstructed; they require ethnic cores, homelands, heroes, and golden ages if they are to survive. Small, breakaway nations rooted in particularist, quasi-religious visions are the most common new nationalist projects today.[112] Nonetheless, this tendency towards the production of many new small nations is contained, Smith suggests (writing before the events of 1989–92 in Eastern Europe, the Soviet Union, and Africa), by the existing framework of nation-states.[113] In sum, "modern nations and nationalism have only extended and deepened the meanings and scope of older ethnic concepts and structures. Nationalism has certainly universalized these structures and ideals, but modern 'civic' nations have not in practice really transcended ethnicity or ethnic sentiments."[114]

Smith does not claim that ethnicity is natural, rather than socially constructed. His argument, rather, is that ethnicity is very slow to change. He acknowledges also that premodern ethnic boundaries were not sharply fixed, though he does claim that they maintained a level of integrity. Above all, Smith suggests that it is possible to trace a "genealogy of nations" in which both cultural and social structural variables can be introduced to account for which *ethnies* become nations. The crucial moment in such genealogies, he suggests, is the transformation of the members of an *ethnie* into citizens. This is a cultural transformation of the character of membership, stressing the lateral ties that link members despite class divisions, and that form the basis for potential political mobilization.[115]

Smith stresses the continuity in ethnic groupings and the relations of cultural similarity that define them. In a clear contrast, Brass offers an account of ethnicity as the product of manipulation, or at least recurrent invocation.[116] Ethnic groups "are creations of elites, who draw upon, distort, and sometimes fabricate materials from the cultures of the groups they wish to represent in order to protect their well-being or existence or to gain political and economic advantage for their groups as well as for themselves."

Imagined communities and categorical identities

It is tempting to explain national identity as a transformation of ethnic or cultural similarity wrought by state-building. Certainly a crucial difference between ethnicities and nations is that the latter are envisioned as intrinsically political communities, as sources of sovereignty, while this is not central to the definition of ethnicities. There are, however, a number of obstacles to seeing this as the whole of the issue. First, nationalisms do not vary neatly with the success of efforts to create consolidated states. As Gellner points out, there are vastly more languages and ethnic or cultural groups than there are nationalist movements or states. This is not just because some lost out in a struggle for national identity or autonomy.

> For every effective nationalism, there are *n* potential ones, groups defined either by shared culture inherited from the agrarian world or by some other link . . . which *could* give hope of establishing a homogenous industrial community, but which nevertheless do not bother to struggle, which fail to activate their potential nationalism, which do not even try.[117]

Beyond this, nationalism is not simply a claim of ethnic similarity, but a claim that certain similarities should count as *the* definition of political community. For this reason, nationalism needs boundaries in a way premodern ethnicity does not. Nationalism demands internal homogeneity throughout a putative nation, rather than gradual continua of cultural variation or pockets of subcultural distinction. Perhaps most distinctively, nationalists commonly claim that national identities "trump" other personal or group identities (such as gender, family, or ethnicity) and link individuals directly to the nation as a whole. This is sharply contrary to the way in which most ethnic identities flow from family membership, kinship, and membership in intermediate groups.

Nationalism, in short, involves a distinctive new form of group identity or membership. It is a new rhetoric of belonging to large-scale collectivities. This depends on new forms of collective imagination, and also on communications capacities and social organizational conditions that encourage a sense of identity with large populations of distant and largely anonymous others. It also depends crucially on modern ideas of individual equivalence.

Individualism

In nearly all premodern patterns of social organization, people were members of polities and other social groups primarily by virtue of their occupation of a variety of ascribed statuses based on descent, kinship, age, gender, and the like. Their membership in larger groups, like clan, was based on and grew directly out of smaller groups like lineage segments, and out of specific interpersonal relationships like father–son.[118] This was true, despite otherwise dramatic differences, for relatively small-scale African societies and for such extremely large-scale polities as imperial China. The modern notion of self as individual changed this. Personal identity came to be seen increasingly as the attributes of a self-contained individual – what Taylor has characterized in Locke's writings as the "punctual self."[119] "The alternative to playing the role of so-and-so's son, so-and-so's brother, so-and-so's wife was," as Schwarcz has written of protagonists in China's largely nationalist New Culture movement, "to gain a positive sense of one's own individuality."[120] Such thinking made it common to understand social groupings as sets of equivalent persons (as in the idea of class as well as in liberal individualism) rather than webs of relationships among persons or hierarchies of positions.[121] The modern idea of nation, despite its roots in notions of descent, has been nearly always such a category of equivalent persons.

So, despite more relational roots, is the prevailing modern usage of "ethnicity." This is revealed in the way in which censuses have been constructed and conducted, quantifying the members of ethnic, racial, and national categories.[122] It is revealed also in the ways in which Western social scientists have sometimes hypostatized notions like caste and lineage segment or corporation.[123] Terms with at least in part a relational usage are recast as though they were simply collectivities of equivalent individuals. Similarly, Ekeh has noted a tendency to abandon the use of tribe in social anthropology and African studies, and to replace it with "ethnic group."[124] But this has the effect of imposing a categorical notion – a collection of individuals marked by common ethnicity – in place of a relational one. Where the notion of tribe pointed to the centrality of kin relations (all the more central, Ekeh suggests, because of weak African states from whose point of view "tribalism" is criticized), the notion of ethnic group implies that detailed, serious analysis of kinship is more or less irrelevant. In part, this is a response to recognition of the contested nature of ethnic identities; it involves an attempt to move away from substantive claims to identify ethnicity on the basis of the "real" shared descent of the members of a group. Weber defined an ethnic group as one whose members "entertain a subjective belief in their common descent because of similarities of physical type or of customs or both, or because of memories of colonization and migration."[125] Barth took this logic a step further and abandoned even the notion of subjective belief in common descent, replacing it simply with the existence of recognized group boundaries.[126] Here the triumph of a categorical logic is complete: an ethnic group is simply a bounded set of individuals, not necessarily characterized by any internal pattern of relationships, much less one of kinship or descent. Once ethnic groups are treated in this purely categorical way – as they are in much everyday contemporary discussion as well as in academic studies – similarities rather than relationships form the defining connection among members. This opens the door to new pressures for conformity.

The categorical nature of national identities is linked strongly to ideas of purity and normalizations of the "correct" way to be a member of a nation. Nationalisms linked to state power are often repressive, thus, not only of the members of "alien" nations or ethnic minorities (like Jews in Europe) but of their own members. Thus European nationalisms have commonly been strongly colored by ideas of middle-class respectability, particularly in the realm of sexuality.[127] National identity has been an eroticized identity, and one that carried prohibitions of deviant sexualities as sharply as on deviant ethnicities.[128] Nationalism has also been a distinctly gender-biased ideology in many settings.[129] Valuing the family as the source of the nation's continuity in time, nationalist ideologues have seen men as future martyrs, women as mothers. Beyond this, however, nationalists resist women's movements because accepting the domination of male interests and perceptions merely perpetuates a taken-for-granted, monolithic view of the nation, while encouraging women to identify their distinctive interests and views opens claims that gender has autonomous status as a basis for personal identity which does not pale into insignificance before the commonalties of (male-dominated) nationhood.

Individualism exerts another influence on ideas of nation. Nations are generally seen as logical equivalents, and themselves as individuals. Just as liberal political theory suggests that employer and employee, rich man and poor woman, are equivalent political persons, so liberal international theory suggests that nations like San Marino and Singapore are formally equivalent to China and Germany.[130] As individuals, nations may also be understood as unitary subjects in historical time. In Fichte's word, "nations are individualities with particular talents and the possibilities of exploiting those talents."[131] Nations not only could take action but could experience abuse; especially after 1848, Poland was conceived as "the martyr-nation";[132] Russian nationalism was colored and driven by a constant "*ressentiment*."[133] Marx's contemporary, Friedrich List, "pronounced nations to be 'eternal,' to constitute a unity both in space and time."[134] This did not preclude the idea that nations were capable in some sense of making themselves, forging a higher individuality out of heterogeneous constituent parts.

Anderson has seized on just this aspect of individuality as central to the modern understanding of nation: "The idea of a sociological organism moving calendrically through homogenous, empty time is a precise analogue of the idea of the nation, which also is conceived as a solid community moving steadily down (or up) history."[135] As Anderson has stressed, the category of nation thus unites the living and the dead. This is a crucial explanation for why the nation can demand such extraordinary sacrifices and commitments from its members. It joins the biographies of individual persons and of the nation as a whole in a common historical narrative. Not only does the nation locate individuals temporally in relation to past and future generations, and in the global context as members of one among many nations, the nation also locates each individual's biography and quotidian narrative as one among the many comparable biographies of the members of the specific nation.[136]

Imagined communities and indirect relationships

As a category of equivalent persons, a nation is, in Anderson's evocative phrase, an "imagined community." Rather than treating nationalism as a genre of ideology comparable to liberalism or fascism, Anderson suggests that we regard nationalism as a distinct mode of understanding and constituting the phenomenon of belonging together, comparable to kinship or religion.[137] A nation, thus:

> is an imagined political community. . . . It is imagined because the members of even the smallest nation will never know most of their fellow-members, meet them, or even hear of them, yet in the minds of each lives the image of their communion. . . . The nation is imagined as limited because even the largest of them, encompassing perhaps a billion living human beings, has finite, if elastic, boundaries, beyond which lie other nations. It is imagined as sovereign because the concept was born in an age in which Enlightenment and Revolution were destroying the legitimacy of the divinely-ordained, hierarchical dynastic realm. . . . Finally, it is imagined as a community, because, regardless of the actual inequality and exploitation that may prevail in each, the nation is always conceived as a deep, horizontal comradeship.[138]

Much of Anderson's book (perhaps the most original, if not the most systematic contribution to the large recent literature on nationalism) is devoted to trying to account for the rise of this distinctive way of imagining community. In addition to the account of distinctive temporal location already touched on, Anderson offers three main arguments.

First, Anderson takes up the notion of language as the essential cultural condition of nationhood. He notes that nationalism did not arise simply out of long-standing traditions of linguistic commonality. On the contrary, in many settings nationalism involved the privileging of vernaculars in place of Latin and other previously widely used languages of high culture and administration (and of cross-regional sharing). It sometimes involved the recovery of little-used languages. It often depended on the integration of more or less distinctive dialects or members of language families into new common languages. And in many cases nationalist imaginings took place in the language of colonial powers. What gave language its efficacy in relation to nationalism was the coincidence of print technology and capitalism.

By pushing for ever-larger markets, capitalist cultural production (in the form of books and newspapers) called forth "unified fields of exchange and communication below Latin and above the spoken vernaculars."[139] That is, in early modern Europe, capitalists sought markets larger than the small number of elite readers of Latin, and larger than the number of speakers of nearly all local vernaculars. They thus pioneered the creation of the specific linguistic communities associated with eventual national identities. In addition, print-capitalism gave a new fixity to language, encouraging a stable orthography, grammar, and form in general. This encouraged the image of antiquity conducive to the notion of long-standing national identity by obscuring the extent to which languages gradually evolved and successive members of putative nations spoke mutually unintelligible tongues. Not least of all, print-capitalism standardized usage of certain administratively sanctioned languages, thus disadvantaging within each realm the speakers of other languages. Where Latin had previously united dozens of local dialects and languages within Hapsburg domains, for example, increasing reliance on German disadvantaged Hungarian elites (among others) and created a pressure for nationalism within and eventually against the empire. At the same time, this gave incentives (not always equally taken up) for elites to make common cause (and common culture) with non-elites. Where premodern society had been divided especially into vertical layers, modern politics (including the politics of language) encouraged the overcoming of vertical divisions and the substitution of horizontal borders. As Gellner described this transition, "a high culture pervades the whole of society, defines it, and needs to be sustained by the polity. *That* is the secret of nationalism."[140]

In addition to helping to sort out the role of language in the creation of ethnic foundations for nationalism, Anderson's formulation of "print-capitalism" also helps to make sense of the new kind of imagining of community more directly. The readers of the same novels and news-papers were joined in imagining communities of other such readers, and of imagining communality with the protagonists of the stories they read.[141] The readers of daily newspapers not only learned the same news as each other, they learned "wholly new ideas of simultaneity."[142] They learned to situate themselves in terms of the activity of many individuals (and nations) taking place in the same temporal moment, not solely in a linear development. This also allowed for a sense of shared paths, which "could arise historically only when substantial groups of people were in a position to think of themselves as living lives *parallel* to those of other substantial groups of people – if never meeting, yet certainly proceeding along the same trajectory."[143] In place of direct relationships among people meeting face to face, thus, print technologies (proliferated by capitalist production relations) encouraged the creation of a new kind of indirect relationship, a social link existing only by virtue of the new medium of communication and its supporting social organizations. Much the same was true of markets, which joined distant and anonym-ous populations in indirect and sometimes invisible but clearly powerful social relations.[144]

The importance of communications media to national integration has certainly been noted before (notably by Deutsch).[145] In most earlier treatments, however, the categorical identity of the nation is presumed and research is focused on how the development of communications capacity enhances the social and political integration of the nation. Anderson's central contribution is to explain how communicative forms figured in creating the categorical identity or imagined community of the nation itself. In addition to media, Anderson creatively analyzes the car-eer trajectories of creole officers of colonial states. He locates an impor-tant and early source of nationalism in their movement around colonies, and the limits placed on both their upward and lateral movement out of the colony in which they served.

These bounded imaginings were given graphic and synoptic expres-sion in the proliferation of maps. Early maps had been either cosmogra-phies, locating a dynastic or religious realm in relation to heaven and the netherworld, or travelers guides, working by landmarks from one loca-tion to another. In the nineteenth century, maps not only began to pro-liferate by virtue of mechanical reproduction, they began to register the whole world as a set of bounded territories, different colors for different empires or autonomous countries.[146] They became the visual representa-tion of a world organized into a system of states. They also offered maps of individual countries as "logos," the image of their territorial shape giving a definite form to the imagined community. In something of the same way, museums, like history-writing, gave temporal depth to nationalism.[147] Colonial powers deployed archaeology to unearth the tangible (and preferably monumental) remnants of ancient cities and sacred sites; these in turn were transformed into tourist attractions and objects of photographs, recordings of a tradition constituted in its distinctness from the modern state. In cosmopolitan museums artifacts from far-flung contexts were (and are) displayed within classifications ordering the world into nations. In national museums, artifacts from disparate temporal and spatial settings are arranged into national narratives. The crucial link was the production of replicable series of artifacts available for classification into types or periods (as distinct from temples still seen as singular in their sacredness, or modern "auratic" works of art imbued with the singularity of an individual creator). The idea of nation is itself an instance and an archetype of this classifying logic of categorical identities.

Conclusion

The relationship between nationalism and ethnicity is complex. Neither is vanishing as part of an obsolete traditional order. Both are part of a modern set of categorical identities invoked by elites and other participants in political and social struggles. These categorical identities also shape everyday life, offering both tools for grasping pre-existing homogeneity and difference and constructing specific versions of such identities. While it is impossible to dissociate nationalism entirely from ethnicity, it is equally impossible to explain it simply as a continuation of ethnicity. Numerous dimensions of modern social and cultural change, notably state-building, individualism, and the integration of large-scale webs of indirect relationships, all serve to make both nationalism and ethnicity salient. Nationalism, in particular, remains the preeminent rhetoric for attempts to demarcate political communities, and claim rights of self-determination and legitimate rule by reference to "the people" of a country. Ethnic solidarities and identities are claimed most often where groups do not seek "national" autonomy but rather a recognition internal to or cross-cutting national or state boundaries. The possibility of a closer link to nationalism is seldom altogether absent from such ethnic claims, however, and the two sorts of categorical identities are often invoked in similar ways.

4

Nationalism and civil society
Democracy, diversity, and self-determination[1]

In 1989, the self-declared "free world" reveled in the collapse of communism. Capitalism and democracy seemed simply and obviously triumphant. The Cold War was over. Everyone would live happily ever after.

Of course, there would be "transitional problems." Word came of fighting in Nagorno-Karabak. It crossed some minds that many residents of Soviet Central Asia might find fundamentalist Islam more appealing than American capitalism. Enthusiasm for Lithuanian nationalism was occasionally dimmed by memories of Lithuanian fascism and anti-Semitism. But in an efflorescence of faith in progress not seen since the nineteenth century, most Western politicians and intellectuals confidently saw "excesses" of nationalism as at most minor detours on the road to capitalist democracy. Even thinkers on the left joined the enthusiasm and, embarrassed by seeming association with the losing side, hastened to forget the lessons of history and the need for serious analysis.

Somewhere between 1989 and 1992, anxiety regained intellectual respectability. Still, it took quite dramatic events, from Ethiopia to the former Soviet Union and especially Yugoslavia, to focus attention on the possibility that nationalism might be more than a passing problem. Serbian talk of "ethnic cleansing" brought shudders of recollection, yet many treated it – like the Nazi ideology it recalled – as a throwback to the premodern. It is no accident, however, that "ethnic cleansing" is the project of academics and technicians, not of peasants, just as Nazism was rooted in scientific discourse and technological dreams as well as old hatreds. Both are fundamentally and horribly modern. And if nationalism is a central problem of post-communist transitions, this is because it is a central way of organizing collective identity throughout the modern world.

Academics have repeatedly announced the death of nationalism, but like that of Mark Twain's demise, the reports have been greatly exaggerated. In one of the most recent waves of such assertions, analysts correctly observe that states are having difficulty organizing and controlling global markets, multinational corporations, large-scale migration flows, and internal "tribalism." Yet these analysts seldom consider the possibility that, rather than spelling the end of nationalism, all these trends and difficulties are its occasion. All encourage the renewal and continuing production of nationalism because nationalism is the rhetoric of identity and solidarity in which citizens of the modern world most readily deal with the problematic nature of state power and with problems of inclusion and exclusion. Rather than following state-building in a neat correlation, nationalism is most an issue where the boundaries and power of a state do not coincide neatly with the will or identity of its members or the scale of action undertaken by other collective actors.

Nationalist claims are one genre of answers to the question of what constitutes an autonomous political community capable of "self-determination." These claims come in two main versions: one places crucial stress on the ethnic or cultural similarity of the members of a political community; the other on their common citizenship in a specific state (with its characteristic modes of political activity). But in both versions, nationalist answers to the question of what constitutes a political community underestimate the importance of the institutions, networks, and movements that knit people together across lines of diversity internal to nations and states; they underestimate, in other words, the specifically sociological problems of social integration.

Nationalism appeared in the post-1989 discourse on transitions to democracy – and in theories of democracy generally – primarily as a hazard to be avoided, not as a central dimension of the subject. Yet nationalism is directly and fundamentally involved in questions about the social foundations for democracy. Leaving nationalism to one side theoretically – and often to anti-democratic activists in practice – the discourse on transitions did sometimes take up the question of what social foundations enable a collectivity of people to organize their institutions through popular political participation. It did so most prominently under the rubric of "civil society." This concept was invoked to account for the various resources outside direct state control that offered alternatives to the state organization of collective life. In many invocations, thus, the role of more or less self-regulating markets or processes of capital accumulation was not distinguished from the roles of networks of interpersonal relations, social movements, and public discourse.

The significance of this became apparent when the economic challenges of post-communist transition began to compete with efforts to increase democratic participation. Various different programs for the rapid creation of "free-market" economies, thus, were all claimed by their proponents to strengthen civil society whether or not they increased the capacity of ordinary people to join together in associations and movements or otherwise to create a public sphere capable of shaping social and political decisions on the basis of rational-critical discourse. Many of these programs of economic privatization, in fact, did relatively little to increase the extent of popular participation in decisions regarding investment and economic structure. While some did seek to increase opportunities for entrepreneurship and the development of new small businesses, others focused more on transferring large-scale state enterprises to "private" owners. The link between the two was faith in the importance of subjecting as much as possible of the formerly "administered" economies to the discipline of the market. The market, however, was understood as an abstract, impersonal, and self-regulating force, and moreover one that either did or should transcend national and state boundaries.

A tension was created, in short, between the pursuit of democratization and the pursuit of economic development. The former was seen as essentially a matter of domestic institutions and actions while the latter involved participation in an increasingly global economy. The constraints and demands imposed by the effort to compete in this global economy were and are frequently cited as reasons for limiting or postponing the project of increasing democratic participation. Indeed, perhaps paradoxically, voters in the new electoral democracies have even been persuaded on several occasions that voting their pocketbooks meant voting against democratization. The prestige of the cadres of international economic consultants brought in to replace the cadres of communist central planners has often been placed behind such conclusions. The result often has been to replace the imperatives of party and state bureaucracies with the imperatives of impersonal market forces as interpreted by technical experts and politicians.

In confronting so dramatically the tension between economic globalization and the pursuit of democracy through domestic institutions, the ex-communist and newly independent states of Eastern Europe highlight an issue faced much more generally in the contemporary world. A broad range of commentators and pundits have pointed to globalization and suggested that the era of the nation-state is at an end.[2] The mobility of capital and impossibility of containing economic activity within the bounds of state control allegedly suggest that states are no longer crucial units of organization and power. This misrepresents, however, the nature and significance of economically driven globalization. First, this is not an entirely new trend, but a continuation of the historical pattern of the whole modern era. Second, this economic globalization may reduce certain of the capacities of states, but it does not make them less important or imply that in general they are likely either to break up or amalgamate. Modern states have always existed and derived much of their significance from their contraposition to other states in a "world-system" that has always been too large for any single state to control. States have existed in part to manage economic – and also military – relations that cross their boundaries. What is most distinctive about the current globalization is not that it creates a level of global integration that states cannot readily manage, but that it brings close to completion the process of continuously incorporating more and more parts of the world into the capitalist world-system.[3]

The travails of Eastern Europe reveal that incorporation into the global economy does not stop states from being crucial arenas of struggle. States remain the organizations of power through which democratic movements have the greatest capacity to affect economic organization. Given the current organization of the United Nations, states remain the highest level of institutional structure at which programs of democratization themselves can consistently be advanced. And states remain the most crucial objects and vehicles of efforts to achieve "self-determination" or autonomy as a political community. As states remain of crucial importance, so too does the ideology of nationalism. Characteristic of the whole modern era, this reflects the constitution of the modern world-system as a system of states. The primacy of national identity is implicit in both sides of the Eastern European transition. It is what gives force to the notion of using domestic institutions to attempt to position a people in the global economy. It is also what constitutes the most basic notion of a people capable of claiming rights over and against a government. This is equally the case whether the claims are those of secession or more simply of self-governance without change of borders. The definition of boundaries and constitution of a collective identity are crucial components of the constitution of a political community in the modern world-system of states.

The problems of collective identity formation are commonly ignored by democratic theory. They are, however, endemic to modern political life. Nationalism, as the most potent discourse of collective identity, appears alike in projects of unity and division. It may be an irony of history, thus, but it is not a sociological contradiction that Western Europe is pursuing the path of unification at the same time that Eastern European countries are being rent by nationalist splits. By the same token, however, this reveals that nationalism is not itself an adequate explanation of such processes of integration or disintegration so much as it is a political rhetoric in which many of them are pursued.

Discussions of the idea of nation and of social integration need therefore to be joined. The theory of democracy needs to deal with both of the two senses in which they raise the question of how political communities are constituted. The first is the bounded nature of all political communities, and the embeddedness of all claims to constitute a distinct and autonomous political community in relationships of contraposition to other such communities or claimants. The second is the web of relationships that constitutes a people (or nation) as a social collectivity existing independently of common subjection to the rule of a particular state.

Civil society

It is not mere coincidence that the opposition to totalitarian role and the transition to democracy have brought ideas about civil society to the foreground. The language of civil society – though often sociologically underdeveloped – has been the most prominent way in which claims to peoplehood and self-determination have been grounded in appeals to social integration. The events of 1989 catapulted this concern from academic circles to the broader public discourse. The phrase is now on the lips of foundation executives, business leaders, and politicians; it seems as though every university has set up a study group on civil society and the phrase finds its way into half the dissertations in political sociology. Too often, the phrase is invoked without sorting out whether civil society means Milton Friedman's capitalist market policies or social movements like Solidarity or the sort of "political society" or "public sphere" beloved of thinkers from Montesquieu to Tocqueville and Habermas, and once thought to exist mainly in cafes and coffee houses.[4]

Two basic questions are raised in discussions of civil society. First, what counts as or defines a political community? Second, what knits society together, providing for social integration? There are several contenders in each case: state, market economy, cultural similarity (e.g. nationality), social networks, political participation by autonomous agents. The idea of civil society entered political philosophy and social theory as a way of describing the capacity of self-organization on the part of a political community, in other words the capacity of a society to organize itself without being organized by a state. If society had such capacity, then "the people" integrated in that society could better be seen as the source of political legitimacy rather than merely the object of rule. In some early uses – notably the Scottish moralists including Ferguson and Smith – the notion of civil society referred to all such non-state capacities for social organization. The economy was not only included, it provided a key example. To these early capitalist thinkers, the self-regulating character of markets demonstrated the possibility for social organization without the direction of the state.

As Charles Taylor has argued, however, it is crucial to distinguish two different branches of the discourse of civil society.[5] While one followed Ferguson and Smith in stressing the economic-systemic character of civil society, the other followed Montesquieu, Rousseau, and Tocqueville in stressing social relations entered into by autonomous agents. The Eastern European discourse of the 1980s and much of the recent usage blurs important distinctions between the two.[6]

The issue is not solved by declaring that civil society must be kept conceptually distinct from capitalist economic organization. On the contrary, capitalism itself appears in both voluntary and systemic guises. On the one hand, capitalist ideology typically asserts that capitalist economic life *is* precisely the realm of free social relations. It offers a model of capitalist life as quintessentially the activity and relationships of owner-operators of small businesses and individual consumers. One might object that these are relations only among buyers and sellers, but one cannot deny that capitalism offers certain genuine freedoms. At the same time, capitalist ideology itself negates its proffered freedom by reference to the immutable "laws" of the market. It claims that the systemic character of markets dictates that interference from states or other collective actors (unions, social movements, etc.) must be kept to a minimum so that the capitalist system can organize itself. This kind of limit on free collective action is asserted by capitalist ideology itself, even when it refuses to recognize the salient distinctions between giant corporations and human individuals, or the inevitable dependence and mutuality between capitalist economics and certain forms of state support.

Nonetheless, capitalism *did* historically and can still play a special and crucial role in the growth of a civil society. The early growth of capitalist business relations provided essential support to the development of a sphere of political discourse outside the realm of state control. This is not to say that business people were the primary protagonists of the bourgeois public sphere. On the contrary, various state employees from ministerial clerks through university professors, and dependents of aristocratic sponsors played far more central roles in the eighteenth-century "golden age" of the public sphere. But the development of a public discourse in which private persons addressed public issues was made possible, in part, by both the policy issues posed by the growth of the non-state dominated market activity, and the creation of settings for such discourse in coffee houses, journals, and other forums operated as businesses.[7]

It is crucial not to accept capitalist ideology uncritically, and therefore to imagine that capitalism is somehow by itself an adequate support for democracy or a viable alternative to state power. It is equally crucial not to ignore the role of certain kinds of at least quasi-autonomous business institutions in facilitating the development of a sphere of public discourse and capacity for social organization outside the immediate control of the state. Above all, we must look beyond capitalism (and more generally beyond the narrow realm of the economy as a putatively self-sufficient and self-regulating system) to seek (a) the extent to which societal integration can be accomplished through webs of interpersonal relations, and (b) the extent to which both these social relations and the more abstract ones of the economy can be organized voluntarily through public discourse. Only when these possibilities are addressed do we have a conception of societal integration that can serve as a foundation to a theory of democracy.

In other words, from the point of view of democracy, it is essential to retain in the notion of civil society some idea of a social realm which is neither dominated by state power nor simply responsive to the systemic features of capitalism. The public sphere of civil society cannot be simply a realm in which representatives of state authority vie for attention with economists claiming to predict the economy like the weather on the basis of its reified laws. It must include an institutionally organized and substantial capacity for people to enter as citizens into public discourse about the nature and course of their life together. This capacity depends not just on formal institutions, but on civil society as a realm of sociability.

In this conceptualization, civil society must also be a realm of intermediate associations. Communities, movements, and organizations (from churches to political parties and mutual aid societies) are all potentially important. Though the nationalist impulse is sometimes to condemn these as intrinsically "partial," this needs to be affirmed as one of their major virtues. For it is precisely in such partial social units that people find both the capacity for collective voice and the possibility of differentiated, directly interpersonal relations. Such intermediate associations are also the crucial defenses both of distinctive identities imperiled by the normalization of the mass, and of democracy against oligarchy.[8]

Hidden in this discourse – in two centuries of public discourse as well as in the last few paragraphs – is the problem of identifying "the people" who may be members of a discursive public or a civil society. From its earliest instantiations, from classical Athens through revolutionary America or Enlightenment Europe, the democratic public sphere has been marred by exclusionary tendencies. Not just slaves, but non-natives, aboriginals, propertyless men and all women have been excluded at various points from both direct political participation (e.g. voting) and from participation in the discourse of the public sphere.

Some other exclusions seem more justifiable, though the theoretical status of the justifications is complex: the participation of children, criminals, and the mentally incompetent is almost universally restricted. In short, "the people" have not all been citizens.

That democracy has always been restrictive has certainly been noticed. But there is an equally basic version of the question "who are the people?" which is less often posed. When we say, for example in relation to the break-up of Yugoslavia, that we believe in the right of "self-determination," just what self is involved? The notion of self-determination is basic to democracy and yet both neglected by democratic theory and shrouded in illusions of primordiality. The problem of self-determination is that for every socially relevant self we can see internal divisions and vital links to others. There is no single, definite, and fixed "peoplehood" which can be assumed in advance of political discussion.

Moreover, as "no man is an island unto himself," no nation exists alone.[9] Each is defined in relation to others and exists within a web of social relationships that traverse its boundaries. Supposed historical autarky was never complete, and modern attempts to close borders have had only partial and temporary success.[10] Conversely, claims to indivisibility are always at least partially tendentious and often (as in the United States pledge of allegiance) recognitions of the successful application of force to preserve unity. In short, do we speak of Macedonians, Croats and Serbs, of Yugoslavians, of Slavs, of Christians and Muslims, or of Europeans? The answers are obvious only from particular and partisan vantage points. Too often it is only forcible repression which makes us sure we see a true national identity. We lack a theory of the constitution of social selves which will give descriptive foundation to the prescriptive notion of self-determination. We are poorly prepared to talk about national identity or nationalism.[11]

Nationality and nationalism

Ideologists of nationality almost always claim it as an inheritance rather than a contemporary construct. This is true whether the inheritance is conceived as a "primordial" identity, rooted deep in the mists of ancient history, or as deriving from a more recent founding moment like the French Revolution.[12] The notion of inheritance is not by any means simply false, for national identity is something that shapes individuals – a Durkheimian social fact, external, enduring, and coercive – not a matter of completely free individual choice. Claims to ancient origins and especially primordiality are, however, problematic. At the very least, they nearly always radically oversimplify the complexities of national identity and history. The issue is not just whether people are members of one or another nation, or whether a particular claimed nation has the right to self-determination, but what it means to be a member of that nation, how it is to be understood, and how it relates to the other identities its members may also claim or be ascribed.[13]

Such notions of primordial inheritance are among the bases for the widespread illusion that somehow earlier traditions and identities can just be picked up and the communist era treated as an inconsequential interregnum. Among some groups in Russia, for example – and in a good deal of Western discussion of Russia – the idea is current that the "real" Russia is that of the Czars. To some this means an ancient spiritual identity, preserved through long travails and waiting to flower again as beacon to all Slavs. To others, this means a political and cultural development, moving forward rapidly in the late nineteenth and early twentieth centuries, when Russia could aspire to European leadership. Protagonists of each interpretation imagine that somehow when the pall of communism is lifted, the Russians of the late twentieth century will begin to write like Tolstoy, and pick up the torch of an interrupted political development. In this remembered history, the struggles against Orthodox religion, against Czarist rule and rural landlords, and between narodniki, bourgeois democrats, and various stripes of socialists are somehow submerged and communism becomes something both alien and accidental, not an outgrowth of national history.

In Hungary, it is easier to make the case that communism was something imposed from outside, but it is still not obvious that the nation can simply go forward in 1992 as a direct extension of that of 1945's imposed communism or 1921's repression of revolution. Is national identity simply ancient and timeless? Or has it been forged and remade in centuries of struggle? What is the relationship between the Hungary which struggled against Hapsburg rule – and flowered under it; the Hungary which struggled to maintain independence and build a modern state in the early twentieth century; that of Nazi rule and resistance to it; that of communism, both domestic and imported; that of the Georg Lukacs who lived in Budapest and the one who lived in Moscow; that of 1919 (just after the collapse of the Austro-Hungarian empire); 1956 (rebellion against communism and its crushing) and 1989 (communism's collapse)? Different answers to these questions flow from different visions of what it means to be Hungarian. There are similar questions in every country's history, and they are central to the reasons why nationalism is always caught in an intimate but ambiguous relationship with history. Nationalist movements always revere martyrs and cherish sacred dates; they always give nations a history. But as Ernest Renan wrote in perhaps the most famous essay ever written on the subject,

Forgetting, I would even go so far as to say historical error, is a crucial factor in the creation of a nation, which is why progress in historical studies often constitutes a danger for [the principle of] nationality. Indeed, historical enquiry brings to light deeds of violence which took place at the origin of all political formations, even those whose consequences have been altogether beneficial. Unity is always effected by means of brutality.[14]

The issue goes further. History is problematic for nationalism and the tacit assumption of national identity because it always shows nationality to be constructed not primordial. The history which nationalism would write of itself begins with the existence of national identity, continues through acts of heroism and sometimes struggles against oppression, and unites all living members of the nation with the great cultural accomplishments of its past. It is usually not a sociological history, of diversity forged into unity, of oppression of some members of the nation by others, of migration and immigration, and so forth. Precisely because it is not a sociological history, it allows all present-day Russians to identify with nineteenth-century novelists, and for the Westernizing efforts of Peter the Great to make him now a nationalist hero. And even in cosmopolitan Budapest it encourages some Hungarian patriots to identify with Magyar horsemen, accept centuries of international influences, and yet think of Hungarian Jews as members of an alien nation.

So nationality is not primordial but constructed. It is, moreover, a construction specific to the modern era and to the emergence of a modern world-system in which claims to statehood became crucial bases for standing in world affairs, and potentially for autonomy, and in which claims to statehood can be justified most readily by professions of nationhood. This does not make nationality or the sentiments of nationhood any less real. But, by the same token, nationality is not *more* real than many other identities which people may claim, or feel, or reproduce in their social relations. The nationalist claim is that national identity is categorical and fixed, and that somehow it trumps all other sorts of identities, from gender to region, class to political preference, occupation to artistic taste. This is a very problematic claim.

It is not easy to define nationalism. There are important variations where different cultures are at issue, where conquest has subordinated one group of people to another, where older ethnic groupings are being recast in terms of the idea of nation, and where an attempt is being made to forge a new unity out of previous diversity. It seems better to see nationalisms in terms of family resemblances (following Wittgenstein) rather than to search for an essentialist definition of nationalism. When we speak of nationalism, thus, we speak of a somewhat arbitrary subset of claims to identity and autonomy on the part of populations claiming the size and capacity to be self-sustaining. For the purpose of any specific analysis we may want to include, say, the religious and political struggles in Northern Ireland or keep them distinct; there is no perfect boundary, no criterion of selecting nationalisms which includes all the familiar cases we are sure we want to consider without also including a variety of dubious outliers.

With more confidence, we can address the underlying factors which gave rise to nationalism and made it a major genus of identity-claim and source of political mobilization in the modern era. Indeed, by noting these underlying factors we can see why in a strong sense only the modern era has produced nationalism. People have always been joined in groups. These groups have derived their solidarity from kinship and other forms of social (including economic) interconnection, from a common structure of political power, from shared language and culture. But in the modern era, cultural and social structural factors have converged to create and disseminate the notion of national identity and make it central.

Culturally, the most decisive idea behind nationalism (or national identity) is the modern notion of the individual. The idea that human beings can be understood in themselves as at least potentially self-sufficient, self-contained, and self-moving is vital. It is no accident that Fichte is crucial to the histories of both individualism and nationalism. For Fichte's notion of self-recognition, of the person who seemingly confronts himself (or herself) in a mirror and says "I am I" is inextricably tied to the notion of the nation as itself an individual. Just as persons are understood as unitary in prototypical modern thought so are nations held to be integral. As Benedict Anderson has indicated this involves a special sense of time as the history through which the nation as perduring and unitary being passes rather than as a differentiable internal history of the nation.[15] The process of individuation is important not just metaphorically, but as the basis for the central notion that individuals are directly members of the nation, that it marks each of them as an intrinsic identity and they commune with it immediately and as a whole. In ideology, at least, the individual does not require the mediations of family, community, region, or class to be a member of the nation. This is a profound reversal of the weight of competing loyalties from the premodern era (and much of the rest of the world). In this we see the sharp difference of nationalism from the ideology of honor of the lineage, and the chilling potential for children to inform on their parents' infractions against the nation.[16]

Nineteenth-century ideologists of nationalism emphasized a world-historical (or evolutionary) process of individuation in which the world's peoples took on their distinctive characters, missions, and destinies. Or at least the world's "historical nations" did so; others lacked sufficient vigor or national character; they were destined to be failures and consigned to the backwaters of history. Not surprisingly, this is typically how dominant or majority populations thought of minorities and others subordinated within their dominions. This was another conceptualization, in effect, of the Springtime of Peoples. It was the period when France took on its *mission civilisatrice*, Germany found its historical destiny, and Poles crystallized their Romantic conception of the martyr-nation.[17] Each nation had a distinct experience and character, something special to offer the world and something special to express for itself. "Nations," wrote Fichte, "are individualities with particular talents and the possibilities of exploiting those talents."[18]

It is no accident, thus, that philosophers like Fichte emphasized simultaneously the individuation of the person and of the nation. The two notions remain inextricably linked.[19] This very linkage, however, could create tensions. The great cultural geniuses of a nation's history were widely celebrated in the nineteenth century; the proliferation of individual geniuses was proof, especially for the Romantics, of the greatness of the nation. Though Norway had but recently gained an independent cultural status (and was not yet independent politically) her production of geniuses in the late nineteenth century, from Munch to Grieg to Ibsen, was proof enough of her standing even for the German intellectuals of the period. But being cast as the bearer of national identity was not always entirely comfortable for geniuses (or others) with their own individual identities. Writing to Ibsen on his seventieth birthday in 1898, the Norwegian poet Nils Kjoer tried to recover something of the autonomy of the person from the demand for representation of national character: "But a people's individuality is manysided, sufficient to explain any peculiarity of the mind and therefore it explains nothing."[20] If recognized geniuses could feel a tension with the demand that they serve as icons of the nation, pressures of a much more troubling nature were (and are) brought to bear on cultural deviants and minorities.[21] Though nations are ideologically composed of individuals, they are not generally promoters of individual distinctiveness. In the formative phases of nationalism, heroic individuals – cultural as well as military and political heroes – figure prominently, but often in the established nation, conformity to the common culture becomes a central value. The character of nationalism is changed as it shifts from insurgent movement to dominant ideology, though even insurgents can be sharply intolerant of diversity. It is easier to admire heroes from afar, and easiest to claim them when they are dead.

The key structural change which makes it possible to conceive of the nation as unitary is the rise of the modern state. Previous political forms neither demarcated clear boundaries nor fostered internal integration and homogenization. Cities dominated hinterlands; sometimes particularly powerful cities dominated networks of others together with their hinterlands. The various kinds of military (and sometimes religious) elites we call "feudal" controlled substantial territories but with a minimum of centralization of power and limited ability to remake everyday life. Though empires could call on subject peoples for tribute and sometimes foster substantial interaction among diverse subjects, they posed few demands for cultural homogenization. Yet the rise of the modern state involved remarkable administrative integration of previously quasi-autonomous regions and localities. This was true both for purposes of military contest with other states and for internal economic activity and political rule.[22] Eventually, state power could be exercised at the farthest point of a realm as effectively as in the capital. Not only could taxes be collected, but roads could be built, schools run, and mass communications systems created. Linguistic standardization is a common measure of national integration, and historical research reminds us how recent such standardization was in most European countries. Most French people did not speak French before the second half of the nineteenth century.[23] Even demographic behavior – fertility rates, for example, which once varied from locality to locality – become strikingly uniform within nineteenth- and twentieth-century European nation-states.[24]

The capacity of states to administer distant territories with growing intensity was largely due to improvements in transportation and communications infrastructure, on the one hand, and bureaucracy and related information management on the other. It was part of a general growth in large-scale social relations. More and more of social life took place through forms of mediation – markets, communications technologies, bureaucracies – which removed relationships from the realm of direct, face-to-face interaction. In addition to facilitating state power, this growth in "indirect" and large-scale relationships directly facilitated nationalism. It encouraged, for example, increasing reliance on categorical identities rather than webs of relational identities.[25] This transformation was closely related to the growth of capitalism. In the first place, a growing division of labor and intensification of trade relations knit localities and regions together in relations of mutual dependence. Capitalism continually drove its agents out beyond local markets, established competitive pressures around the globe, and demanded coordination of ever-growing supplies of labor and raw materials – even before the generation of increasing consumer demand became an obsession. Capitalism thus both depended on and continually increased the capacity for large-scale and indirect social relations. Because more and more of the activity on which lives and livelihoods depended was taking place at a distance from immediate locales, attempts to conceptualize the commonalties and connections among locales were increasingly important. Beyond this, connections established only through markets and the commodity form were especially prone to reification and representation in categorical terms. The nation became the domestic market, other nations international competitors or clients.[26]

Partly (though not entirely) under pressure of capitalist expansion, the entire world was divided into bounded territories. Every inch of land was declared the province of one state on another. No longer were there hinterlands in which people could follow their ways of life relatively undisturbed by pressures to conform to one or another state's dominant culture. Attempts to preserve local tradition now required active resistance. Where empires demanded mainly political loyalty, states imposed pressures for multifarious forms of cultural loyalty and participation. The opportunity for a people to be self-organizing was increasingly limited to those who could mount a successful claim to state sovereignty. Whatever the actual form of government claimants anticipated, from the moment that sovereignty came to be a claim from below, by the people, rather than from the rulers above, the modern ideal of the nation-state was born. Even Hobbes, in justifying the absolute sovereignty of kings, required first a body of citizens – a nation – capable of granting the right to rule in explicit or implicit social contract. And these citizens were, perforce, basically interchangeable as members of the nation.

This is a crucial contrast between the empire and the nation-state, or, as Weintraub has shrewdly noted, between the cosmopolitan city and the polis. The creation of a political community called for a new kind of interrelationships, and something more than a "live and let live" urbanity. In the cosmopolis or empire, since "heterogeneous multitudes were not called upon to be citizens, they could remain in apolitical coexistence, and each could do as he wished without the occasion to deliberate with his neighbors."[27] In both the polis and the modern nation-state, membership in a common polity requires more than tolerance and common subjection to an external sovereign. It requires mutual communication. This poses an impetus for erasure of differences among the citizens. One of the crucial questions of the modern era is whether meaningful, politically efficacious public discourse can be achieved without this erasure.

The claim to be a nation was a claim to be entitled to a state (or at the very least, to special recognition in the constitution of a state). Though the reciprocal claim was not logically entailed, it was common. By the nineteenth century it was thought not only that every nation deserved a state, but that each state should represent one nation.

Nationalism, as Ernest Gellner writes, held that nations and states "were destined for each other; that either without the other is incomplete, and constitutes a tragedy."[28] One of the features of this new way of conceptualizing sovereignty was that it treated all nation-states as formally equivalent, whatever their size or power. It was no longer possible to conceive of derogated levels of partial or subordinate sovereignty – kings and dukes below emperors, autonomous cities under the protection of prices, etc. Either Burgundy was part of France or it was an alien state; if part of France, it was merely part and not nation in itself. In the mid-nineteenth-century United States, extreme claims to "states' rights" in a weak confederacy of strong subsidiary parts were not so much the claims of one or more alternative nationalisms as claims against nationalism itself. The "country" to which Confederate soldiers owed a duty was conceived from the immediate family and local community outward (and largely through a hierarchy of aristocratic connections, not laterally). It was not conceived primarily as a categorical identity, coterminous with a single polity and culture.[29]

Just as the spread of capitalism created a world-system in which only capitalist competition could be effective, so the division of the world into states created a continuing pressure for the production of nationalisms. Claims for greater autonomy or greater unity could gain legitimacy primarily as claims to create a nation-state, that is, to create a new state to match a pre-existing nation. This is why the single term nationalism encompasses both fissiparous or secessionist movements and unificationist or "pan-"nationalist movements. Croatian or Ukrainian nationalism and pan-Slavic nationalism are dimensions of the same process. Programs for the unification of Europe draw on new histories which emphasize the commonalty of the European experience and identity; the specificity of Europe is counterposed to the rest of the world, rather than the specificity of France being counterposed to Britain or the Netherlands. At the same time, fringe nationalist movements (and claims for regional autonomy) flourish within the European Community. And on Europe's eastern border, Yugoslavia and perhaps other countries seem set to splinter into tiny nation-states. Indeed, nationalist struggles in Eastern Europe reveal the continuing relevance of nationalism in a Western Europe whose publicists had claimed it had moved beyond it. Divergent visions of the European Community and divergent interests have been brought out not just by German unification, but by fighting in Yugoslavia and appeals from Poland, Czechoslovakia, and Hungary for community membership. Not least of all, East to West migration both results from nationalist strife (and nationalist protectionism which creates economic strife), and contributes to xenophobic nationalist responses.

Contrary to some over-glib journalism, there is no global reason for nationalism to be more integrating or disintegrating. The same rhetoric can as readily be deployed to claim unity across separate states (all Slavs or all Arabs) as to demand autonomy for a region of one (e.g. Slovakia or Ruthenia). But there are global reasons why national-ism remains the central form of identity in which people pose their claims to sovereignty. The most important of these is simply the cre-ation of the world-system as a system of states. Though some analysts predict the dissolution of such states in a postmodern welter of local identities and global corporations, the states do not yet seem to have given up the ghost. Nationalism remains important in part because claims to state sovereignty do matter – not least of all because states remain the central organizational frameworks within which democracy can be pursued.

Of course, as state administrative power was growing, and the world was divided into bounded territories, not all potential national-isms thrived.[30] A variety of factors helped. One was simply the history and development of nationalist discourse itself. As Anderson points out, nationalist discourse was not simply a product of simultaneous inven-tion around the globe. It was, at least in part, diffused; in his view it originated in certain colonial experiences and was exported to Western Europe and thence re-exported.[31] The nationalist discourse has grown during the last 300 or so years; more is available as resource to late-comers. Within any putative nation as well, there may be greater or lesser history of nationalist discourse. There may be richer and more evocative discourses on national history and culture to provide particu-lar content to nationalist aspirations. Specific experiences of external challenge or oppression may help to promote national consciousness, providing a clear and significant other for self-identification by contrast. It may be more or less possible to frame other discontents within the nationalist idiom. And other organizing bases, class above all, but also religious organizations, may be either absent, or congruent and supportive rather than competitive.

By the same token, not all nationalisms take the same form. They are shaped in different international contexts and from different domestic experiences. Some grow in response to histories of direct colonialism, others in response to present weakness in the world-system without any specific colonial antagonist to shape them.[32] Some are elite, others democratic. Some seem to absorb an entire culture, claiming everything from language and literature through political practices and agricultural methods as specific to the nation. Others are more narrowly political movements, recognizing common participation in a broader culture. And last but not least, nationalist movements are shaped by the periods of their flowering: it was easier to believe in a happy fellowship of nations in the 1840s than it is today.

Nationalism as successor ideology

As recently as the early Gorbachev years of the mid-1980s, the leadership of the Soviet Union was still propounding a modified vision of the happy fellowship of nations. The condition of this fellowship was the elimination of the social antagonisms which set capitalist nations against each other and made nationalist conflicts an attractive distraction from class struggle. As a book in Novosti's series on "the Soviet Experience" put it,

> as social antagonisms disappeared under socialism, so did national strife and racial inequality and oppression in every form. . . . The socialist multinational culture has been enriched through an intensive exchange of cultural and intellectual values. The socialist nations that have emerged in the USSR have formed a new historical community of people – the Soviet people. . . . Today it would be no exaggeration to say that a feeling of being members of one family prevails among Soviet people.[33]

On the one hand, such lines from a work entitled *How the Soviet Union Solved the Nationalities Question* seem laughably divorced from reality. On the other hand, a moment's reflection on the rapid return of nationalist conflict to what was once the Soviet sphere of influence reminds us why for so long Soviet ideology claimed the resolution of "the nationalities question" as one of the central accomplishments of communism.

Nationalism enters contemporary politics most strikingly in the wake of communist crisis and retreat. As obviously in Ethiopia as in Eastern Europe, this has much to do with conditions which preceded (and sometimes coincided with) communism. Contemporary nationalism is, in part, a direct continuation of old struggles for autonomy from neighbors and stature among nations. This is accentuated in much of Eastern Europe (and Western or Central Asia) by the extent to which communism appeared in the guise of Russian domination. But Russian nationalism is also resurgent, so this cannot be the whole story. Similarly, communism was in many cases imposed on people who had not made a commitment to it through struggles of their own. This too has probably made nationalism more likely as a successor ideology, but its effects should not be exaggerated, for the countries in which communism had most indigenous strength before becoming a Soviet-supported state ideology do not seem markedly less prone to nationalism than those for which communism was more clearly an external imposition.

Communist regimes were perfectly prepared to try to mobilize nationalist sentiments to bolster their legitimacy. The Romanian state made a massive enterprise of reproducing folklore in ways it could both claim and control.[34] The reconstruction of historical buildings was a major part of postwar rebuilding in both Poland and Hungary. Enormous resources and prestige were invested in production of international athletic successes. At the same time, Communist states acted in ways which highlighted national identities in arenas where they officially denied or minimized their significance. Thus, Stalin sought to build "socialism in one country," and his Chinese counterparts still pursue "communism with Chinese characteristics."[35] Russia imposed its language as primary in the Soviet Union and secondary throughout the Warsaw Pact countries. In Yugoslavia, the very stratagem of holding the country together by balancing national groups (and even making sure each nationally defined state contained regions with substantial members of other nationalities) reaffirmed infra-Yugoslavian national identities at the same time that it temporarily held nationalist rivalries in check.[36] Not least of all, the Soviet Army's occupation of much of Eastern Europe could hardly fail to stir some nationalist resentment, especially when coupled with political interference.

Indeed, the most basic reasons for nationalism to flourish in the wake of communism have to do with political repression not socialist – or statist – economics. Communist states repressed most forms of subsidiary identities and discourses on alternative political arrangements. Faced with pressures or opportunities for collective action, people were thrown back on pre-existing bases for identification and collective action. This worked in two ways. First, when people chafed under centralized misrule their national identities were the most readily available ways to understand and respond to abuse. Second, when communism collapsed, nationalism was available to take its place. The latter was true especially where communism collapsed without the development of strong indigenous movements of resistance and counterculture. In Poland, Solidarity offered an alternative arena of cultural production and discourse – though of course Solidarity had a strong nationalist current of its own. In varying degrees other Eastern European countries had both opportunities for cultural creativity and public discourse, and movements which both challenged the existing order and offered an alternative cultural discourse. In much of the Soviet Union, by contrast, repression was more severe, and insurgency from below less developed. One result was that in many settings – the Transcaucasus, for example – nationalism could emerge as the primary form of identity and the basic medium through which people expressed their aspirations for a better life (though nationalism was also closely tied to religious identity).[37]

Communist states did not encourage the cultural creativity and free flow of discourse which could have both knit them together and opened a variety of bases of identity. This had several effects. It meant that in large and heterogeneous countries like the Soviet Union, only state-sponsored cultural productivity could work to unify the country as a whole. When the state lost its credibility, so did much of the cultural basis for unity at the largest level. Behind this suggestion is the general postulate that for populations to achieve some unity as citizenries, they need to be knit together by a common discourse. This does not mean that they are knit together simply by similarity of ideology. On the contrary, mere ideological similarity is a fairly brittle and easily fractured form of cultural unity, particularly when confronted with problems outside its familiar range. A shared discourse of problem solving provides a stronger foundation for confronting new challenges. More generally, culture is a stronger source of unity when it is open to rich and varied forms of creation and discussion. When discussion and creativity are foreclosed in order to maintain ideological conformity, it becomes difficult to achieve the manifold continuous cultural adjustments which are essential to both legitimation processes and sense of common membership in a political community. So, ironically, the very attempt to maintain complete conformity undermined identification with the whole, left it superficial and easily forgotten.[38]

At the same time, the absence of an open cultural sphere or political discourse meant that the development of multiple bases for individual identity was impeded. Outside the range of authoritarian rule and strong nationalism, it is common for people to gain their identities from a range of cross-cutting group affiliations (as Simmel suggested), and from membership in a variety of different salient cultural categories. Thus a woman in the United States may feel a strong sense of identity stemming from her occupation, her gender, her family, her community, her political activity, and her religion as well as and partially in competition with her nation. Though national identity may be a source of inspiration or pride, or of a sense of obligation to help others by pursuing the common good of the United States ahead of the general good of humanity, it is unlikely to be an identity which "trumps" all others. Of course, it is an open question how long this would last if the US ever came under severe external pressure, or wars were again fought on American soil. Nationalism comes to the fore under a variety of historically specific circumstances – like war – as well as perhaps being comparatively stronger in some cultural traditions than others.[39]

In the face of such pressure – and its immediate memory, as in Eastern Europe – liberalism may seem a fairly thin ideology. Liberal capitalism is, however, the main ideological option offered by the West

today. There is of course the Catholic church, with its resurgent con-
servatism on the one hand (abetted by a Polish Pope) and the remnants
of liberation theology on the other. The left remains relevant mainly
by pursuing a variety of ameliorative reforms within the framework of
welfare state capitalism, and defending various special interests of subordinated groups. But it is in disarray overall and no longer seems to
offer a very compelling positive vision to complement its critique of
liberal capitalism. Indeed, the Western Left's failure of vision is directly
related to the resurgence of nationalism in Eastern Europe, as the Left
has not been able to make much significant connection with advocates of
a "third way" or a more robust notion of civil society. Westerners "on
the Left" found East Germany's "New Forum" group appealing, thus,
but were unable to connect with it in very deep or sustaining ways which
would help to provide a viable electoral alternative to the vision of unity
promoted by the Christian Democrats (largely because their own social
democratic vision had been narrowed to a series of ameliorations of
capitalist ills). The weakness of the Western left (not least its defensive
posture in the US) helped to open the way to a discourse in which liberal
capitalism and versions of nationalism are the main contenders for
succession to communism. These contenders, as the German example
reveals, are not as antithetical as has sometimes been thought. Many
forms of nationalism can thrive quite happily on a capitalist foundation
and put forward their claims in the rhetoric of liberalism. Indeed, liberalism's strengths run to the enunciation and preservation of certain
liberties, not to the constitution of strong social or cultural identities.
Nationalism can be its complement – rooted in the same individualism –
as readily as it can be dissolved by liberalism's advocacy of the individual
as the basic unit of analysis.

Nationalism and democracy

Nationalism is not an intrinsically "bad" ideology. It has been and
remains an important source of inspiration. Any account of the political
problems attendant on nationalism which does not recognize the achievements of poets, painters, and composers who were moved by nationalist
sentiments misses an important part of the story.[40] Any account which
imagines that citizens or human beings could be rational actors unmoved
by cultural commitments and pre-rational identities loses touch with
reality. In the political realm itself, nationalism is not intrinsically pernicious or anti-democratic. In the first place, there needs to be some
culturally constructed identity behind the word "self" in the idea of self-
determination. It is worth recalling too that in the 1840s nationalism
often appeared as a progressive, liberal ideology in which a domestic

push for democratic expression was coupled with a respect for other nations. Even more than respect, Romantics of the early nineteenth century were sufficiently inspired by heroic nationalist struggles to offer their own lives on behalf of alien nations. Yet even this phrase reveals a tension. To the strong Romantic humanist – to Byron, say – there were no alien nations, only many expressions of a common humanity striving for freedom and creative voice. Yet in extremes Romanticism (like its current postmodernist successors) had as much trouble making sense of difference as Enlightenment rationalism; neither grappled well with the problem of incommensurable practices, with the reasons why differences become hostilities.[41] And the exclusivity implied by the word alien is more common in the rhetoric of nationalism. Nationalism is all too often the enemy of democracy rooted in civil society.

In the first place, nationalism in power is very different from nationalist resistance to alien rule. Not unlike authoritarian regimes as I described them above, nationalists too often tend to promote the pseudo-democracy of sameness instead of the recognition and respect of difference. Ironically, like communism, nationalism often stifles cultural discourse – not in the name of the state or even necessarily by the imposition of state power; it can work by a closure of the mind. Nationalism in power is often a repressive ideology demanding strict adherence to the authority of the official embodiments of national tradition – and very unlike nationalism in opposition which is generally a strong stimulus to cultural productivity. The problems arise with the assertion that there is only one right way for any individual to be a Pole, or a Russian, an Azeri or an American.

Repression is wielded not just against diversity of cultural expression but against the variety of alternative bases for personal identity which might compete with the nation. Thus the common antagonism of nationalists to autonomy and equality for women is not just a continuation of sexist traditions. Nationalism encourages this sexism by internal (and I think non-essential) cultural traditions – e.g. valuing the family as the source of the nation's continuity in time, and seeing men as future martyrs, women as mothers. Beyond this, however, nationalists resist women's movements because accepting the domination of male interests and perceptions merely perpetuates a taken-for-granted, monolithic view of the nation, while encouraging women to identify their distinctive interests and views opens claims that gender has autonomous status as a basis for personal identity which does not pale into insignificance before the commonalties of (male-dominated) nationhood.

In this sense, nationalism has totalitarian potential. It can be treated as a categorical identity more fundamental than other personal identities, even able to override them, and as fixed in both biographical and historical time. This is what I mean by saying that nationalism is used to "trump" other identities or values.[42] Nationalists often want the sentiment or sense of national identity to go beyond the feeling of being more at home in one place than another, beyond placing a special value on the traditions with which one grew up, beyond focusing one's attention more on one subset of humanity than on the whole. In its extreme forms, nationalism, like religious fundamentalism, often involves claims to monopolize the sources of legitimate identity. As Hannah Arendt wrote, we are apt since Tocqueville to blame conformism on the principle of equality, but "whether a nation consists of equals or non-equals is of no great importance in this respect, for society always demands that its members act as though they were members of one enormous family which has only one opinion and one interest."[43]

The decisive question about nationalism, therefore, is whether it can thrive with the nation open to competing conceptualizations, diverse identities, and a rich public discourse about controversial issues. These issues were faced in France in the late nineteenth century; in the Dreyfus affair victory went to the forces of openness and heterogeneous civil society as the basis for democracy. There have been attempts to revoke the victory, notably by World War II-era collaborationists and the contemporary radical right, under the leadership of nationalists like Jean-Marie Le Pen. But in Central and Eastern Europe there have been few such signal victories and, as Adam Michnik has suggested, the issue is a very current one:

> In both France and Poland the question was whether the nation was to be open and the state tolerant and multicultural, or whether the state was to be based on authoritarian principles and nationalistic doctrine. And I think this has been the central question ever since. Whenever the shadow of anti-Semitism arose in Polish public life, it was an unmistakable signal that people with antidemocratic, intolerant views were on the political offensive.[44]

It would be good, but not enough, to say that tolerance should reign within states. Even multinational, multicultural states require more than simply tolerance among subsidiary peoples. They require public discourse. Citizens from different nationalities, as from different regions, religions, or occupations, need to be able and willing to engage each other in discourse about the social arrangements which hold them together and order their lives – in brief, about the common good. Moreover, the same is crucial within nationalities. There is no reason to accept monolithic conformity within any one nation or people (insurgent or in power). Not only may states be multinational or multicultural, nations themselves must – if they are to be allies of liberty – admit and encourage internal diversity whether they are coterminous with states or exist as subsidiary identities within states. It is necessary, in other words, that the nation be open to democracy and diversity whether or not the close link between nation and state is severed. In power, extreme nationalists do not just repress other peoples, they repress the diversity and creativity of people within the very nation they cherish.

Without diversity, democracy is hardly distinct from a dictatorship of the mass. Indeed, it is hard to imagine how such a monolithic mass could be sustained beyond an ephemeral uprising except by means of centralized totalitarian power. Nationalism is only benign when it does not tend towards this pseudo-democracy of sameness. And this is where civil society comes in. Civil society is the locus of diverse groups and individuals and more importantly of their contact with each other. Division of labor and other sources of difference may arise within civil society or be brought into it from the family or other less public realms. But in civil society, the exchange not only of goods but of ideas can take place. Advocates of democracy in the late twentieth century are called upon to discover whether the virtues of diversity, sociability, and tolerance associated with the ideal of the cosmopolis can be combined with the self-governing political community of the polis. Can political arguments be considered on their merits, at least partially autonomous from the identities of the arguers?[45]

The *locus classicus* of such public life lay in European cities of the eighteenth centuries. It may be that current trends in Europe – especially the integration of the European Community but also perhaps the creation or restoration of states in the East – may actually restore some of the early modern prominence of cities in public life and social organization. Links among cities and/or regions may partially replace those among states. But major improvements in the nature of modern public discourse cannot come about simply through direct interpersonal relationships in cities. They must happen also through television and newspapers. They must happen on the scale of millions of people in powerful states. Political parties with their patronage, bureaucracies, and public relations staffs will mediate the relations between groups as much as cafes with their intellectual arguments.[46] These parties must remain open to diversity for they are crucial means of achieving not consensus so much as reasonable compromises where consensus is impossible. If democracy is to flourish, nationalism must not become the enemy of difference.

The events of 1989 showed the power of mass media to further an internationalization of culture and politics. I was in Beijing that spring, and watched with amazement. Chinese students deliberately echoed Poland's Solidarity movement, and within days protesting students in

Eastern Europe marched with headbands and placards proclaiming their sympathy with the Chinese. And today Chinese democrats – and nationalists – look to Eastern Europe for inspiration. The nationalism which figured centrally in these movements is an international phenomenon – as nationalism was in 1848. Not only is it shared through mass communication, it is driven by global processes that value and privilege nations as categories of identity between the immediately interpersonal and the local. It is often repeated that the twin tendencies of the present era are towards globalization and localization. This has an element of truth, but it is an overused mantra. It neglects the importance of states as arenas for democratic struggles, and agents for contesting an economic power which has not ceased to be concentrated as it has become global. And it suggests that the division of the world into ever smaller units of putative internal sameness is the only way to achieve happiness in our immediate lifeworlds. It is as though someone decided that Durkheim's mechanical solidarity is the only kind that works.

Nationalism encourages the identification of individuals not with locality per se, not with the webs of their specific interpersonal relationships, but with an abstract category. This category of nation may be a helpful mediation between the local and the global. Indeed, I think this is one crucial reason why nationalism is unlikely to disappear any time soon. Globalization, where it occurs, is likely to call forth new and different nationalisms and more generally politics of identity. Far from producing a cosmopolitanism somehow antithetical to nationalism, the massive international migrations currently underway are apt to accentuate in both predictable and unpredictable ways the salience of cultural divides and identities in many people's everyday lives. Simply getting rid of nationalism is thus not a viable response to its disagreeable features.

Contrary to much received wisdom, I have argued that both states on the one hand, and nationalism and the discourse of national identity on the other, are likely to remain of central importance in an increasingly globalized world. Much of the question of how this will affect human life turns on the extent to which and manner in which institutions of civil society provide social foundations for democracy. Whether claims to national identity will be used to override other identities, either within or across national boundaries, will be determined not just by the cultural content of nationalist ideologies or the choices of nationalist ideologues. It will be determined also by the presence or absence of cross-cutting social ties and mediating institutions.

Is it possible to build states and even confederations of states in which cohesion and self-rule is established through public discourse across lines of difference? Can we conceive the growth of a cultural unity within such states or confederations that does not devalue or demand the obliteration of other sources of personal and political identity? Or must we fall back on nationalism alone as our shelter in a world grown too frightening, or as the one immediately satisfying identity with which to confront the globalization of capital?

5

Nationalism, political community, and the representation of society
Or, why feeling at home is not a substitute for public space

In both social science and public discourse, our most basic understand-ings of what count as societies are shaped more than we usually care to admit by the modern era's distinctive rhetoric of nations and national identity. This "discursive formation" (in Foucault's sense of the term) is implicated in the usage that constructs societies as bounded, integral, wholes with distinctive identities, cultures, and institutions.[1] The tacit assumption of nationalist rhetoric reinforces our acceptance of state-centered conventions of data-gathering that make nation-states the predominant units of comparative research – even when the topics are cultural or social psychological, not political-institutional. Charles Tilly has referred to the "pernicious postulate" that societies are bounded and discrete, but his critique has hardly ended the usage, partly because it is so deeply embedded in the way we speak and think.[2] This is not an unmotivated error by social scientists; it is a participation, perhaps unwitting, in the nationalist rhetoric that pervades public life and con-temporary culture. This rhetoric presents nations with a decontextualized autonomy that hampers academic understanding and has impacts on practical affairs.

This notion of society has a history and a rich meaning. A particu-larly salient root lies in seventeenth- and eighteenth-century discourses about political legitimacy and collective prosperity (joined in the notion of commonwealth). These brought forward arguments about the dis-tinctiveness of "the people" and of civil society as self-organizing entities with existence distinctive from particular rulers.[3] Arguing a case for legitimacy and rights ascending from the people rather than descending from God or inherited office, thinkers from Locke and Montesquieu through the Scottish moralists to Althusius and Gierke made a case for the priority of societies to political regimes. It was common, if not quite crucial, that "society," in this usage, be represented as self-moving and whole. Put another way, society was rendered autonomous, made the "text" against which all else was "context." It was but a short step to nationalism, with its treatment of nations as themselves individuals – beings capable of action and existence through history, autonomous and operating in the context of other independent beings of like kind, true Leibnizian monads.

Internally, nationalist rhetoric typically treated nations as categories of individuals, units of membership for persons equivalent in their common relation to the whole. The latter notion in turn strongly inflected the idea of citizenship. To be a citizen was to fit properly into such a categorical notion of the nation-state, and to be the equal of other citizens. This could, of course, be a radical notion – as during the French Revolution – and it should not be thought that nationalism is in any sense inherently conservative. It is as basic to the idea of revolutionary action as the action of an entire people (represented, of course, by a few and by distinctive cultural devices) as to the struggle for democratic citizenship rights against monarchs. Nationalism thus emerged alongside modern states as a discourse for understanding questions of legitimacy and more generally the "match" between people and state.

From this account of nations as the basis for states we derive crucial features of our understanding of society. Various contributory streams to the discourse helped also to give rise to sociology itself. Sociology has always had contrary tendencies, to be sure, including a number of efforts to proceed, as it were, "upwards" from directly interpersonal relations, refusing the macrosociological assumption of society as a whole. Notions of social system and institutions have a different provenance, of course, but still depend in most usages on nationalist rhetoric for their tacit assumptions of bounded, autonomous, and decontextualizable units.

Similarly, the discourse of political community is deeply shaped by nationalism but has not included much critical examination of the implications of its nationalist inheritance.[4] We use terms like "community," for example, as though there is no problem in making them refer simultaneously to local, face-to-face networks and whole nations conceived as categories of culturally similar persons.[5] We neglect, or at least fail adequately to explicate the difference between, social self-organization through movements, collective action, and public discourse, on the one hand, and relatively impersonal processes operating mostly "behind the backs" of social actors. In this way, we fail to make some of the important contributions we might to understanding citizenship and more generally to grasping democracy as a social and cultural project.[6] Debates on nationality and citizenship need to problematize not only the contrast among territorial, civic, and ethnic models, and the questions of how to understand immigrants, minorities, and aboriginal populations, but also the very way in which a rhetoric of nations and nationalism shapes the representation of political community.

Membership in a society is an issue of social solidarity and cultural identity as well as legally constructed state citizenship. This is all the more important to recognize in an era shaped both by new cultural diversities and new challenges to the abilities of states to maintain sharp and socially effective borders. We need not leap to the conclusion that globalization is fatally weakening the nation-state to see the prominence of both solidarities and activities that cross borders and ways in which transnational organizations and links may work to empower subnational regions or other groupings.[7]

Discourse about citizenship is impoverished and sometimes confused, I want to contend, when multiple meanings of solidarity and identity are not addressed. A minimal notion of socially decontextualized, individual jural entitlement has increasingly been found wanting, e.g. by both feminist theorists and communitarians.[8] Several scholars have attempted to broaden understanding of citizenship, but these otherwise valuable efforts are marred by lack of attention to distinctions among different modes of social belonging. Specifically, because of its centrality to democracy, I want to argue for the importance of keeping a conception of public space – a space of discourse but also the space within which jural entitlements can be enforced – distinct from both webs of interpersonal relationships and large-scale categories of cultural identity. Citizenship in this sense is metaphorically located between the locally different and the nationally same. It is not a replacement for either, but it is potentially a protection against both – that is, against the demands of extremely dense and binding local networks (say, kin groups) and against calls for cultural conformity on a national scale.

In the present chapter, I shall develop this theme primarily with regard to the implications of cultural diversity. Please bear in mind, however, that I mean to do so against the background of the larger issues just evoked and especially the slippage in the notion of community between the local world of directly interpersonal relations and broad cultural identities like nationality. One important dimension of all these issues is the ways in which a rhetoric or discursive formation rooted in the idea of nation shapes the relevant understandings of collective identity. Nationalism has helped to produce a way of conceiving of society that lends itself to specific approaches to citizenship. Both confusions and argumentative advantages for certain ways of thinking follow.

A confusing tendency to intermingle different notions of social belonging has become prominent in communitarian rhetoric. The term community has come to be used in a misleading omnibus manner that obscures the distinctions among different kinds of groupings:

(a) Communities – relatively small groups that are not primarily constituted through formal political-legal institutions but through informal, directly interpersonal relationships;

(b) Categories based on the putative cultural similarity or jural equivalence of persons, and commonly comprised of large numbers of people with a low density of directly interpersonal ties; and

(c) Publics – quasi-groups constituted by mutual engagement in discourse aimed at determining the nature of social institutions including states.

The confusion is wider than communitarian theory, of course, as is the sentiment attached to the word community. The English language itself helps obscure the distinction among different senses of citizenship and nationality: jural status, cultural identity, and civic participation. In French, by contrast, the distinction of citizenship as a Republican idea from nationality and being the subject of a monarch is clearer.[9] Citizenship, by contrast to community or categorical nationality, is a specific mode of belonging directly dependent on public space. Among citizens, political participation is distinctively possible:

(a) because the unit of membership is in fact a polity (and not simply a community or a nation);

(b) because its collective affairs are to some considerable extent organized through public discourse; and

(c) because citizens are empowered to enter effectively into that discourse.

The limits to the pure jural notion of citizenship become apparent when we consider the extent to which a democratic polity depends on social solidarity and a shared sense of belonging rather than merely on force, and when we ask what social or cultural conditions empower citizens.

The slippage among community, category, and public is prominent not only in what we usually call communitarian writing, but in many arguments on behalf of minorities and other "communities" marked by oppression or difference. It has been proposed, for example, that culturally or socially distinct subgroups within larger polities – say the Quebecois or aboriginal populations in Canada – be granted special constitutional status.[10] Arguments for such special statuses, and for group rights more generally, need to attend to different understandings of identity and belonging.

In particular, where such arguments are made on behalf of potentially autonomous and self-sustaining populations and their ways of life, they may portend a severing of the link between social solidarity and citizenship. Special statuses may, for example, encourage in-group solidarity at the expense of intergroup solidarity. This raises questions about whether a Durkheimian "organic" solidarity based on recognition of interdependence is endangered by merely "mechanical" jural linkages among fellow citizens living in parallel societies. Constitutional arrangements recognizing such special statuses might then be thought to require balance by attempts to encourage cross-cutting social ties.

Similarly, the notion of special status tends to enshrine a categorical notion of membership. This may be proposed on behalf of a community, perhaps one characterized by a "traditional" way of life. But enactment inescapably transforms this by the logic of a jurally defined category, much as the rise of the national state transformed traditional polities in early modern Europe. Questions inevitably arise about the criteria of membership, since a binary in/out criterion is apt to be needed. More basically, individuals are presumed to be identified quite strongly by their membership in such a group. Whatever multiple, overlapping, and shifting patterns of identity may obtain for the rest of the population would be inhibited or at risk within such special status categories. Moreover, the particular patterns of power relations that constitute a community and way of life would tend to be presumed into its new legal special statuses. It would seem incumbent on any grant of social status to minimize this. If a traditional community excludes women from public life, for example, ways should be sought in any grant of special status to provide legal resources for members seeking to overcome such disabilities.[11] This would presumably extend to changing the culture of the group with special status. This implies a difficulty – large, though perhaps not insurmountable for attempts to ground the grant of special status solely on the virtues of preserving a traditional way of life. The alternative, however, is for the state that grants such special status to treat each group to which it applies as essentially fixed and immutable. This would make the state as much an advocate of cultural ossification as of living tradition, and potentially the support of a particular inequitable power structure. After all, no cultural patterns simply "continue." Rather, they are reproduced in human action, and in every cultural context, the capacity for influence over such reproduction is unequally distributed and patterns of culture reflect, among other things, social power.

At the same time, individualist arguments against such claims about group rights often fall short of truly joining the issue in question. Many, for example, reduce the issue to a matter of individual particularities yielding different interests before the state. But all such individual particularities inherently produce categories of persons with similar particularities. Even if not previously joined as a subsidiary society, members of these may mobilize, and form social bonds and common culture. In an important American example, thus, it has been argued that deafness is a matter not simply of physical difference (let alone disability) but of culture – complete with an arguably separate language.[12] Where pre-existing cultural commonalities and social bonds are at issue the individualist conception captures matters even less well.

In general, the rhetorics of culture and community are problematic ones by which to grasp political rights. Most basically, they encourage reification of the unity and uniformity of what are everywhere, in principle, and inevitably internally diverse entities, and of the politics of representation by which such internally diverse phenomena as cultures and social groups are made to appear as integral. The currently existing power structures involved in the representation of groups or ways of life as autonomous and distinct tend to be favored by formal recognition of the collective identities with which they are joined.

Arguments for the public recognition of culturally diverse groupings often start by claiming those groupings to be "natural" or "essential," while presuming the broader public forums in which the claims are brought forward to be artificial or constructed. Multiculturalism thus commonly appears as an argument for diversity rooted in a claim to integral singularity – not unlike nationalism. The premise of many multiculturalist arguments is that people "naturally" feel at home in one culture that is either smaller than a nation-state or cuts across the boundaries of nation-states. This follows nationalism in privileging one sense of belonging – that of membership in a categorically distinct culture. There are, however, different senses of belonging, and multiple modes of social solidarity.

We may "feel at home" with people whom we know personally, to whom we are committed in the networks of social relationships that make up community. It is a mistake to equate this with sharing largely similar cultural styles. The two may overlap, but cultural similarities are used to demarcate very large categories of people not knit by dense interpersonal relationships and represented (often falsely) as sharply bounded. Communities and categories are, then, distinct. Both differ sharply from solidarity forged through public discourse in which distinct individual or subgroup positions may be articulated and draw their meaning, motives, and power from their embeddedness in the larger, but differentiated, whole. At the local and small-scale level, community, cultural categories, and public discourse easily overlap. But on a larger scale, community in the sense of dense, multiplex networks of interpersonal relationships becomes impossible. We are left with similarities – a very different matter – or publics. The two are not opposites. Indeed, cultural similarity may grow out of public discourse and public discourse may be grounded in cultural similarity. But the analytic distinction is important.

We may feel at home in a certain public discourse – as intellectuals inhabit particular arguments with a comfortable feeling of being at home, especially when returning from abroad. We are, in other words, comfortable with particular ways of expressing ourselves and with particular sorts of differences from others, as well as with sameness or identification with "people like us." We even enjoy, I would posit, particular ways of feeling *different* from others, and one of the unsettling things about entering new cultural contexts is that we lose some of those familiar differentiations, not just familiar identifications. One who has always thought of himself as a left-wing outsider or cultural critic, for example, may be suddenly uncomfortable when traveling abroad. Not only is he apt to be seen by others as a representative of the dominant national culture with which he considers himself to be in some tension (and perhaps rightly so). There may be an unsettling loss of personal identity in discovering that the cultural cues that locate one's distinctive differences no longer operate.

Nonetheless, though they may overlap, the activity of engaging in a public discourse is distinct from the activity of finding commonality in pre-established cultural similarity.[13] Public discourse depends on articulating differences – crucially differences of opinion; potentially but not necessarily also differences of group identity.[14] "Articulating" is a key word here. What we know as "public" discourse is that in which ideas, opinions, and identities are made clear and subjected to more or less open discussion – ideally, perhaps, to rational-critical discussion. It is an arena of debate and acknowledged attempts at persuasion. Public discourse in this sense is distinct from collective representations that invoke the common identity of the whole as a trump card against the internal differentiation of identities and interests.

Such public discourse is also one way in which culture is transmitted or reproduced, and indeed new culture may be made and identities created or changed in public interaction. People do not emerge fully formed from private life into the public sphere (as Habermas seems sometimes to imply). However, public discourse is distinct from much of what goes on in families, communities, and other settings – especially face-to-face ones – in which we transact much of the business of our lives – fall in love, raise children, play sports, read poetry, listen to music. These latter settings are distinct by virtue of scale, but also – partly for reasons that scale facilitates – by virtue of the extent to which common understandings can be taken for granted and produced, tested, or altered unconsciously, or at least imperceptibly, as a by-product of other activities, without rational-critical codification or publicness. Above all, these arenas of familiarity are distinct from public settings by virtue of the (relative) absence of strangers. Publics, by contrast, are arenas in which people speak to each other at least in part as strangers. This need not mean that they have never met, but that they are not bound by dense webs of common understandings or shared social relations, that they have to establish rather than take for granted where they agree and disagree. While an element of "publicness" may enter into familial or communal realms of familiarity – one may engage in a rational-critical debate about kinship and descent when inheritance is at stake – very much of it would radically disrupt daily life and undo what we mean by community or family.[15]

We need to be attentive, then, to three distinct modes of relating to each other and to culturally produced and encoded information: community, categories, and publics. Too much communitarian and multiculturalist discourse (whatever its other merits) follows nationalist discourse in representing large-scale categories in which people are in fact quite different and are often strangers to each other on the model of small-scale familial or communal groupings. In arguing the case for strengthening community, thus, Etzioni emphasizes "affective attachment." But affective attachment means something different when it is a bond between concrete persons and when it binds persons to large-scale cultural categories such as nations.[16] More generally, communitarian and multicultural discourses often coincide in presenting nations, cultures, peoples, genders, etc. as realms of familiarity and sameness, not as categories within which heterogeneous members have rights of participation. This is one reason why the category of public is only weakly developed in such discourse. It makes a great deal of difference, for example, whether one talks about a Black public sphere in which different ideas connected to race are critically debated among Black people, or a Black nationalism in which the identity of Black people with each other is more uncritically assumed.[17] What makes us feel at home, in other words, may not coincide precisely with what enables us to articulate and rationally-critically debate our differences of opinion.

Surprisingly often, multiculturalist visions celebrate out-group difference and deny the relevance of in-group difference. They describe the interplay of putatively discrete collective (and individual) identities. They offer suggestions about how people of different colors, or religions, or ethnicities, or sexual orientations might better live together within single societies. But they presume that these labels define meaningful social groupings, that the members of these groups accept the dominance of a single label over their identities, and that their identities are relatively settled. In other words, these simplistic multiculturalist visions share with monocultural visions the notion that the world can be divided neatly into categories within which individuals are largely similar by virtue of the identifying traits they share, and between which there are consistent and significant differences. The distinguishing claim of multiculturalists, then, becomes simply that people of different cultures can live together peaceably and to mutual benefit within the same country. It is a sort of domestic equivalent to the optimistic, cosmopolitan nationalism of the early nineteenth-century "Springtime of Peoples."[18] Such a view does little to challenge or even to analyze critically the underlying notion of discrete and internally homogenous cultures that has been widespread, powerful, and largely pernicious throughout the modern era. This is a vision of the world pioneered by nationalism, and reinforced by much in the broader current of modern individualism.

As individualism posits discrete and integral personal identities, with unique biographical trajectories, so nationalism posits sharply bounded and internally unified nations with unique histories. One of the central paradoxes of modernity, indeed, is that this international rhetoric of national identity has become the preferred, nearly universal, mode of claiming autonomous local cultural identity. Countries claim their local distinctiveness or uniqueness, in other words, by claiming to be tokens of a more universal type: nations.

Nationalist discourse involves an attempt to constitute identities in sharp, categorical terms, to render boundaries clear and identities integral even while the processes of capitalist expansion, slave trade, colonization, war, and the globalization of culture all have ensured the production of ever more multiplicities and overlaps of identities. It is fashionable to characterize modernity as involving standardization, routinization, and the elimination of differences. It is opposed thereby both to prior local heterogeneities – the differences of dialect and craft that distinguished European villages before industrialization and modern communications technologies – and to postmodern celebrations of differences. But modernity is more contradictory than this. For every spatially localized "difference" that is eradicated by McDonald's or television there are increased confrontations with difference created by the juxtapositions of diverse cultures in media and cosmopolitan cities. New hybrid identities are created by international migrations – including the slave trade (which was just as integrally modern as the campaigns to abolish it that are more often treated as modern by self-congratulatory Western thinkers). Peasant economies never were in all respects models of heterogeneity – consider the remarkably common routines of most peasant farmers and the remarkable diversity of occupations today. Nonetheless, though modernity brought new differentiations and new juxtapositions of people different from each other, dominant patterns of thought attempted to order difference by relying on categorizations of those presumed to be essentially the same. The phenomenon of "double consciousness" that W.E.B. Du Bois analyzed in the situation of those who were both Negro and American was a resistance to this dominant pattern in the construction of identities.[19] It was an assertion that in the politics and experience of identity, "both/and" is true at least as often as "either/or." But it was in more than one sense a minority voice.

However common, even ubiquitous, double consciousness really was, the prevailing rhetorics of identity, agency, and citizenship sought singular, integral subjects. Thus lines were drawn on maps and populations understood – at least ideally – to fit as unambiguously as possible within them. Moreover, the loyalties and obligations of individuals to nations were commonly described as unmediated and direct. Traditional kinship systems reckoned identity in a series of nested groups from families outward to larger lineages and clans, often cross-cut by age-sets and other groupings.[20] Modern thought, by contrast, has understood individuals to be immediately members of a nation, as though nationality were inscribed in their very bodies. Nationalism launched a war on traditional intermediate associations. And ways of constituting local identities throughout the world, from China to India to Turkey to Spain were all influenced by this discourse of individuals and nations. Even in the manifestly international culture of what Paul Gilroy has called "the Black Atlantic," produced by the slave trade and maintained by later migrations of people and cultural products, there was a tendency to construct Black identities in essentialist terms:

> original, folk, or local expressions of black culture have been identified as authentic and positively evaluated . . . while subsequent hemispheric or global manifestations of the same cultural forms have been dismissed as inauthentic and therefore lacking in cultural or aesthetic value precisely because of their distance (supposed or actual) from a readily identifiable point of origin.[21]

Nowhere, however, was the formation of national unity really apolitical or entirely a matter of distant past history – not even in the countries that form paradigmatic Western cases of nations by implicit reference to which the claims of others are judged. The countries where republican and sometimes democratic constitutions took root – and the countries with the clearest acceptance in international forums – commonly have been ones where the history of unification itself could be kept at a distance. As Ernest Renan said of France,

> Forgetting, I would even go so far as to say historical error, is a crucial factor in the creation of a nation, which is why progress in historical

studies often constitutes a danger for [the principle of] nationality. Indeed, historical enquiry brings to light deeds of violence which took place at the origin of all political formations, even those whose consequences have been altogether beneficial. Unity is always effected by means of brutality.[22]

The consequences of the pursuit of national unity by strategies of both forgetting past brutalities and forging ahead with new ones included an implicit repression of differences within such identities and differences cross-cutting them. As Gilroy puts it, "where racist, nationalist, or ethnically absolutist discourses orchestrate political relationships so that these identities appear to be mutually exclusive, occupying the space between them or trying to demonstrate their continuity has been viewed as a provocative and even oppositional act of political insubordination."[23] The insubordination is resented and often repressed not only by established states and agents of institutionalized power, but by those who would organize social movements and popular struggles on behalf of oppressed or disadvantaged groups.

Nationalism was not the whole, but only the most important part of the tacit consensus forged in the late nineteenth century as to what would count as politically appropriate identities. It played a central role in the development of "essentialist" thinking that was also basic to the way class, race, gender, sexual orientation, and other modalities of collective identities came to be constituted.[24] In all cases, the assumption has been widespread both in social theory and in more popular discourses that these cultural categories address really existing and discretely identifiable collections of people – and more surprisingly that it is possible to understand each category by focusing on its primary identifier rather than on the way it overlaps with, contests and/or reinforces others.

Put another way, as I suggested near the beginning, it has been the tacit assumption of modern social and cultural thought that people are normally members of one and only one nation, that they are members of one and only one race, one gender, and one sexual orientation, and that each of these memberships describes neatly and concretely some aspect of their being. It has been assumed that people naturally live in one world at a time, that they inhabit one way of life, that they speak one language, and that they themselves, as individuals, are singular, integral beings. All these assumptions came clearly into focus in the late nineteenth century in ways closely linked to nationalism; all deeply shape contemporary multiculturalist discourse; and all seem problematic.

The underlying issues are hard to get at because social and cultural theory did not consistently study the constitution of nations, races, genders, or other categories. Rather, a variety of putatively neutral terms – society, culture, subculture – were introduced. Their seeming neutrality obscured the extent to which they reflected the presumptions about categorical distinctiveness that were forged especially with sex, race, class, and nation in mind. Social scientists came to a remarkable extent to take for granted the objects of their study – notably societies – without reflecting on the extent to which their view of what societies were had been produced largely on the foundation of nineteenth-century nationalist reasoning.

The nineteenth-century discourse of nationalism still shapes much of our vocabulary for thinking about these issues – and identifying the subjects of democratic projects. From Bosnia to the South Bronx, the question of European unification to that of Canadian division, this mode of understanding identity and difference remains basic to contemporary politics and culture. Yet politicians – and for that matter some influential social theorists such as Jürgen Habermas – act often as if these questions are settled in advance, in some sort of prepolitical prehistory to our contemporary struggles. Habermas's recent proposals for a "constitutional patriotism," for example, though honorable are basically idealizations of the "civic nationalism" model, with the same presumption of an underlying "natural" nation always already there.[25] To such presumptions, sociologists respond with an idea of constructionism that makes any identity seem equally plausible, but this robs us of a grasp on why some of these identities have the power they do, and underestimates the importance of the enduring rhetoric within which struggles over identity are conducted. Poststructuralist celebrations of difference resist uniformity but too often abandon the search for explanation and the prospect of giving normative guidance against the violence of simple expression of will.

Two tacit guiding assumptions to much modern thinking on matters of identity are that individuals ideally ought to achieve maximally integrated identities, and that to do so they need to inhabit self-consistent, unitary cultures or lifeworlds. It is thought normal for people to live in one culture at a time, for example; to speak one language; to espouse one set of values; to adhere to one polity. But why? Not, I would suggest, on the basis of historical or comparative evidence. On the contrary, throughout history and still to a considerable extent around the world we find multilingualism common; we find people moved simultaneously by different visions of the world (not least, religion and science); we find people able to understand themselves as members of very differently organized collectivities at local and more inclusive levels, or at different times or stages of life. Think of the extent to which civilization has flourished in polyglot and more heterogeneous empires and in cosmopolitan trading cities. Consider the extent to which nationalist visions of internally uniform and sharply bounded cultural and political identities have had to be produced by struggle against a richer, more diverse and more promiscuously cross-cutting play of differences and similarities. The pursuit of "integrity" in personal identity may be important, but it is a project responding to the challenge of multiple values and desires and often complexly varying external contexts.

Modernity, ironically, has brought both the attempt to "clarify" and "consolidate" identities, and the production of an enormously increased field of cultural differences. Conquests, extension of markets, migrations, and expansions in the reach and ease of use of communications and transport technologies all played a role. So did new freedoms in cultural creativity and a new diversity in material occupations. The last several hundred years have been an era not of simple growth in sameness but of conflicting tendencies. The idea that people need "naturally" to feel at home in a taken-for-granted and internally homogenous community contends with the creation of polities and cultural fields too large and differentiated to be organized as communities. Within such larger settings, it is not an adequate response to human differences to allow each person to find the group within which they feel at home. It is crucial to create public space within which people may engage each other in discourse – not just to make decisions, but to make culture and even to make and remake their own identities.[26]

6

Inventing the opposition of ethnic and civic nationalism
Hans Kohn and *The Idea of Nationalism*

The contrast of ethnic to civic nationalism, organic to liberal, Eastern to Western is so habitual today that it is hard to recall that it was invented. Like nationalism itself, it seems almost natural, a reflection of reality rather than a construction of it. But while the distinction does grasp important aspects of modern history and contemporary politics, it does so in a specific way, shaping evaluations and perceptions, reinforcing some political projects, and prejudicing thinkers against others. And it was invented. Hans Kohn was the most influential source both of the opposition of civic to ethnic nationalisms and of its association with a parallel opposition between Western and Eastern versions of modernity.[1] *The Idea of Nationalism* is the most important statement of Kohn's view, and it occupies a central place amid his voluminous writings as the main general statement of his mature perspective. It is of interest not only because Kohn was an important scholar and public intellectual, and because his contrast of civic and ethnic nationalisms has been deeply influential, but also because his book is an enlightening window onto the more general relationship between liberalism and nationalism.

The Idea of Nationalism has in one sense an odd organization. After a general introduction to the "nature" of nationalism, Kohn traces the development of the idea of nationalism in Western history, from Israel and Hellas through Rome, the Middle Ages, the Renaissance and the Reformation to the late eighteenth-century emergence of fully developed modern nationalism.

> The continental Europe of the seventeenth century and of the first half of the eighteenth still lived in the prenationalistic age. But in the growth of centralized states, in the secularization of political life, in the rise of individualism with its faith in liberty and its confidence in man's power, with the acceleration of economic life demanding the

loosening of the static forms of traditional organization – the foundations were laid for the rise of nationalism.[2]

France took the lead on the European continent, though Kohn acknowledges that England's seventeenth-century revolution was not just a precursor but the first real flowering of modern nationalism. The American and French revolutions were pivotal, crowning the Age of Enlightenment. The story of nationalism is thus embedded in an account of the development of Western Civilization. The account culminates with the production of a new kind of liberal universalism and appropriate political structures for this by means of revolution, transformation of absolutist monarchies, and creation of new countries in the "new world." "Modern civilization was molded into its definite form in the eighteenth century."[3] Then there are two chapters on "Stirrings in the Old World" tracing developments in Central and Eastern Europe. These start out promising cultural revitalization but end up anti-modern or at least reactionary.

Kohn initially planned to write a second volume. This would have extended the discussion of Europe further into the nineteenth century and added more on nationalisms which developed elsewhere on into the twentieth century. He never did, though he published numerous studies of later European nationalism and nationalism in Asia, Africa, and elsewhere.[4] But in a sense the very omission is telling. His story of nationalism is a story of liberal achievement and an illiberal challenge to it. It is a story in which the West – represented principally by England, France, and the United States – represents the universal and the rest of the world, frequently identified with the East, represents innumerable particularisms. But it is also a story which refuses to cede nationalism to mere backwardness, atavistic loyalties, or traditionalism.

The idea of nationalism, in Kohn's view, developed specifically in the West as part of the pursuit of a social order based on reason and universal justice. It was central to liberalism and liberalism central to it – until it was appropriated and transformed, mainly in the East, by Romantics, traditionalists, mystical irrationalists, and those pursuing a different *raison d'état* governed not by universal ideals but by the desire to claim an equal or even dominant place in the world remade by the West. But the good, liberal version of nationalism was not irrevocably lost, Kohn suggested; it could be recovered, claimed by Western Europe and the US, and even potentially spread throughout the world as part of the West's gift to humankind. Liberal nationalism could still serve as a valuable step on the path to cosmopolitan global integration,[5] as Kohn ended *The Idea of Nationalism*, summing up its message:

> From Hebrew and Greek ideas the age of nationalism drew many of its initial and fundamental inspirations, but from Jerusalem and Athens

shine also the eternal guiding stars which lift the age of nationalism above itself, pointing forward on the road to deeper liberty and to higher forms of integration.[6]

Greece and Israel are the crucial sources of the Western inheritance of universalism, humanism, reason, and liberty. "It is significant that in antiquity only the two nationally conscious peoples developed a conscious cosmopolitanism and universalism."[7]

Kohn's story of the idea of nationalism, in other words, is situated in the heroic version of the story of the rise of Western Civilization and its gift to the world of Classical, Judeo-Christian, and Enlightenment versions of reasoned universalism. It is as much an account of the flourishing and importance of liberalism as a study of nationalism. But it is not simply triumphal. Though Kohn seems to have been of generally optimistic character, and found reasons for hope not always apparent to his contemporaries, *The Idea of Nationalism* is informed by the rise of Naziism and the Second World War, and indeed by Kohn's fear for the future of liberalism. Kohn had already been worried by illiberal nationalism, especially in new states such as Turkey, and by Soviet Communism. He was well aware of the potential for dominant groups to harness nationalist ideology to projects that oppressed minority nationalities and indeed freedom more generally.[8] But the rise of the Nazis prompted Kohn not only to turn his attention back to Europe but to try to warn his fellow Americans of the threat National Socialism posed.[9]

The 1940s must have been an extraordinary time to write about nationalism. They were perhaps a still more extraordinary time to take up the challenge of showing that nationalism and liberal democracy were compatible, and indeed that enlightened nationalism was inseparable from liberalism. The tendency to equate nationalism with its worst excesses was already widespread (it continues to shape liberal discussions). The other most prominent early twentieth-century analyst of nationalism, Carlton J.H. Hayes, portrayed it as a kind of religion, emphasizing the irrational rather than the rational.[10] Much more extreme examples of the effort to distinguish essentially bad nationalism from the broader and more benign consciousness of national identity abound. Frederick Hertz, for example, argued that the term nationalism should be reserved "for political movements characterized by a one-sided, intolerant, and often fanatical accentuation of one's own nationality . . . the striving for power and domination, and the subordination of all other values to these aims."[11] Kohn by contrast stressed at length how nationalism grew in close relationship to Enlightenment liberalism and cosmopolitanism, and should not be equated with the ethnic variants that grew in nineteenth-century response, inspired in part by Rousseau and Romanticism. Each version shared in the common history of nationalism, though they revealed that it was Janus-faced. Ethnic nationalism was not merely late, however, but different in kind, and representative of a branching off of intellectual lineage.

Though Kohn only presented his fully crystallized view in *The Idea of Nationalism*, he had been developing it throughout his life, on the basis of personal experience and public commitment as well scholarship. Kohn was born in Prague on September 15, 1891, near the end of the long nineteenth-century European peace and just before the Continent's convulsive political crises. He grew up in a prosperous and cosmopolitan Bohemia but lived to see the collapse of the Austro-Hungarian Empire, the struggles of the Czechoslovakian Republic and its German invasion, and the reconstruction of Czechoslovakia as a communist state after the ruinous World War II. He died in 1971 in Philadelphia.

As formative for the young Hans Kohn as this cultural and political context was the project of "cultural" or "ethical" Zionism. He studied at the German University in Prague, eventually receiving a doctorate in law. While there, he became active in Zionist student organizations. For him, as for many others, a visit from Martin Buber was transformative. Indeed, Buber's reception by the Prague students was enthusiastic and recruited a number of devoted followers to cultural Zionism. If there was a single fundamental tenet to this alternative to Theodore Herzl's statist version of Jewish nationalism it was the notion that Judaism itself required an internal renewal. It was not enough to change the external conditions faced by Jews, or even to create a new state to give Jews a secure place to live. If both Jews and Judaism were to flourish there must be a transformation of Jewish culture and indeed a spiritual revitalization. Buber thus brought to Kohn and others his own version of the cultural Zionism associated with Ahad Ha'am, who clashed famously with Herzl over just these issues.[12] Herzl focused on saving Jews, Ha'am and Buber on saving Judaism. Herzl promoted a straightforwardly Western secular modernization program, emphasizing the state as such and not focusing directly on dynamics of identity, social cohesion, or religious values. By comparison, Ha'am and Buber were more interested in what made Jews Jews, and what made Judaism valuable. Interestingly, they were also far more conciliatory towards the Arab population of Palestine.

In fact, Herzl had recruited Buber to edit a Zionist paper in Vienna, but they grew apart over the issue of Jewish identity. The same happened with others, including Israel Zangwill, a British Zionist who by his own account worked slavishly for Herzl before breaking with him on precisely this issue. For Herzl, "Jew" was largely a biological, a racial category, and Jews were people to be protected by seeking the power of a state.[13] But for Buber and Zangwill, Jews were bound spiritually and culturally. Moreover, the cultural Zionists saw in Judaism a moral message which should change the outside world, and faulted Jewish inwardness that blunted this message – which amounted roughly to human brotherhood, or the essential relationality Buber would evoke with the language of "I" and "thou" (anticipating in some ways Levinas's more philosophically sophisticated account of "alterity").[14] As Kohn would do a little later, Zangwill explicitly called for joining the Jewish message of justice and solidarity to Greek universal culture, though Zangwill emphasized Greek esthetic ideals more than Kohn.[15]

In the early twentieth century, Ha'am's cultural Zionists were often seen as "Jewish particularists" in opposition to Herzl's advocates for a secular, state-centered Jewish realpolitik. As the case of Kohn reveals, though, the "particularist" label can be misleading. The cultural Zionists certainly called for a stronger sense of the special identity of Jews, not merely as a race or descent group, but as bearers of a moral and cultural mission. Kohn would later emphasize messianism as a distinctive component of Jewish nationalism – but also as a contribution to the broader development of nationalism. "Side by side with this nationalistic Messianism," Kohn wrote, "there developed from the very beginning the tradition of universalistic Messianism."[16] And he would interpret messianism not only in terms of the belief in the coming of a Redeemer, but as an aspiration to make a better world. He thus linked messianism to liberal nationalist faith in the possibility of transforming the conditions of social life to achieve universal ends. "The future kingdom never was expected outside this world, in Heaven, but was always regarded as a phase of human history, whose stage was the earth, sometimes a transfigured earth, but still the earth with life purified and clarified but still human. . . . It was a stage of national or universal history."[17] For Kohn, Zionism must not stand for backward-looking historical claims, nor only for the inward-looking self-concern of "the chosen people." It must contribute to what he would later analyze as liberal nationalism's advance of global justice and global integration. "Jewish nationalism stood as a moral nationalism – duty and not law; responsibility for humanity."[18] Of course, in the end Jewish particularism came to be associated less with such outward looking reformers and more with the Orthodox and with a range of immigrants to Israel who sought to defend received understandings of Jewish identity, particular interpretations of the law, and even exclusive definitions of who was a real Jew. Not only did Israel become more religious than early secular Zionists imagined, its religion was shaped less by the spiritual renewal Buber, Ha'am, Kohn, and others advocated.

In this context, it is curious that Zangwill should be famous for two phrases that seem to embody contradictory messages. It was his play, *The Melting Pot*, which popularized that understanding of America, promising transcendence of the ethnic diversity of immigrants, to Theodore Roosevelt's great pleasure. But it was the same Zangwill who influentially and misleadingly described Palestine as "a land without people for a people without land."[19] It was important to many Zionists to conceive of Palestine as all but empty – as European settlers had earlier thought of North America, Australia, Southern Africa, and other potentially desirable territories. But of course Palestine was already occupied and when he approached it less abstractly, Zangwill recognized it was relatively densely occupied and that this would be a problem for Zionism. Indeed, he broke with the dominant currents of Zionism and became a leader in the pursuit of a non-Zionist approach to a Jewish territory.[20] He was among those tempted by the offer of Uganda – though of course it too was hardly empty. But central to the transformation in his thought and the development of Kohn's was the notion that a territorial solution for Jews need not be a racially or ethnically ordered state, and perhaps must be a multicultural state.

In general, the cultural Zionists from Ha'am on were sympathetic to the Arab population already in Palestine. Their preoccupation with Jewish ethics and the relations of Jews to the larger world was a factor in this. When Buber, for example, wrote that the Arabs are the test God has given Zionism he didn't mean simply that Arabs were trouble for Jews, though he has been quoted as if that were the sense of his remark. He meant that the project of Zionism would have to be judged on how well it accommodated the interests of Arabs as well as Jews, and how well it met the moral standards of Judaism. Such thoughts were widespread in the Brit Shalom (Covenant of Peace) movement. As Kohn's friend Robert Weltsch put it in 1918, "Zionism is not only a political movement; it is above all a spiritual and moral opportunity."[21] Cultural or ethical Zionists felt that all Jewish immigration to and settlement of the land must only be done in brotherly conciliation with the Palestinian people. Anything they would regard as an immoral imposition should not be attempted.

Kohn in particular was deeply troubled by the ways in which Palestinian settlement put Jews in the position of dominating others by power alone, rather than cultural renewal and a dialogical exchange. He was especially unimpressed with arguments based on "historic right" (just as he would be in his writings on nationalism years later). "With the term 'historic right'," he suggested, "one can rationalize every kind of injustice."[22] As he wrote to Buber in 1929:

We have been in Palestine for 12 years now and have not once seriously tried to secure the acceptance of the people or to negotiate with the people that live in the country. We have relied exclusively on the military power of Great Britain. We have set goals that inevitably and in themselves had to lead to conflicts with the Arabs and about which we should say that they are reason – and justified reason – for a national uprising against us.[23]

Kohn was by this time living in Palestine. During World War I, he had been a prisoner of war and was interned in Soviet prisons in Samarkand and Khaborovsk, Krasnoyarsk and Irkutsk until 1920. He learned Russian and later returned to the Soviet Union as a journalist for the *Frankfurter Zeitung*. His writings on Russian nationalism and the USSR are much influenced by personal observation and are not without sympathy. He also spent a great deal of time in Paris and London, working for Zionist organizations and combining an increasing commitment to scholarly writing with both activism and journalism. He had married Jetty Wahl in 1921, and then in 1925 moved to Palestine, where he worked until 1929. Quickly, though, Kohn grew frustrated both with the limited success of cultural Zionism compared to more ethnonationalist variants, and with the growing tensions between Jews and Arabs. The dominant Zionist approach worried him not just because of the conflicts it engendered with Palestinian Arabs but because it at best ignored and at worst was directly contrary to the spiritual and cultural renaissance of Judaism he sought. The Arab riots of 1929 shook him, and helped to precipitate his move to the United States. At the same time, Kohn's growing frustration with the dominant currents in Zionism led him to look further at the nature of nationalism.

Kohn also grew more and more engaged with historical research into European nationalism – not least because European affairs seemed determinant for global affairs. After the riots of 1929 he left Palestine and in 1934 started teaching Modern History at Smith College in Northampton, Massachusetts. From 1949 until 1961, he taught at the City College of New York, intermittently at the New School for Social Research, and as a Visiting Professor at Harvard, Chicago, and other universities. He was also a member of the Institute for Advanced Study in Princeton. But Kohn never became simply an academic historian. For all his academic appointments and his prominence among historians, Kohn remained in important ways as devoted to public intellectual life as to scholarship. Or rather, his scholarship was always in the service of a public agenda. And while that agenda had a variety of specific foci from Zionism to alerting the American public to the dangers of Naziism to shaping Western response to the anti-colonial nationalisms of the postwar era, it had an enduring theme. The theme was rational enlightenment liberalism, and more specifically the possibility of a growing unity of humankind in which nationalism was not the enemy of cosmopolitanism but a crucial if temporary mediator between individuals and global citizenship. Until the end of his life, Kohn was engaged both in writing the history of nationalism and in trying to guide it.

Kohn was steeped in Central European intellectual traditions and exemplified the command of multiple languages and breadth of learning that so astonishes us about many nineteenth- and twentieth-century German thinkers.[24] And, as was typical of these thinkers, he saw the Greeks as the fundamental source of Western Civilization. It was somewhat more distinctive to give equal weight, as he does in *The Idea of Nationalism*, to the Jews. Certainly Judea and Hellas were small countries and the ancient world was a broad terrain, but they stand out against the background of all the rest of Antiquity. Indeed, "for the European consciousness, this background was no more than a distinct and obscure setting which by contrast served to illuminate even more brightly the two great protagonists of ancient history, Israel and Hellas."[25] In general, Kohn probably exaggerates the extent to which appreciation and appropriation of the "Old Testament" heritage was basic to early European nationalism. But it was not without importance.

The Greeks and the Jews shared two basic traits that set them apart in the ancient world: individuals mattered, and they achieved national consciousness. The two are commonly opposed – or at least they have been in recent years, especially by liberals but also by more than a few conformity-minded ethnonationalists. But Kohn clearly wants from the outset to make the point that they need not be. Among the Greeks and Jews, the "natural group-sentiment of tribalism" which is common to all ethnic groups was transformed into something more. And the something more of Greek and Judaic nationalism makes no sense without the complement of the more active engagement and dignity of each member of the group. Jews and Greeks developed "a new consciousness which gave every member of the group the knowledge of a special mission entrusted to it and distinguishing it from all other peoples. This consciousness, shared by every individual, raised him to a new personal dignity, and prepared the spiritual foundations of democracy."[26] Or again,

> the masses of the other peoples appeared, to Greeks and Hebrews alike, as without individual dignity, subject to the will of their despotic rulers, without participation in a national mission, and without an active share in the cultural life reserved to the priestly class. . . . With the other peoples of antiquity, only rulers and empires left their traces

on history. With the Greeks and the Jew, it was the national character and the spiritual creative energy of the people which endured.[27]

Kohn's theme flows as directly from his heritage in cultural Zionism as from the crisis of Europe that culminated in World War II. As Wolf remarks, there was something naive about the cultural Zionist hope for a bi-national state in Palestine, since there was not much support for this idea among either Jews or Arabs.[28] This is an instance of the idealist's hope for the abstract ought without much regard for the concrete tendencies. And indeed, Kohn appeals to religion for an account of how the Greeks and Jews achieved their distinctive mix of individuality and nationalism in an appeal at once terribly tendentious about the actualities of the two religions and yet not without its insight.

> God is the reconcilitation of multiplicity to unity. The Greeks arrived at this conciliation by contemplation and a wisdom full of moderation; they never doubted that all men would love virtue if they could but contemplate it. The Jews found conciliation not in the contemplation of knowledge but in the exertion of the will.[29]

Greek philosophy is here elided rather easily into an account of religion, and the specificities of Greek religion seem to matter hardly at all. Whether Kohn refers to the Homeric pantheon or Neoplatonism is never made clear.

Kohn is clear, however, that there are important differences among great Greeks with regard to his key concerns of individual dignity and national identity. He claims the Sophists as incipient humanitarians against the "absolute precedence of the state over the individual" urged by Plato's *Republic*, which he saw as simply a military despotism.[30] The Sophist "enlightenment" started an emancipation of the individual from the narrow traditions of family, clan, and city and prepared the way for a broader "community of individuals held together by intellectual instead of tribal or local bonds."[31] This seems to have been most realized in the Hellenism following the Alexandrine transcendence of the Greek city-state. But while this makes clear Kohn's emphasis on the difference between mere cultural commonality – ethnicity – and mutual intellectual engagement that could be part of a transformative project leading eventually to world community, it raises deep questions. In what sense, for example, was there a Hellenistic "community"? Certainly there were far-flung intellectual connections among those who wrote in Greek. And there were some links by travel and trade. There was arguably a Hellenistic *oikoumene* around the Mediterranean,[32] but this was not in itself the basis for any *political* community. On the contrary, the Hellenistic intellectuals survived partly by keeping their distance from politics and partly by virtue of the protection of an imperial peace. But they did not organize or for the most part run the empire. It is certainly true that the Stoics helped to promulgate a vision of world community. Kohn quotes Plutarch's summary of Zeno: "that all the inhabitants of this world of ours should not live differentiated by their respective rules of justice into separate cities and communities but that we should consider all men to be of one community and one order common to all."[33] He reports Alexander's refusal of Aristotle's advice to think of himself as leader of the Greeks – as it were, a nationalist – and he avers that "as a result of Alexander's attitude the universalistic philosophy of the Stoics had a practical example set before it."[34] But it is a little chilling to think that the practical example is one of conquest.

It is easy to fault Kohn for overreaching as he tries to sustain the pairing of Hellas and the Hebrews. But it would be a mistake to dismiss entirely the importance of the combination of universalism and messianism to some nationalisms: France's *mission civilisatrice* and America's sense of being a "city on a hill" perhaps most notably. And it would be a mistake also to miss the importance of nationalist projects that founded on ideals of transformative self-improvement. Americans my age will always remember the opposed slogans of "America: Love It or Leave It" and "America: Change It or Lose It." Among other things, Kohn is grasping for ways to remind his readers of the potential of the latter approach to nationalism and patriotism.

Over time, Kohn's outlook was shaped more and more by Enlightenment rationalism and the distinctively American version of liberalism. Both get pronounced emphasis in *The Idea of Nationalism*. But among Enlightenment rationalists and American liberals, Kohn is unusual for his sustained and largely positive attention to nationalism. Liberals have more commonly sought to debunk nationalist claims as mere historical errors or inventions of opportunistic politicians.[35] Many have rejected nationalism as a fundamentally illiberal imposition of the collectivity over the individual, of ethnic loyalty over human rights, and of tradition over reason. And even more commonly, liberalism has swept its own tacit reliance on nationalist thinking under the carpet, failing to analyze why the population of any one country belonged there and why the state was entitled to keep others out. Liberalism generally took up questions about how to advance justice and liberty within "societies," didn't much examine what made a society a society, and (except when prodded by war) was vague on the relationship between a world of such distinct societies and sovereign states and the rights of individuals in the world as a whole. These issues have come to the fore recently in response to globalization, with many liberals struggling with national identities and state boundaries and proclaiming adherence to a more cosmopolitan ideal. The same issues came to the fore after World War II, as liberals sought to organize the United Nations and promote "modernization" in less "developed" countries. Kohn's was an important voice informing the "nation-building" agenda of modernization theory and practice. But he was considerably ahead of the wave of postwar modernization projects, and his synthesis of values from cultural Zionism with Enlightenment liberalism is a key reason. In this regard, Wolf is right that "throughout his life, Kohn remained a prophet of the cultural Zionist ideals: world unity, individual liberty, and a humane ethical nationalism."[36] At the same time, Kohn lived through a fundamental crisis of the traditions that formed him.

Rome and Christianity, like the Middle Ages and the Renaissance, are for Kohn mostly conduits through which the essential ancient heritage of Greece and Israel is passed on to modernity, when once again intellectual, cultural, and moral creativity begin to nurture improvements in the common inheritance.[37] The conduits nonetheless shape the history of nationalism.

Rome, first of all, provided an organizational context in which the Stoic idea of cosmopolitanism could become a reality. Kohn sees this as an essentially Greek idea taken up by the Romans and, together with the Greek idea of *philanthropeia* or love of mankind, reworked to make the ideal of *humanitas*, "a compound of the qualities of the human and the humane, that quality which makes a man a man. . . . This new meaning of *humanitas* found its outward expressing in the Roman Empire which Caesar founded by his revival of the idea of Alexander."[38] Rome bequeathed to the subsequent history of nationalism, thus, mainly the "universalism of the Empire."[39] But Rome was only imperfectly able to realize the ideal it embraced: there were Barbarians without and there was inadequate integration within. "Only many centuries later, in our own days, has the march of technical progress made it objectively possible to unify mankind without leaving any barbarians at its frontiers or entirely outside its orbit."[40] Nonetheless, Kohn suggests, the memory of the Roman Empire offered hope to sustain Europeans through the ensuing Dark Ages.

Christianity appropriated the hope, but transformed it, partly by also appropriating the Jewish idea of a chosen people. At the same time, Christendom was explicitly conceived as multinational. Kohn notes the difference between Eastern Orthodoxy, with its structure of national churches, and the Western overlay of Catholic universalism and a congeries of more local polities. He identifies Byzantium with a new spirit of authoritarian despotism introduced into the Roman imperial heritage by Constantine, and significantly links this to a transition from a "this-worldly civilization of liberty" which he imagines to have obtained under Augustus to "an otherworldy civilization of authority."[41] Church was subordinated to state in the East.[42] In the West, at this time, "the decentralization and differentiation within those bodies which were later to form the future nations in no way allowed the growth of that political and emotional integration which is the basis of modern nationalism."[43] Moreover, "the political thought of the Middle Ages was characterized by the conviction that mankind was one and had to form one community. . . . The main conflict of the Middle Ages was not between universalism and the desire of separation of individual groups, but between two forms of universalism, *Sacerdotium* and *Imperium*."[44] Indeed, however much the power of the Holy Roman Empire might fade after Charlemagne, the inherited notion of continuing Roman, Christian universalism remained strong. Even figures like Dante who expressed profound love of country were not nationalists. "What he wished was not the unity of Italy, but the peace of Italy and the peace of humanity in a unified world."[45] There were very local solidarities, rooted not only in territory and polity but in autonomous occupational communities. But these are as different from nationalism as the pan-national Church. It is only from the thirteenth to sixteenth centuries that the formation of nations got underway in Europe, and it took form as a struggle against the Church (and indeed, against the autonomy of local groups).

It was Renaissance and Reformation that brought nationalism back onto the Western European stage. "The rise of nationalism demanded a new attitude of this-worldliness and affirmation of nature, the birth of individualism, and a new interpretation of history."[46] Renaissance and Reformation provided these. At the same time, they contributed to a breakdown of the ostensible universal order that had overlain medieval localism (Kohn's account here centers especially on the Holy Roman Empire). Yet, neither actually was typified by or even directly produced nationalism; they paved the way. During both Renaissance and Reformation there were appeals to something like nations, not least in literature, but the nascent nations were torn apart from within. Indeed, most of the humanist writers of the Italian Renaissance, however much they might appeal to larger ideals, were employed in the service of local princes or cities. Machiavelli was the first to transcend this, though even he wrote less as a nationalist per se than as an advocate of a secular state. And it was indeed the absolutist states that succeeded in unifying the disparate local powers – except of course in Germany. The modern nationalism of the West, what Kohn would later describe as the good "civic" variant of nationalism depended crucially on this precedence of the state over ethnocultural appeals to solidarity. And indeed the contribution of absolutist monarchs was not just to dominate feudal lords and other local powers, but to integrate and homogenize affairs throughout their realms.[47]

In England, thus, the rise of the Tudors exhausted the feudal barons and brought an integrated commerce. And then it was in England's seventeenth-century civil war, a rebellion against attempted extension of that very "absolutism" that "the first great surge of nationalism . . . embraced a whole people."[48] "Here we find the first example of modern nationalism, religious, political, and social at the same time, although it was not yet the secularized nationalism which arose at the end of the eighteenth century."[49] Milton and Cromwell were both deeply religious yet in important ways, Kohn suggests, they emphasized reason as well as faith.[50] It was no accident, moreover, that England gave rise to science in the same era. For science embodied, not least for a utopian like Bacon, the prospect not just of riches but of transformation of the conditions of human life. It marked a new and forward-looking, progressive orientation which Kohn wanted to claim for liberal nationalism – an expectation of society continually improved. This in turn informed a changed orientation to history, in which the history of the nation could appear largely as yet to be made. It was not unrelated to the fact that English nationalism "never made the complete integration of the individual into the nation the aim of nationalism; it always put a great emphasis on the individual and upon the human community beyond all national divisions."[51] It was, in other words, just as Kohn wanted nationalism to be.

What Kohn wrote about English nationalism he would have wished for Zionism:

> A nation had come into being, directing its own destiny, feeling responsible for it, and a national spirit permeated all institutions. It sprang from a unique consciousness of the identity of divine, natural, and national law, based upon the dignity and liberty of every individual as God's noblest creature, upon his individual conscience inspired by the inner light of God and reason alike.[52]

English nationalism was, however, early on the European scene. On the Continent, the more general trend was for the consolidation and secularization of states to proceed without the level of popular participation seen in seventeenth-century England. "Etatism, not nationalism, emerged from the disintegration of medieval universalism." Politics became increasingly rational, but "the masses continued to live in the emotional forms of religion." There were movements to rationalize religion as well as politics, of course, such as pietism. But in general these sought to dissociate religion from politics – and states returned the favor, claiming a *raison d'état* grounded in instrumental rationality not religious values. Only in the late eighteenth century did nationalism begin to rival religion as a source of "emotional warmth." This met a need of the secular states, however, which could no longer rely so readily on religion for their legitimation. "Nationalism made the new State legitimate and implanted it deeply in the hearts and wills of its citizens."[53]

Kohn is interested in two senses of the "idea" of nationalism. On the one hand his concern is for how "nationalism," as an idea, developed in history. On the other hand, he is concerned for how each nationalism – that is, each cultural movement of nation-forming – formulated its distinctive national "idea" and why these diverge.[54]

The former concern is evident when Kohn distinguishes nationalism from nationality. Nationalism is not a natural extension of nationality but involves its transformation by ideas of sovereignty, popular participation, and ideals.

> Nationalism is a state of mind, permeating the large majority of a people and claiming to permeate all its members; it recognizes the nation-state as the ideal form of political organization and the nationality as the source of all creative cultural energy and of economic well-being. The supreme loyalty of man is therefore due to his nationality, as his own life is supposedly rooted in and made possible by its welfare.[55]

While this is a plausible account, it is a rather compound definition with shifting parts, not a singular idea. Indeed, part of what Kohn brings out is that there is not a singular idea of nationalism, but rather multiple clashing ideas that share a good deal of vocabulary and reference.[56] This is in fact one reason why he – and after him much of the literature – became increasingly reliant on the value-laden distinction between ethnic and civic nationalism.

The latter concern comes out most clearly in Kohn's discussion of the United States, though it is also basic to the account of the various less liberal nationalisms contrasted to it in the latter part of the book:

> Though (or rather, because) the American nation was to be a universal nation – not only in the sense that the ideal which it pursued was universal, valid, and applicable to the whole of mankind, but also in the sense that it was a nation composed of all racial and linguistic strains – it was to be strongly integrated around allegiance to the American idea, an idea to which everyone could be assimilated for the very reason that it was a universal idea.[57]

We see in this important features of liberal nationalism generally, which

Kohn had initially expressed in his accounts of cultural Zionism. Substitute the word "Jewish" for "American" in the passage just quoted. It then evokes precisely the cultural Zionist claim which the more ethno-racial Zionists rejected.

Liberal nationalisms center on universal ideas, especially freedom and justice. These also provide liberal nations with universal missions: "Thus America became the vanguard of mankind, full of a proud and blissful faith in its mission. This faith of the American people in itself and its mission made it a nation."[58] Clearly the assimilationist, universal dimension of American nationalism was different from what would develop in most of Europe – along with a more forward-looking, less historical orientation and greater individualism that deeply inflected the version of liberty Americans would claim. These were not merely coincidental differences, however, they were dimensions of self-understanding. The nation's idea of itself could repeatedly be clarified in the contrast. "Each national idea gains its emphasis by contrasting itself with and differentiating itself from another concept; in the case of America, this concept was Europe."[59] American nationalism was a "cultural nationalism" but not in the sense of claiming ethnic culture. Rather, it was cultural in the sense that education and cultural production were to play a "sorely needed" role "in the young nation to cement the loose ties binding the distant communities and colonies with their divergent traditions and backgrounds" into a common whole.[60] In addition, of course, freedom demanded knowledge. In Jefferson's words, "If a nation expects to be ignorant and free, in a state of civilization, it expects what never was and never will be."[61]

America provided an exceptionally promising environment for the realization of the ideals of the French Enlightenment. Indeed, Kohn begins his discussion of the US by emphasizing this connection, not simply the direct lineage of English ideals. He is justified in this both by the admiration many French thinkers showed for English liberties and by the importance of the American example for the French, but he probably does underestimate the influence not only of English thinkers but of the Scottish moralists. In any event, what is important to Kohn is that in the North American colonies the struggle for civic liberty could lead directly to the foundation of a new nation.[62] Here, too, the historical role of the middle classes as protagonists of liberal nationalism was renewed (after a slide towards greater aristocratic dominance in Restoration England). American patriotism, on Kohn's reading, was typified by the cosmopolitanism of Thomas Jefferson and Tom Paine. In different ways each emphasized that the freedoms of Americans were not simply English historical liberties but natural rights of all men.[63] "For by the end of the Revolution the American colonies had emancipated themselves from the past so completely that they did not regard common descent or a common root as the foundation of their community."[64] The common foundation was the constitution, a this-worldly human action, based on ideas and ideals and showing their efficacy in the world (as against mere realpolitik). "The American constitutional laws of 1789 have lasted because the idea for which they stand was so intimately welded with the existence of the American nation that without the idea there would have been no nation."[65]

The US is the setting for creation of a "new man" as well as a new nation. Kohn's emphasis on the newness of American nationalism leads him to see little common culture, identity, or social integration uniting the thirteen colonies before the Revolution. This underwrites his view of the US as achieving an almost purely civic nationalism. Likewise, he says little about the ethnocultural construction of American identity that would later be termed "WASP."

Kohn emphasizes the melting-pot character of the United States in terms comparable to (and including quotes from) Zangwill. Crèvecoeur emphasized "that strange mixture of blood, which you will find in no other country" and along with mixed descent the attitude of "leaving behind him all his ancient prejudices, and manners, receives new ones from the new mode of life he has embraced."[66] Kohn quotes John Adams with approval: "this radical change in the principles, opinions, sentiments, and affections of the people, was the real American Revolution."[67] Not unlike Hannah Arendt, he finds in the Revolution and the founding of the United States a paradigmatic exemplification of the human capacity to create something new and good in the world, going beyond the exigencies of necessity and narrowly instrumental interest.[68] Unlike Arendt, he would extend much of the same enthusiasm to the French Revolution, dwelling little on the slippery slope towards totalitarianism she thought it revealed.[69]

Kohn's discussion of American national identity and self-understanding also reveals how much his ideas about liberal nationalism depend not only on the themes of universalism, active individual participation, and an ethical orientation but also on a notion of creative self-fashioning. In Christian terms, it is not Christ's suffering body as portrayed in the crucifix, but the redemption – and perhaps the Pentecost – that liberal nationalism claims. This also suggests one of the reasons why Kohn sees an implicit affinity with Protestantism. The transformation from an externally imposed order to a continual sense of the self as a moral project – what so troubled Foucault about modern individualism – is central to Kohn's embrace of liberal nationalism.[70]

While Kohn is adamant that nationalism is a state of mind, he is clear that this state of mind is produced not just by inheritance of an "idea" or the labor of intellectuals (though *The Idea of Nationalism* is mainly an intellectual history). Partly because nationalism is so importantly about what ordinary people think and feel, Kohn is well aware that it has roots not just in the reading of high theory but in the experience of everyday life and communication. He anticipates the stress placed a generation later by Karl Deutsch on communications media as a basis for nationalism, noting for example that French road building and transportation was very advanced,[71] and more generally how important communications and transport technology was not only to nationalism but to cosmopolitanism.[72]

A deep problem for the new socio-political order that arose with nationalism and the centralized, secular state was reconciling "the liberty of the individual with the exigencies of social integration."[73] It is a problem familiar to sociologists in Talcott Parsons's classical evocation of the Hobbesian problem of order at the beginning of a treatise on how voluntary social action could produce social structure.[74] As stated, it is slightly less familiar to political theory, because questions of social integration have not figured prominently in that tradition, though the opposition of the individual to the state has. This is not quite the same thing, because the liberty of the individual is counterposed here not only to state or collectivity but to social integration. Above all, this is the problem taken up by Rousseau, whose solution is maddening, not least for trying to bring together what political theory generally keeps asunder. As Kohn suggests, Rousseau was seeking "amid much confusion and contradiction, a new community starting from, and based upon, the free individual."[75] Kohn too.[76]

Reconciling individual liberty, a sense of felt community, and ethical universalism is for Kohn at the heart of nationalism. And here the problems started, which would lead Kohn eventually to distinguish civic from ethnic nationalism. As a Zionist, Kohn had opposed cultural or ethical nationalism to "merely" political. Now, influenced both by deeper study of liberalism and by the rise of Naziism, Kohn opposed two kinds of political nationalism. One retained individual liberty and ethical universalism and underwrote the nationalism of the Allies in World War II. The other focused more on culture, but in irrational ways and without the ideal of self-transcendence Kohn valued; embodied in fascism it transmuted ethical universalism into mere imperialism.

Rousseau appears as the last great thinker crucial to the development of both civic and ethnic nationalism. Claiming Rousseau, at least in part, for Enlightenment rationalism, and for his version of civic nationalism, Kohn insists that "a nation that expressed itself through the general will, could for Rousseau not be a product of nature."[77] Indeed, Rousseau did suggest in *Of the Social Contract* that "the mere promptings of appetite are slavery, while obedience to a law which we impose upon ourselves is what constitutes liberty."[78] This was in accord with Kohn's opposition (already clear in his writings on Zionism) of mere self-interested power politics to the transformative, ethically higher notion of the nation. But Kohn wants to extend the distinction to dissociate his Rousseau from later Romantic readings:

> [The Romantics] established a distinction between state and nation: they regarded the state as a mechanical and juridical construction, the artificial produce of historical accidents, while they believed the nation to be the work of nature, and therefore something sacred, eternal, organic, carrying a deeper justification than works of men. Nothing could be further from Rousseau's thought; for him the nation and the nation-state were nothing "natural" or "organic," but a produce of the will of individuals.[79]

Rousseau was certainly no conservative nostalgic for the feudal order, but Kohn's reading does not confront Rousseau's distinction of the "will of all" from the "general will."

Nor does Kohn deal adequately with Rousseau's worry over what happens when the normative ideals of the small community are transposed to the large-scale society, though he notes the rural and isolationist bias implicit in his proposed constitution for Corsica.[80] It is true that "Rousseau envisioned a world federation of small independent and peaceful states and the extension of the rule of law from the national city-state to the city of man."[81] But Kohn without comment treats this as identical to the problem of national states in the modern global order. The problem lies however not simply in the question of whether free peoples will attack one another and thus whether perpetual peace is possible, but also in the sociological shift from the local, largely face-to-face community to the much larger and more abstract nation.[82] Elsewhere, indeed, Kohn is at pains to make the distinction, precisely because he disagrees with Romantic nationalist assertions that the nation is simply an extension of home and family to a larger scale.[83] He recognizes that nations must be associations among strangers. But scale is an issue not only for ethnic nationalists who claim an illusory identity between kinship and nationality. It is also an issue for civic nationalists who propose that shared political forms should be adequate to support the mutual commitments of citizens to each other – an issue that has famously resurfaced recently with Jürgen Habermas's call for a "constitutional patriotism."[84] Nonetheless, in Kohn's eyes, "Rousseau provided the modern nation with its emotional and moral foundations."[85] And, though nationalism with Rousseau was almost religious feeling of an entirely new intensity and of an all-pervading intimate nature, it was fundamentally opposed to any intolerance or hostility to other nations. Its basic aim was to render life more moral, more peaceful and happy for all men, to establish firmly and protect the dignity and liberty of every individual, and ultimately to replace the state of nature, in which men are subject to passions and appetites, by the rational order of law.[86]

It was an important catch that the Romantic reading of Rousseau which Kohn disputes was widespread and influential.[87]

The absence of a sustained chapter on the French Revolution and its aftermath is the signal lacuna of *The Idea of Nationalism*. After his approving account of the American founding, Kohn turns to the stirrings of nationalism in the Old World, by which he means mainly Central, Eastern, and Catholic Europe other than France. In the course of this he introduces the distinction between civic and ethnic nationalism that will become so influential, though he does so not by taxonomic announcement but by the very organization of the book. As I noted at the outset, the distinction is framed in several more or less homologous oppositions and associated strongly with geography.[88] That it is represented in a whole series of specific histories, rather than announced as an analytic apparatus, makes it appear all the more as simply part of the empirical record. But the missing French Revolution is the pivot on which this turns.

Perhaps the more detailed treatment was intended for the second volume, though that seems anachronistic. In any case, it is not that Kohn doesn't think the French Revolution important, for his opening paragraph declares it "the first great manifestation" of nationalism, which in turn "gave the new movement an increased dynamic force."[89] One might suggest that the reason the French Revolution doesn't get sustained treatment is that it did not contribute directly to the *idea* of nationalism. This is why Kohn's Rousseau-centered chapter on the French Enlightenment seems to stand in for it. Such an argument would depend on a sharp separation between philosophical contributions to the idea of nationalism and those from practical politics, public discourse, and everyday life. Indeed, Kohn does not maintain such a sharp distinction elsewhere, though his bias like that of most intellectual historians is towards high culture. But surely the *levée en masse*, the participatory politics of the Paris clubs, factions, committees, and *quartiers*, and the numerous ritualizations of revolutionary citizenship – like the use of *citoyen* and *citoyenne* as terms of address, and even the "family drama" of the treatment of the royal family – all contributed to the idea of nationalism.[90] The Revolution itself – as event and as myth – is clearly pivotal to the French national idea, the national self-understanding of French public culture. In fact, of course, this reliance on the traditions and celebrations of the Revolution introduces a significant element of historicism, traditionalism, and cultural nationalism into France's vaunted civic nationalism. Likewise, the *philosophes*, whom Kohn rightly seeks to reclaim for the story of nationalism, were not simply rationalist enemies of tradition. Voltaire gave France an important national narrative in the *Henriade*, extolling Henry IV as a man who put national unity ahead of party or religion.[91] To treat France as simply "civic" is to indulge too much its own national self-understanding, reproduced in ritual and a pedagogical narrative that is not quite simple fact, and also in a characteristic opposition to Germany.[92]

Kohn's thin treatment of France masks trouble at the core of the concept of civic nationalism. The problem is one that runs back into Zionism as well. Indeed, one might think of it as the fundamental paradox of liberal nationalism: the need to account for the particularity of belonging. That is, Why should French nationalism apply to the French, or Zionism (cultural or otherwise) to the Jews? Why should Americans be privileged to live in one of the world's richest and freest countries and others kept out?

The problem with the maximally universal construction, in other words, is that it makes poor sense of particularism – and yet relies on it. One response is simply to abandon particularism and with it any defense of nationalism. This is the route taken by some extreme cosmopolitans.[93] Whatever its other merits, it suggests that any strong feelings of membership in a more particular community are at best temporary expedients, probably suspect, and to be tolerated morally only so long as they do not imply favoritism for fellow members or otherwise get in the way of more universal ethics.[94] When Kohn writes of nationalism as merely a way-station on the path to a unified world, he expresses ambivalence towards it. And this ambivalence informs the introduction of the distinction between civic and ethnic nations – effectively good and bad nationalisms.

The French case is central in a variety of ways. On the one hand, France figures (alongside the US, but in the literature on nationalism even outweighing the US) as demonstrating the paradigmatic civic nationalism. On the other hand, the main cases of "ethnic" nationalism developed partly in response to French invasions and imperial projects, especially in the Napoleonic Wars. And the French Revolution itself is a dramatic but troubling exemplification of extreme civic nationalism in action. It does not appear unequivocally as "liberal."[95]

Part of the issue is that civic France was so imperial. It became explicitly imperial with the rise of Napoleon, of course, but it also retained old colonies and conquered new dominions while it retained republican form. Certainly republican France proved unable to accept a Republican Haiti. It was the Directory that sent General Napoleon to Egypt, thus, and it presumably agreed with his liberal universalist speech to his troops on May 9, 1798, just as they prepared to attack. "The genius of liberty, which has since its birth rendered the Republic the arbiter of Europe, is now headed toward the most distant lands."[96] The troops responded "The Immortal Republic forever!" and planted a Tree of Liberty. The French Republic of Egypt was governed by its own Directory (the Diwan) on the model of that in Paris. Popular sovereignty was announced, but it manifestly did not include national self-determination. If "the growth of nationalism is the process of integration of the masses of the people into a common political form,"[97] this would seem to count as a variant. But it might also simply be called imperialism, though an imperialism at least somewhat different from those that put only an umbrella of common form over the retention of local structures of authority.[98]

Arguably this imperialism was rooted in messianism.[99] Kohn is right not to shrink from the direct connections between nationalism and imperialism; too often the two are simply opposed, as though France were only imperialist when formally an empire rather than a republic. But, in common with nearly all analysts of nationalism, Kohn does not think through what imperialism means for understanding Republican France and its vaunted civic nationalism. "French nationalism was born," he writes, "(as English and American had [been] before it) in a wave of generous enthusiasm for the cause of mankind; the opposing nationalisms lacked this initial inspiration of a disinterested humanitarianism – from the beginning they were directed to laudable but narrower goals, self-centered and antagonistic."[100] Yet the distinction between France – the Hexagon – and its dominions was real, if masked by republican ideology, as were the racial distinctions that informed colonial policy and helped to give rise to modern anthropology in concern over *métissage*. And surely the export of universalistic ideas by force carries problematic implications.

That imperial France was still France and not simply the flowering of universal reason was also felt by many in the European countries invaded by Napoleon's armies. Of course, this didn't bother everyone equally. Hegel and a host of other intellectuals welcomed the French Revolution, and some even the Napoleonic invasion which they hoped would usher an era of progress and liberty into German history. Goethe remained unimpressed by German nationalist appeals even after France was defeated. But at least from 1813, German nationalism was ascendant among intellectuals (though it is unclear how much this mattered to the rest of the population).[101] The story belongs perhaps to "the age of nationalism" – the concern of Kohn's projected second volume – but the way it played out was shaped by a distinctive version of the idea of nationalism. This is the subject of the last two chapters of the book Kohn actually finished.

Germany is the overwhelming model for ethnic, Eastern nationalism – for Kohn as for most others – though it is a merit of Kohn's account that he pays significant attention to other European traditions. It is common to stress four factors which encouraged an "ethnic" nationalism in Germany: because it was politically disunited, cultural and linguistic commonalties mattered more; because it developed late, compared to France or England, it had less chance to develop rational political institutions and relied more on traditional loyalties; because the power of rural elites was entrenched and the peasantry less free participatory politics was impeded and top-down nationalism encouraged (an argument applied even more in regard to Russia); and because the Napoleonic invasion in particular and the threat of domination by France and Britain more generally stimulated German nationalism it was essentially reactive.

Kohn accepts each of these arguments, but doesn't think them fully adequate. Part of what he wants to show is how a different national idea took shape, sharing some philosophical roots but taking a different intellectual course. The *idea* giving form to nationalism matters, Kohn suggests, not just the circumstances in which politicians develop nationalist strategies. If the Western nationalist idea – at least in its idealized form – stressed universalism, rationality, and self-transcendence, the Eastern stressed particular national identities, an emotional connection to history, and development rather than transcendence. Central and Eastern European nationalists drew on myths of the past, dreams of the future, and distinctive intellectual traditions to imagine "an ideal fatherland, closely linked with the past, devoid of any immediate connection with the present, and expected to become sometime a political reality."[102] It is important that in the eighteenth and early nineteenth centuries this nationalism was not informed by close relationships to actually existing states or social institutions. Where English or French nationalism was about transforming an existing state, nationalism in Central and Eastern Europe focused on developing culture and thus was initially more remote from projects of practical reform. The development of centralized state institutions preceded and informed English and French nationalism – not least with concerns for individual liberty in relation to those states. Though he is not explicit about it, I suspect Kohn would argue the same was true for the United States, albeit in more complicated form because the existing centralized state was British and a new one had to be created in America. But neither the old Hapsburg Empire nor the scattered German dominions offered the same capacity to put the project of rationalizing the relationship between people and government in the forefront. As Kohn writes:

> Nationalism in the West was based upon a nationality which was the product of social and political factors; nationalism in Germany did not find its justification in a rational societal conception, it found it in the "natural" fact of a community, held together, not by the will of its members nor by any obligations of contract, but by traditional ties of kinship and status. German nationalism substituted for the legal and rational concept of "citizenship" the infinitely vaguer concept of "folk."[103]

The issue remains current, as this quotation from Jürgen Habermas, informed by German history though formulated in general terms, makes clear:

> The nation-state owes its historical success to the fact that it substituted relations of solidarity between the citizens for the disintegrating corporative ties of early modern society. But this republican achievement is endangered when, conversely, the integrative force of the nation of citizens is traced back to the prepolitical fact of a quasi-natural people, that is, to something independent of and prior to the political opinion-and-will-formation of the citizens themselves.[104]

Habermas writes in exactly the terms of Kohn's argument, and is concerned to achieve – throughout Europe but not least in Germany and the East – a "constitutional patriotism" in which the loyalty of citizens is based on the reason, justice, and universality of the constitution they have chosen for themselves and agreed to in democratic fashion. In other words, Habermas's project is the realization of the civic ideals Kohn describes. But Habermas is also aware – more than Kohn though it remains an unsolved problem for his theory – that "the question arises of whether there exists a functional equivalent for the fusion of the nation of citizens with the ethnic nation."[105]

The "nation of citizens" is a product of politics and collective will, it is a creature of choice and contract. The "ethnic nation" is prepolitical, the product of history (and perhaps nature), found in already-existing community, though not necessarily static and possibly amenable to nurture and development. The contrast of the two ideas is clear enough, with Habermas raising to theory the historical typology presented by

Kohn. But rather than opposing the two types of nation, it might be better to ask how the two dimensions of solidarity and identity, and the two sorts of claims to membership and rights figure and relate to each other in specific national histories. There certainly are differences of emphasis. Some nationalisms – the Japanese and Chinese – rely on ethnic ideas fused with racial typologies.[106] Some may be more matters of rhetoric than actual behavior or policy. Rogers Brubaker, for example, shows how despite France's long-standing rhetoric of assimilationist civic inclusion and Germany's famous ethnic nationalism, the two countries receive immigrants at about the same rate and grant them comparable benefits (though Germany does make it harder for them to become citizens).[107] But even the most "civic" of nationalisms demand an account of the particularity of their relationship to the larger world.

For Herder, "the national community was the necessary medium between mankind and the individual."[108] Kohn seems to have thought much the same thing as a cultural Zionist, but to have become unsure as he contemplated fascism. Or perhaps the necessity of the mediation was temporary – only until the world as a whole could be ordered on the liberal, Enlightenment principles he advocated. But in any case, what he described as the ethnic nationalism of the East was different because of a deep investment in the idea of an essential diversity of nations. And although Herder was no nationalist in the modern sense – and "his love for nationality embraced all nationalities and their national life"[109] – he was central to the development of this line of thought. "Herder was the first to insist that human civilization lives not in its general and universal, but in its national and peculiar manifestations."[110] Language was paradigmatic.

Kohn shows a considerable sympathy for Herder (despite his general remarks on German and more generally ethnic nationalism). Indeed, much of Kohn's discussion of Old World nationalism is focused on what at least its eighteenth-century forebears shared with Western Enlightenment, revealing the resources for a civic, cosmopolitan nationalism even in Germany.[111] Of course this makes one wonder just when and how Germany became "Eastern."

For most German intellectuals, at least, it was certainly not in the eighteenth century. Speaking of Schlözer, Kohn suggests that "like all representative German thinkers of the age, he never thought of himself as a German; and he never envisaged a common nationhood for Germany."[112] Schiller declared it "a poor and trifling ideal to write for one nation; such a limitation is totally unbearable for a philosophical mind. It cannot find satisfaction in such a changing, accidental, and arbitrary form of mankind, a mere fragment. . . . It can have no warm feelings for it except in so far as a nation or a national event appears important for the progress of mankind."[113] Kant concurred, visualizing a universal society of free individuals. Writing of the French Revolution, he suggested that "such a revolution . . . arouses in the minds of all spectators . . . a desire to participate, one which almost verges on enthusiasm, and which as its expression was dangerous, could therefore have no other cause than a moral faculty in mankind."[114]

While some made reference to national cultural traditions, no eighteenth-century thinker regarded the *volk* as natural and unchangeable.[115] Appeals to the fatherland were apt to be more or less "utilitarian" as they sought to mobilize the loyalty of subjects to their rulers.[116] But if there was one crucial theme that foreshadowed the later divergent construction, it was the proto-Romantic reception of Rousseau's emphasis on the indigenous originality of each nation. Even this, however, was part of a broader European current – Rousseau was, after all, a Genevois writing in Paris, and as Kohn notes the vogue for national legends was also exemplified by the Ossian scam in Scotland and a variety of more honest Celtic discoveries.[117] But the notion of the distinctiveness of national cultures was taken up with particular enthusiasm and intellectual depth in Germany, and linked eventually to ideas of national "genius" and to the distinction of "historical" nations from those lacking the capacity to survive.

Early versions of this thinking focused on the issue of a national spirit that should connect contemporaries with each other as well as with the past. In Moser's phrasing, "we do not know ourselves any longer, we are estranged from one another, our spirit has departed from us."[118] Indeed, the Rousseauian theme of "estrangement" was taken up in a variety of projects for achieving new kinds of community as inherited ones grew weaker; Marx was a crucial inheritor of this tradition but it equally informed nationalism. Kohn notes in passing but doesn't develop the point that concern for "new ties for the integration of society" went well beyond political unification into more sociological concerns.[119]

Where patriotism, cosmopolitanism, and liberalism had been inseparable, as the century progressed the first element became dominant. While Italy's Risorgimento revealed its roots in Western thought by moving from rational cosmopolitanism to liberal nationalism,[120] in Russia, as in Germany, there was a turn from liberal cosmopolitanism to narrow nationalism.[121] But it was not just the narrowness of nineteenth-century nationalisms that would distinguish these for Kohn. It was the widespread embrace of irrationalism: "The reasonableness of the eighteenth century gave way to a fanatic enthusiasm from the depth."[122] Kohn may be looking forward to Wagner and others beyond the precise time frame of this book. In any case, his formulation enables him to see ethnic nationalism as an Eastern revolt against the West – and specifically against Enlightenment – rather than as a dimension of all nationalisms and indeed as a reflection of a crisis within Western thought and politics.[123]

Herder employed all the traditional claims that became typical of German nationalism in the nineteenth century. Yet, he remained insistently liberal and cosmopolitan, a humanitarian and a democrat. A protean thinker (like Rousseau) he could be claimed by opposing intellectual and political traditions. Kohn is left ambivalent, I think, partly because Herder suggests three ingredients crucial to Kohn's vision of progress and missing from much Enlightenment rationalist philosophy. The first is the relationship of being to time implicit in his notion of becoming. "Humanity is the character of our race," Herder wrote; "we receive it only as a potentiality, and we must develop it."[124] Herder's ideas of potentiality and becoming resonate with Kohn's notions of self-transcendence. Likewise, Herder's emphasis on language connects him to Ha'am and an important thread in cultural Zionism. Finally, Herder is insistent on an active participation in national self-development: "the happiness of one people cannot be forced upon any other. The roses for the wreath of each nation's liberty must be picked with its own hands, and must grow happily out of its own wants, joys, and love."[125]

But Herder's strong sense of the uniqueness of nations is troubling. He articulates a constitutive role for language and culture that Kohn can only see as worryingly relativist, anticipating what in the twentieth century would be called "incommensurability."[126] "No individual, no country, no people, no history of a people, no state is like any other. Therefore, the true, the beautiful, and the good are not the same for them."[127] As Kohn recognizes, Herder sees each nationality as embodying an original version of a common humanity, a humanity which because of culture and creativity has a tremendous potential for variation. To eliminate this variety – even in the name of rational order or equality – would be to lose much of what is distinctively human. The problem is that eighteenth-century rationalism and later liberalism rely heavily on notions of the human individual that do not acknowledge this constitutive role for culture, that are often atomistic, and that match with universalism by presuming equivalence. So there is a real difference, already in play with Herder, even though he doesn't draw the illiberal conclusions from it that some later nationalists will.

A key question – unresolved to this day – is whether granting culture this constitutive role can be reconciled with either individualism or universalism. Habermas, for example, reacted vehemently to Charles Taylor's advocacy of multiculturalism precisely because it seemed to him to challenge universalism and thus a necessary foundation for liberalism – and to echo this troubling German tradition for doing so.

The constitutional state can and should tolerate cultural differences, Habermas suggests, but these should not be introduced into either the intellectual or the legal basis for such a state.[128]

Kohn recognizes both the innovative character of Herder's thought and the extent to which it offers an answer to the question of "why a nation?" that other versions of liberal thought find more difficult. He sees in Herder, moreover, a strong echo of Moses and much that he had praised in his earlier discussion of ancient Hebrew nationalism. "Herder's nationalism, an ethico-cultural nationalism, showed deep traces of affinity with the national idea of the Hebrew prophets and psalmists."[129] Yet Kohn is ambivalent because Herder's culturalism (if I may use that word) seems to lead in what history proved were dangerous directions, and because he cannot reconcile it with Enlightenment rationalism and universalism.

A cosmopolitan global order must be built, Herder suggests, in a way that provides for the flourishing of numerous nationalities, each mediating the relationship of its members to humanity at large, each contributing to the fulfillment of human potential in diverse ways.

> Has the world not enough space for all of us? Do not the countries exist peacefully beside one another? Cabinets swindle one another, political machines maneuver until they destroy one another. But fatherlands do not maneuver in such a way, they exist peacefully beside one another, and like families, help one another.[130]

Kohn and others chastened by the late nineteenth and twentieth centuries commonly suggest the world has not space enough for all of us. Think back to the cultural Zionists' recognition, perhaps surprisingly belated in some cases, that Palestine was not "a land without people for a people without land." Think too of the two world wars. Is this not support for a different version of cosmopolitanism, one in which nationality would not mediate but be subordinated, valued only insofar and in so long as it promoted individual rights in a single, rational, universal order?

Kohn envisions a progressive extension simultaneously of the scale of political integration and of the use of reason and justice to order world affairs. Nationalism transcends localism and kinship; cosmopolitanism transcends nationalism. His concern is to vindicate liberal nationalism as part of this general progress, and to keep it from being identified completely with the fascist and other aggressive ethnonationalisms. But he doesn't focus clearly on why or when the claims of country or community rather than only humanity as a whole should carry weight. As a result, when he begins to examine the claims for more particularistic national identities in the second part of *The Idea of Nationalism* he sometimes seems to unravel the case he made in the first part for the positive potential of a civic nationalism joining citizens in common commitment to an ethical project.

Implicitly, of course, Kohn suggests that good nationalism deserves loyalty more than bad, and good nationalism inheres in commitments to reason, justice, individualism, and universality. It therefore is self-transcending. A central problem with organic, historical, or ethnic nationalism thus is that it is not self-transcending. At best it is benign – when it is not coupled to projects of exploiting minorities or conquering neighbors. At worst it lacks the moral orientation required (a) to consider the interests of other nations as carrying comparable moral weight to those of one's own, or (b) to ask that one's nation become better than it is, not merely be preserved.

The key is a conception of politics as rational, self-conscious creation, the making of social order by means of mutual agreements and coordinated actions:[131]

> In the West nations grew up as unions of citizens, by the will of individuals who expressed it in contracts, covenants, or plebiscites. Thus they integrated around a political idea, looking towards the common future which would spring from their common efforts. A nascent German nationalism, unable to find the rallying point in society or in a free and rational order, found it in nature or in the past, not in a political act but in a given natural fact, the folk community, formed by the ties of a hoary past, and later of prehistoric biological factors. This natural foundation was not simply accepted as a fact, but raised to the dignity of an ideal or of a mystery. The political integration around a rational goal was replaced by a mystical integration around the irrational, precivilized folk concept.[132]

In this respect, Kant is a decisive improvement on Rousseau. "Both shared the fundamental respect for the dignity of the human individual, but Kant's ethics never knew any other horizon than the universal one of mankind."[133] And on this even the more Romantic Goethe would agree: "the fatherland of the man who thinks without prejudice, who can rise above his time, is nowhere and everywhere."[134]

But then, just where is the man who thinks without prejudice? Just how far can anyone rise above his time (and still matter in it)? At its most extreme, the civic/ethnic opposition implies the possibility of a purely political, purely rational order, escaping from any constitution by culture or pre-existing social relations. Even in more moderate versions, though, it suggests the radical prioritization of political community over all other senses of community or social solidarity. It suggests that "belonging" can plausibly be based entirely on adherence to an "idea" expressed in more or less abstract forms. And in doing so it begs the question of whether such civic belonging based on adherence to liberal universalist ideals could underwrite the specific loyalty of specific citizens to specific states, or the exclusion of others from those states.

It is not that the distinction of civic from ethnic makes no sense. The problem lies, rather, in using it to construct opposed types of nationalism. This obscures the extent to which "civic" and "ethnic" dimensions are intertwined in all cases, albeit in varying proportions. It also collapses into "ethnic" a variety of notions about why some people belong together, from language and shared culture to attachments to place and participation in a social structure. And it suggests more homology with the series of other oppositions – West/East, peaceful/aggressive, liberal/illiberal, forward-looking/backward-looking – than is warranted. It is worth noting that though Carlton Hayes's idea of "integral nationalism" shares something with Kohn's "ethnic nationalism" it is by no means identical and it is not proposed as distinctively Eastern. Hayes presents it as typified by Barrès and Maurras as much as Mussolini and Hitler – and indeed his label is drawn from their "*integriste*" movement.[135] And it was a Frenchman who wrote famously that "historical enquiry brings to light deeds of violence which took place at the origin of all political formations, even those whose consequences have been altogether beneficial. Unity is always effected by means of brutality."[136] Of course, Renan imagined nationalism a "daily plebiscite" not a binding inheritance. But he recognized the impossibility of a pure polity, free from the original sin of being particular and probably the product of power.

Where does this leave the Jews? As a Zionist, Kohn sought a cultural transformation that would realize Jewish ethical ideals and a nation that would save Judaism not only Jews. Both frustrated with the actual developments of Zionism, and horrified by what nationalism became in fascism, Kohn turned to recovery of a liberal nationalism from a secularized Christian tradition, the Enlightenment, and its appropriation of the Sophists, Stoics, and other Greeks. This centered on individualism, the rights of man, a rational and universal concept of political liberty, and a progressive orientation to the future. He contrasted this to a nationalism founded on particular histories, on "monuments and graveyards, even harking back to the mysteries of ancient times and of tribal solidarity."[137] This stressed the past, the diversity, and the self-sufficiency of nations. The former, he thought, was grounded in the rising middle classes. The latter appealed to the aristocracy and the masses. Each of these was available by the beginning of the nineteenth century, and together they became the poles around which the age of nationalism revolved. Nationalism was to be feared unless it could be Western.

In this conclusion, we see Kohn falling back on the opposition of two types of nationalism. He associates them with different national ideas and understands these to organize the thoughts and feelings of different nations, West and East. The later-developing Eastern nationalisms he will see as derivative, at best participating in the spread of an originally European Enlightenment, but too commonly deviating from it in the direction of claims rooted in ancient and overly fixed ethnicities.[138] The opposition of civic and ethnic nationalisms exerts a powerful influence over the study of nationalism, but like many typologies it obscures as much as it reveals. It not only crowds out a variety of other variables, and leads too many to locate national traditions as wholes on one side or the other of the divide rather than studying their internal tensions. It also encourages misrecognition of the cultural constructions on which ostensibly wholly civic nationalisms rest. It encourages self-declared civic nationalists, liberals, and cosmopolitans to be too complacent, seeing central evils of the modern world produced at a safe distance by ethnic nationalists from whom they are surely deeply different.

Yet in *The Idea of Nationalism* Kohn also performs an important service. He integrates nationalism into the story of Western liberalism (even if he distinguishes ethnic nationalism too sharply from it). He rightly shows nationalism at work in the seventeenth- and eighteenth-century foundations of Western modernity and indeed democracy. He calls our attention to the appropriation of ideas from Classical Antiquity that informed this. And he shows how nationalism could be, at least sometimes, internationalist and even universalist. Kohn's book had its greatest influence through the opposition of civic and ethnic nationalisms. But reading it again can also be an occasion for thinking anew about the relationship of nationalism to liberalism, skeptical about Kohn's problematic dichotomy and perhaps about the overconfidence of mid-twentieth-century liberalism, but attentive to his indications of the pervasive influence of nationalism and the importance and even progressive potential of some forms of solidarity between families and other face-to-face groups and the world as a whole.

7

Nationalism and the cultures
of democracy

If nationalism is over, we shall miss it. Revolution may be the project of a vanguard party acting on behalf of its masses. Resistance to capitalist globalization may be pursued by a multifarious and inchoate multitude. But imagining democracy requires thinking of "the people" as active and coherent and oneself as both a member and an agent. Liberalism informs the notion of individual agency, but provides weak purchase at best on membership and on the collective cohesion and capacity of the *demos*. In the modern era, the discursive formation that has most influentially underwritten these dimensions of democracy is nationalism.[1]

Nationalists have exaggerated and naturalized the historical and never more than partial unity of the nation. The hyphen in nation-state tied the modern polity – with enormously more intense and effective internal administration than any large-scale precursors – to the notion of a historically or naturally unified people who intrinsically belong together. The idea that nations give states clearly identifiable and meaningfully integrated populations, which in turn are the bases of their legitimacy, is as problematic as it is influential.[2] It is of course an empirically tendentious claim. But it is part of a discursive formation that structures the world, not simply an external description of it.

To be sure, nationalism has also been mobilized in sharply antidemocratic projects; it has often organized disturbingly intolerant attitudes; it has led to distorted views of the world and excesses of both pride and imagined insults. It has also been a recipe for conflicts both internal and external. Populations straddle borders or move long distances to new states while retaining allegiances to old nations. Dominant groups demand that governments enforce cultural conformity, challenging both the individual freedom and the vitality that comes from cultural creativity. These faults have made it easier for liberals to dismiss nationalism from their theories of democracy. But this has not made it less important in the real world.

There are of course also many problems that affect everyone on earth – environmental degradation, for example, or small arms trade. Nationalist rhetoric is commonly employed in excuses for governmental failures to address these problems. Transnational movements press for action. But for the most part the action comes, if it does, from national states.

Likewise, there is no non-national and cosmopolitan solution available to "complex humanitarian emergencies" like that in Darfur. International humanitarian action is vitally important, but more as compensation for state failures and evils than as a substitute for better states. More generally, lacking a capable state may be as much as source of disaster as state violence. National integration and identity are also basic to many efforts at economic development and to contesting the imposition of a neoliberal model of global economic growth that ignores or undermines local quality of life and inhibits projects of self-government. Nations also remain basic units of international cooperation.

Though a secular decline in the capacity and importance of nation-states has often been asserted – or at least predicted – as a result of globalization, this is not evident. Certainly nation-states face new challenges: multinational corporations and global markets organize production, exchange, and even real estate markets across borders. It is harder for any state to control its fiscal policy autonomously, for example, and harder for most to control their borders (as not only migrants but money, media, and a variety of goods cross them). The popularity of neoliberal privatization programs has challenged state enterprises and provision of services that sometimes played an integrating role. The extent to which the integration of nations matches that of states, has never been complete, and now faces challenges from calls for greater regional, ethnic, and religious autonomy. Proponents of cultural diversity have often challenged assimilationist approaches to the cultural integration of immigrants. Migration has been organized into diasporic circuits linking communities in several countries and making returning migrants and remittances significant issues in sender states.

Yet nationalism and nation-states retain considerable power and potential. Rather than their general decline, what we see today is loss of faith in progress through secular and civic nationalism and state-building projects. This makes it harder to appreciate the positive work that nationalism has done and still does (alongside its evil uses). Nations provide for structures of belonging that build bridges between local communities and mediate between these and globalization. Nations organize the primary arenas for democratic political participation. Nationalism helps mobilize collective commitment to public institutions, projects, and debates. Nationalism encourages mutual responsibility across divisions of class and region. We may doubt both the capacities of nation-states and the morality of many versions of nationalism, but we lack realistic and attractive alternatives.

Crucially, we are poorly prepared to theorize democracy if we cannot theorize the social solidarity of democratic peoples. Substituting ethical attention to the obligations all human beings share does not fill the void. This effort lacks an understanding of politics as the active creation of ways of living together, not only distributing power but developing institutions. And, accordingly, it lacks a sense of democracy as a human creation necessarily situated in culture and history, always imperfect and open to improvement, and therefore always also variable.

A deep mutual relationship has tied nationalism to democracy throughout the modern era. Nationalism was crucial to collective democratic subjectivity, providing a basis for the capacity to speak as "we the people," the conceptualization of constitution-making as collective self-empowerment, and commitment to accept the judgment of citizens in general on contentious questions. As important, democracy encouraged the formation of national solidarity. When states were legitimated on the basis of serving the commonwealth, when collective struggles won improved institutions, when a democratic public sphere spanned class, regional, religious, and other divisions this strengthened national solidarity. It is a pernicious illusion to think of national identity as the prepolitical basis for a modern state – an illusion certainly encouraged by some nationalists. It is equally true that national identity is (like all collective identity) inherently political; created in speech, action, and recognition. A democratic public is not merely contingent on political solidarity, it can be productive of it.

Of course political community can be and is constructed on bases other than nations. Most people live in multiple, overlapping zones of solidarity. There are varying degrees of local autonomy within nation-states, and varying degrees of integration among neighboring states. And of course nations can be transformed; they need not be treated as prepolitically given but can be recognized as always made – culturally as well as politically – and therefore remarkable. But the idea of democracy requires some structures of integration, some cultural capacity for internal communication, some social solidarity of "the people."

Liberalism within or beyond nations

Political liberalism developed largely in the effort to theorize the transition from pre-national empires, monarchies, and aristocracies to nations. Nations were the primary political structures in which liberal individuals would be equals and have more or less universal rights.

The same liberalism was well attuned, of course, to recognizing the failures of actually existing nations, including especially failures to extend equal rights to all citizens. Liberals generally respond to these failings of nations and nationalism by abandoning reliance on historically achieved solidarities and subjectivities. This tendency has been reinforced by recognition of the ways in which globalization limits states. Seeking greater justice and liberty than actual nations have offered, they apply liberal ideas about the equality of and relations among individuals at the scale of humanity as a whole. But it is not clear that ratcheting up universalism makes it any more readily achievable.

In addition, this attempt to pursue liberal equality and justice at a more global level reveals a tension previously beneath the surface of liberalism. So long as liberalism could rely (explicitly or implicitly) on the idea of nation to supply a prepolitical constitution of "the people" it could be a theory both of democracy and universal rights. But the pursuit of greater universalism commonly comes at the expense of solidarity, for solidarity is typically achieved in more particularistic formations. Since there is no democracy without social solidarity, as liberalism is transposed to the global level it becomes more a theory of universal rights or justice and less a theory of democratic politics.

Liberalism has been pervasive in democratic theory – enough so that its blind spots have left the democratic imaginary impoverished. This shows up in thinking about (or thinking too little about) solidarity, social cohesion, collective identity, and boundaries. With its concerns focused overwhelmingly on freedom, equality, and justice for individual persons, liberalism has had at best a complicated relationship with nationalism. For much of the modern era, liberalism worked within the tacit assumption that nation-states defined the boundaries of citizenship. John Rawls made the assumption explicit:

> we have assumed that a democratic society, like any political society, is to be viewed as a complete and closed social system. It is complete in that it is self-sufficient and has a place for all the main purposes of human life. It is also closed, in that entry into it is only by birth and exit from it is only by death.[3]

This "Westphalian" understanding incorporated a distinction of properly "domestic" from properly international matters that was closely related to the distinction of public from private emerging more generally in modern social thought.[4] It underwrote, among other things, the exclusion of religion from allegedly "realist" international relations, a treatment of religion as essentially a domestic matter (and often by implication a private choice) that has informed not only liberal political theory but the entire discipline of international relations. This has been closely related to liberalism's difficulties with "strong" or "thick" accounts of culture as constitutive for human subjectivity. Liberalism typically presumes a theory of culture that it does not recognize as such, but instead treats somewhat ironically as an escape from culture into a more direct access to the universal – whether conceived as human nature, or human rights, or political process in the abstract.

More recently, pressed by the porousness of state borders in an era of intensified globalization, many liberals have recognized the difficulties with relying uncritically on nation-states to provide the framework within which liberal values are to be pursued. Allen Buchanan stated the case clearly in describing Rawls's version of liberal theory as "rules for a vanished Westphalian world."[5] To be precise, Buchanan challenged Rawls's international argument about a "law of peoples," not all of Rawls's liberal theory. There is in fact considerable controversy among those largely swayed by Rawls's earlier theory of justice over whether to accept his later law of peoples.[6] For many of these, the demands of justice as fairness simply must override both the norm of tolerance that Rawls sees as underwriting a strong respect for different ways of life and the fact that the cohesion of actual existing social life is rooted in different historically created solidarities and ways of life. Others struggle more to reconcile respect for difference with the demands of a universalistic appeal to cosmopolitan justice.

But perhaps Rawls accepted too much from nationalist representations of "peoples" as discrete, culturally integrated entities. Nationalists often make strong claims to ethnic purity and cultural uniformity. But in fact part of the importance of nationalism is the ways in which the national bridges a variety of differences. It does this not simply by providing an encompassing culture but by providing an arena for public debate and culture-making.[7]

Certainly greater global solidarity would be a good thing. But many liberal, cosmopolitan arguments rely on three tendentious assumptions. First, that it will be possible to create strong enough solidarities at a global scale to underwrite democratic mutual commitment (or to do so soon enough that pursuing these should have equal or higher priority to strengthening national solidarities and making them more democratic). Second, that justice, respect, and rights are more effectively secured for more human beings by approaching these as ethical universals than as moral obligations situated within particular solidarities and ways of life. And third, that an interest in or commitment to the universal (or the cosmopolitan) is based on the absence of culture (because culture is particularistic bias) rather than itself being a kind of cultural perspective.[8]

I have argued elsewhere about the importance of seeing cosmopolitanism as the presence of particular sorts of culture rather than the absence of culture, and about the extent to which access to the cosmopolitan is distributed on the basis of privilege.[9] What I want to stress here is the extent to which nationalism and democracy may – together – hold more potential for providing political solidarity across lines of cultural difference.

Structures of integration

A key part of the work that nationalism does is to provide cultural support for structures of social integration. Indeed, it is itself a source of such integration insofar as it structures collective identities and solidarities.[10]

Not everyone would consider this an obvious gain. Starting from the premise that the primary obligation of each human being is to all others, a range of ethical cosmopolitans argue that any smaller-scale solidarity requires specific justification – and starts out under the suspicion of being nothing more than an illegitimate expression of self-interest at the expense of justice for humanity at large.[11] I don't propose to take up such positions in detail here. Let it suffice to indicate that they are reached by starting with "bare" individuals as equivalent tokens of the universal type, humanity; that they treat the particularities of culture and social relations as extrinisic to and not constitutive of these individuals; that they substitute abstract ethics for politics and particularly for a conception of politics as a world-making and therefore necessarily historically specific process such as that developed in the rhetorical tradition; and finally that they lack any sociological account of how humanity is to be integrated such that the abstract norms they articulate may concretely be achieved. Such a procedure may open up some ethical insights, but it runs the risk of substituting a pure ought for a practical politics. It also deflects our attention from the social, cultural, and historical conditions of democracy.

Democracy depends on social solidarity and social institutions. Neither is given to human beings as a matter of nature; they must be achieved through human imagination and action – in short, through history. As a result, all actually existing examples vary and all are imperfect. It is more helpful to approach them in a spirit of "pragmatic fallibalism" than radical ethical universalism, asking about improvements more than perfection, next steps more than ultimate ends.[12] This doesn't mean that there is no value in utopian dreams or efforts to imagine radically better societies; it does mean both that such dreams will be more helpful if they include attention to the social conditions of solidarity alongside the abstract definitions of justice, and that in making abstract norms guides for practical action we will do well to temper them with recognition of historical circumstances.

Nations, and indeed all structures of social integration, have been achieved with more or less violence. This is neither a source of legitimacy nor a disqualification from it. No one gains rights from the blood of fallen ancestors. Neither does bloodshed render the institutions and solidarities that follow it mere results of force. Nations forged partly in war and in projects of remembering heroic dead exert powerful pulls on the living. It is an important project to try to turn national self-understanding in peaceful directions, but a merely illusory project to imagine that moral objections to past bellicosity or domestic repression render national solidarity unimportant.

National allegiances, moreover, are always in some part the result of symbolic violence and imposition, as for example countries are created in part by skewing resources towards capital cities and making provincials embarrassed by rural accents. In other cases the integration of subaltern populations into national projects has been brutal and severely unequal. But this does not mean that there is necessarily a politically sensible project of undoing those allegiances either in favor of the universal or in order to restore prior local identities – or that this might not itself be an imposition involving new symbolic – or material – violence.

Partitions and secessionist wars are almost universally bloody routes to political autonomy, and if they sometimes become inevitable that does not make them praiseworthy. Moreover, they create new nations which may be as repressive of difference as old ones. Far better to remake national identities and institutions to better accommodate diversity and to support both partial local autonomy and intercultural relations.

Many nationalist ideologies – and indeed many versions of the discursive formation of nationalism itself – mislead in this regard. Nationalist rhetoric is commonly employed to produce the image of populations unifying prepolitically, by culture, religion, or territory. This allows those who employ it to judge contemporary politics – and culture and economics – by the standard of a people understood as always already there, constituted in a kind of primal innocence outside the realm of ordinary politics. The people may be understood simply as given, on ethnic or other cultural grounds, or as the creation of martyrs, heroes, and lawgivers acting outside or above the normal politics of individual and sectional interests. Both images may be evoked at the same time. The important thing is the implication that the nation is established in advance of, separately from, the more quotidian developments which may then be judged as serving or failing to serve its interests.

But in reality nations are always the result of at least partially political histories. That is, not merely are they the result of more or less arbitrary historical circumstances – wars won or lost, mountain ranges that slow the spread of evangelism or commerce. They are also the result of self-constituting collective projects in which culture is created and choices are made. Nations are products not only bases of politics, and they are accordingly objects of new political projects.

Saying that the ideal of prepolitical national unity is an illusion does not make the illusion any less powerful, either in its grips on individual imaginations and emotions or in its capacity to constitute a cultural order. People who have read about "the invention of tradition" are still moved by national anthems and soccer teams, enlist in armies, and understand themselves to have "home" countries when they migrate.[13]

Nations are not the only or necessarily the primary structures of social integration of cultural identity. That they are commonly represented as a kind of "trump card" against other identities, exaggerating national unity and giving short shrift to intranational diversity, is a form of symbolic violence. But local autonomy and cultural diversity may be better pursued through improving structures of national integration rather than abandoning them.

National structures are important in the modern era both because they embody historical achievements and because globalization itself – a key ingredient of the entire modern era – creates a demand for mediating structures between humanity as a whole (or inhumanity as a whole, since that is as often what is achieved on a very large scale) and face-to-face interpersonal relations. Nations are important because integration beyond the level of family and community is important. This requires both culture and institutions. There is no reason to want all to be the same. Moreover, nations are not the only form for such integration – religions are also important and indeed sometimes transnational political movements. But the need for such integration means that nations are not simply "optional"; they may be restructured or replaced but there is no viable way simply to abandon them.

The integration nations help to achieve is of several sorts. They help to bind people together across social classes. They bridge regional and ethnic and sometimes religious differences. They link generations to each other, mobilizing traditions of cultural inheritance mutual obligation. They link the living to both ancestors and future generations. They do this not simply in ideology, but in social institutions which matter to the lives of individuals, families, and communities. Nations are integrated in educational systems, health care systems, and transportation systems. Strengthening these is generally a national and often a state project. Certainly philanthropists moved by care for humanity at large also build schools and clinics and sometimes roads. But, for the most part, these are achievements of nation-states and typically are public institutions (though this very public provision for the common good is currently under challenge). Not least of all, national integration is produced in the formation and sharing of new culture and in political arguments.

Nations accomplish all these linkages imperfectly, leaving room for contention. But if nationalism creates peoples, continued politics can transform them. At best, these are peoples in which the sentiment of common belonging is strong enough that it enables citizens to absorb the frustration of losing political battles over particular policies and leaders while remaining commited to the larger structure of integration. For there is little possibility of collective action to make and remake solidarity that is not also agonistic.[14] World-making politics is inevitably contentious politics, but not for that reason without solidarities.

Among the range of solidarities that have been mobilized in political action, national solidarities have been distinctively capable of political self-constitution in the making or transformation of states. Nations, at least sometimes, are peoples able to utter (or believe they have uttered) phrases like "we the people" as it appears in the Preamble to the US Constitution:

> We the people of the United States, in order to form a more perfect union, establish justice, insure domestic tranquility, provide for the common defense, promote the general welfare, and secure the blessings of liberty to ourselves and our posterity, do ordain and establish this Constitution for the United States of America.

Such acts of founding are basic to national histories throughout the Americas and present a distinctive counterpart to the idea of nations as ethnic inheritances, as always already there, which is more common in Europe (though in Europe the history of revolutions is a reminder of the role of active creation in nationalism).

To be sure, the founding of a new nation has never been simply the uncoerced and egalitarian project of all potential citizens. On the contrary, elites have commonly driven national projects and claims to unitary national voice have typically occluded not only the cultural diversity within nations but the subjugation of large populations. Indigenous peoples throughout the Americas, and in many countries slaves of African descent, were thus dominated, marginalized, and often in political rhetoric forgotten by national founders. But if independence was not liberation for many in the Americas – or in postcolonies around the world – the new nations, especially where they embraced democracy, did create conditions for continued struggles for fuller citizenship.

The idea of constituting a new country – making new social institutions to integrate people in a solidarity only partially inherited – has profound significance for democracy. Such acts of founding are reminders that the very structures of integration that constitute countries are subject to making – and potentially to democratic will-formation. Democracy, in other words, is something more than electing the least objectionable leaders.

Hannah Arendt situated such acts of revolutionary founding of new countries within the more general human potential for innovative world-making – "natality" – in every act of political speech.[15] Her argument is rooted in a rhetorical tradition that stretches back to ancient Greece but which has been subordinated by dominant perspectives in philosophy and political theory. Politics has been seen as more about power than persuasion, more about perfecting institutional arrangements than nurturing creativity. But Arendt and the rhetorical tradition remind us of a strong sense in which politics can be the creation of new institutional arrangements and indeed the remaking of the world. Politics in this sense is ineluctably historical, culturally specific, and diverse.

If democracy is, following Arendt's lead, about the ways in which people may creatively develop new ways of living together, choose new institutional arrangements, and even found new countries, then it is necessarily not simply a matter of abstract design or the best formal procedures. It is a matter of discerning ways to make the will and well-being of ordinary people more determinative of the very formation of social institutions as well as of specific decisions within them. This can be informed by abstract, universal political theory but it is also necessarily informed by concrete, historically and culturally specific circumstances.

From one side, nationalism is an internationally reproduced discursive formation full of pressures to make each country into an isomorphic token of a global type. There are pressures for conformity: each country should have a recognizable government with ministers and other officials analogous to those in other countries. Each should have a national museum and national folklore, passports and border controls, an authority to issue driving licenses and postage stamps.[16] Countries also face similar problems and learn from each other. But at the same time, in their more historically and culturally specific dimensions, nationalisms mediate between the isomorphic character of constructing tokens of a global type and the historical particularities of tradition and cultural creativity. Distinctive national self-understandings are produced and reproduced in literature, film, political debate – and political grumbling, political jokes, and political insults. These structure the ways in which people feel solidarity with each other (and distinction from outsiders).

Modernist self-understanding commonly exaggerates breaks with history and cultural traditions. Conscious plans and rational choices are favored – even immediate expressions of emotion are in more favor than adherence to tradition. Nationalism, however, is a way of claiming history within a modernist frame. It is typically misleading for it claims history through units of contemporary consciousness and solidarity that did not necessarily exist in the past.

Thus archeologists may speak of Sweden or Sudan when describing sites and cultures millennia older than either nation. Of course, the history that produced both Sweden and Sudan is a matter of imposition and drawing of boundaries by force, not simply of maturation. In different ways, each is troubled today by the international flows and forces of modernity – migrations, money and commodities, media. Each has difficulty with its internal diversity, and leaders in each are tempted to assert untenable ethnic (and sometimes religious) definitions of "proper" national identity. Sweden was shaped by its earlier imperial ambitions as well as later nationalism. Transnational Protestantism informed its constitution which is now being transformed by European unification. Sudan has long been shaped by both pan-African and pan-Arab projects as it is now by transnational Islam. Sudan is also being remade by a geopolitical crisis reverberating throughout northeast Africa, with issues of trade and diplomacy making distant China an important counterpart and human suffering which has brought a humanitarian response on a nearly global scale.

The stories of Sweden and Sudan do not simply pit long-standing, unquestioned, and culturally defined internal unity against new, troubling, and political-economic external forces. Internal diversity is part of the history of each. Some of the lines of diversity predate the history of each (as there were Arabs and Africans, Nubians and Nuer before there was a Sudan). And the history of each is partly a matter of producing what now are taken as defining boundaries (as seemingly obviously unitary Sweden not only includes territories whose integration was contested but doesn't include its former dominions of Estonia, Finland, or Norway). But it is also a matter of producing language, culture, distinctive social institutions, and personal styles.

Nationality situates persons in time, in the world, and in relation to each other. Of course it is not the only identity anyone has. Nationality may be supplemented by a range of other categories of belonging and may be in tension with some – from religion to class. It could be replaced as a primary dimension of belonging; it could be transformed. But simply to imagine overcoming it without attending to the work it does would be a mistake.

Beyond primordiality vs. invention

National identities are neither simply inherited from a premodern past nor arbitrarily created by elites struggling for power and seeking to enlist followers in their projects. Some nationalist ideologues claim the former. Some debunking academics claim the latter. But thinking just in terms of these dimensions obscures the dynamic quality of culture and social organization. Rather than mere inheritance we need to recognize reproduction that always has room for selectivity, rearrangement, and outright innovation. And cultural creativity is hardly limited to cynical manipulation. It is one of the crucial features of national identities that they contain the potential for self-transcendence. Just as individuals can want to be better than they are – want even to have better wants and desires – so national cultures incorporate norms, values, and understandings that point to better futures.[17] Nations can innovate in ways that transcend their mere immediate existence in other words, and they are pushed to do so by social movements and indeed by art, moral discourse, and sometimes even academic analysis. Even references to a glorious past may be criticisms of the present as much as sources of pride, and may underwrite efforts to make things better.

Academic analysts of nationalism are typically drawn to analyzing the "truth content" of national traditions. Examining received histories, thus, contemporary historians try to correct our views of the past. Nationalist historical claims and myths offer fertile ground for this exercise. To take an example now as familiar to American historians for its falsity as it was once a taken-for-granted truth of school lessons and a doxic part of the culture, there is no credible evidence that George Washington chopped down a cherry tree and confessed because he could not tell a lie. The story seems to have originated in the early nineteenth century with Mason Locke Weems (a clergyman – hence the more familiar name, Parson Weems – who actually made his living as a printer and found his most thriving market with stories of the founding fathers of the young nation). In more important ways as well, establishing clearer knowledge of a country's past, including its interrelationship with other countries, may be helpful in improving the quality of present politics. But while the writing of new histories may be more accurate, the production of common culture continues and is never quite reducible to truth or falsity for it is also a constitute framework for understanding.

Imagining a way out of culture in favor of truth content alone may be an illusion especially common in the modern era, but the idea of actively making culture in ways not reducible to mimesis has been at least as central to modernism. It is an ancient idea, of course, that through speech or artistic creativity or even craft work one may participate in making the world. In the modern era, something of the same idea has animated social movement activists who have sought not only to build "a new Jerusalem" but to imagine Jerusalems of the mind and make them real. Blake's notion of escaping "mind-forg'd manacles" has to do in part with escaping the ways received traditions of thought limit us, and in this it shares much with Enlightenment rationalism. But though Blake was an Enlightenment figure in some senses, he did not mean simply to replace received concepts with logical-empirical truths. He meant to facilitate the imagination and through it to help produce a better reality.

Modern political theory, nonetheless, has tended to focus on interests and values to the neglect of creativity, imagination, or rhetoric. This has obscured the extent to which national culture (like all culture) is neither fixed inheritance nor cynical manipulation but vital precisely because reproduced in ways that include creativity.

Human creativity (what Arendt called natality) opens the possibility of innovation – both in realizing more fully the existing culture and in ways more sharply different to it. Yet, much writing on nationalism and modernism (or modernity) tends to assume uncritically that the last five centuries of history reveal a unilateral decline in human diversity. Part of the problem is that researchers and political activists alike tend to focus on tracing continuities in named groups or nations. This is to some extent built into the discipline of history with its organization as a series of national histories.[18] When these disappear – as many of the ethnie of the past have in fact disappeared – it seems a loss of diversity.

The whole modern era has been shaped by globalization, moreover, and this has created new commonalities based on the central organization and expanded reach of commodity production and exchange. Various media bring common messages to remote sites more or less in real time. But it remains a considerable leap to assume that differences among human groups are simply inherited from the past.

Social scientists have surprisingly often accepted the proposition that nearly all of the important differences among human beings originated in the relatively distant past, and are thus *found* by rather than created in modernity. Here is Ernest Gellner:

> Cultural nuances in the agrarian world are legion: they are like raindrops in a storm, there is no counting of them. But when they all fall on the ground . . . [during modernization] they aggregate into a number of distinct, large, often mutually hostile puddles. The aggregation, the elimination of plurality and nuance anticipated by the internationalists, does indeed take place, but it leaves behind not one large universal culture-puddle, but a whole set of them.[19]

Gellner is disagreeing here with liberal internationalists who imagined that nations would give way to a single world-culture, but he accepts the notion that in the main diversity was produced in the past, and is now being erased (or at least consolidated) by "the tidal wave of industrialization or modernization."

This proposition has been sharply and rightly contested by a number of authors.[20] But it has surprising resilience. It is as though analysts imagine that there was great cultural creativity in tribal and agrarian societies, but that moderns wield only the capacity to homogenize, or manipulate, but not to create – and create differences. This view, I think, is one that early moderns helped to produce by the way they revered the classics and the way they understood both historical time, reason, and the struggle against prejudice. But it is false. And in fact, I don't think most social scientists believe it – that is, they don't really believe that peasant societies are more culturally fertile – they only write about nationalism as though they believed this. What they seem actually to believe is that the sort of "culture" that counts for the construction of deeply felt ethnicity is necessarily ancient, even if obviously created at some point. Oddly, even those who seek to demonstrate the novel and invented character of national culture tend to accept the same assumption. They argue that "invented traditions," in the phrase of Hobsbawm and Ranger, are not as real as those which grow by gradual accretion over the centuries.[21] And it is taken as obvious that the spread of CNN and McDonald's franchises, following the spread of English and global trade, simply betoken growing uniformity of culture.

But globalization and modern life generally are productive of difference and novelty in common culture, not just flattened commonalities. Indeed, ethnic identities themselves are not simply premodern. Ethnicity as we understand it today is not the same as kinship. It is not simply an inheritance from primordial times, whether in the imagery of Wagnerian mists or African jungles. Rather, ethnicity is a product of confrontation among peoples of different group identities and cultural backgrounds. It is a mode of identity forged largely in cities, not in the countryside; in migrations and military service, not in staying home. Migrants to cities developed ethnicity by accenting commonalities with people to whom they would not necessarily have been close in the countryside, people from the "wrong" clan or a distant village. In the context of a city, these could appear as speakers of the same language, practitioners of the same religion, people with whom one could feel at home. But common ethnicity was not primarily a matter of specific relationships of marriage and descent, like those of kin-based societies, nor of place. Though ethnics might marry within their ethnic group, and even try to keep alive more specific norms about proper matches, the ethnic group was in fact a category rather than a network. That is, it was constructed out of cultural similarities salient in the urban context rather than the specific webs of relationships that constituted alliances and rivalries in the countryside. It might contain more or less of those webs of relationships, but it was not defined by them. Ethnic groups were and are defined by their juxtaposition to other ethnic groups and to the state. In the eyes of each other and under the gaze of the state, each tends to be a category, a set within which members are largely equivalent.[22] Ethnicity in this sense certainly existed in the premodern world, with religion often dominant in the ascriptive constructions, as in the Ottoman millet system. But ethnicity also flourished and was constructed anew in the rise of modern cities and states. In this sense, the construction of ethnicity out of kinship continues. New identities are formed. Many, like Asian-American, have no analog "at home" and cannot be understood simply as an amalgamation of prior local identities.

In addition to transforming older identities and helping to produce new identities such as ethnicities, modern life occasions increasing juxtapositions among identities. It brings a new "dynamic density" of intergroup contacts (to borrow Durkheim's under-remarked phrase). Markets, media, migration, state-building, and the growth of cities all bring together people of different cultural and social-organizational backgrounds. This is not radically new; trading cities and the capitals of empires always produced contact across cultural lines. But the contacts are intense, particularly in certain key nexuses of global flows. Even without the production of new identities, therefore, modernity helps to produce in each person a greater awareness of diversity of identities. The world of others is represented to each person in terms of a welter of different groups. As in the past, and perhaps more often, many individuals experience belonging to more than one of these at the same time.[23]

New differences are created, and suppressed differences are given new public voice. Science, for example, may be universalistic, but it produces change and multiplication and diversities of knowledges. The very expansion of what is known – far beyond the capacity of any single human knower – makes it inevitable that the common knowledge of different groups will partake differentially of the ever-expanding whole. Beyond science, literary and artistic activity produces novel culture all the time, and at least as much now as ever before. They also are appreciated in different communities of reception and help thus to contribute to cultural differentiations among groups (as in the way Asian-American novels may help to make, not just reflect, Asian-Americans). There is also an expansion of occupations and economic niches in the modern world. A quick glance at the *Dictionary of Occupational Titles* produced by the US government should give pause to anyone who thinks diversity is being erased, even if most of these exist in capitalist labor markets that commodify labor and establish class differences. So should the inverse thought: wasn't the way of life of traditional peasants impressively uniform, at least within broad ecological and material-cultural zones?

Indeed, local communities vary a great deal today, and at least in the world's richer countries afford the relatively novel luxury of choice of "lifestyles." The differences from one peasant village to another in Vietnam or Burkina Faso are hard to describe in terms of this kind of diversity, but despite widespread condemnation of the homogeneity of suburbs by comparison to cities, there is this sort of diversity – at least up to a point – between one suburb and another in Westchester County. But lifestyle communities are not generally coincident with local government boundaries. Look at the emergence of more strongly self-identified and publicly recognized communities based on sexual orientation. Homosexuality may have existed through history (though there are tendentious issues of definition here that I do not want to try to engage at the moment). But opportunities to form differentiated social groups based on gay lifestyles – or indeed other lifestyles "alternative" to conventional heterosexual family formation – have certainly proliferated more recently. This is an achievement unevenly distributed both among and within "modern" countries.

Finding ways to integrate culturally diverse populations has been central to modern nationalism. Sometimes this amounts to trying to impose new common culture against others, and this of course may be done with both material and symbolic violence. Such repression of difference can mark anti-colonial and democratic struggles, moreover, as they seek to forge new solidarity in the cause of overcoming external power. In the pursuit of Algerian independence from France, for example, the nationalist movement was also an Arabicizing movement. Algeria's Berber populations suffered a double repression. So too throughout Latin America, independence movements let by European and Mestizo elites often failed to acknowledge or actively discriminated against indigenous peoples.

But nationalism is not always simply homogenizing. Nationalists can struggle to develop institutions and cultural practices that facilitate connections across lines of cultural difference without suppressing any. The solidarity of national populations need not depend only on cultural similarity or the categorical identity in which each citizen is a token of the national type. It may also be developed out of the incorporation of mediating communities into the whole, based on recognition of functional interdependence, or embodied in the formation of public culture, discourse, and debate. National arenas for public culture are important and may achieve solidarity amid contest and diversity. Such public life is necessarily culture-forming, not only rational-critical. And while it certainly involves arguments, it also involves other modes of communication and expression.

Cultures of democracy

One reason not to dismiss nation-states as structures of integration is because they embody collective histories of struggle. National liberation movements have fought not only for sovereignty but for the opportunity to build new social institutions. Constitution-making and sometimes revolution have reshaped the conditions of collective life. Relations among specific religious communities and efforts to overcome clashes have forged projects of mutual coexistence that are not grasped by the notion of secularism as the mere absence of religion or toleration as an altogether abstract value. Workers have fought to gain economic rights and security. Democracy itself has been won in collective struggles, not simply designed in political theory, and democratic practices are grounded in different traditions as a result. These histories are resources for further struggles; they are situating and orienting backgrounds to democratic action. These histories, moreover, have been in large part nation-making histories. Nehru's classic *The Discovery of India* is of course also a story of the making of India (and an act of claiming a particular history as part of that making).[24] So too France and America, Russia and Rwanda, Ecuador and Argentina have all been made not simply found. The struggles that have made them may stretch over shorter or longer periods of time, may have been more or less democratic, and more or less violent. But they leave each with a distinctive context for democratic action today.

From eighteenth-century revolutions, to the nineteenth-century "Springtime of Peoples," to mid-twentieth-century postcolonial independence movements, nationalism has often been closely linked to the pursuit of greater self-government. Clearly the idea of "self-determination" puts a great deal of pressure on the idea of "self." This is full of strains for individuals and even more for nations. In each case, though, the idea of self and the further idea of self-determination is basic both to the social imaginary of modernity and to critical engagement with forms of domination.

At the individual level, debates about what constitutes such a self inform and were informed by the emergence of modern ideas of legal personality, a growing emphasis on the autonomy of moral subjects, and psychological concerns for the integration and integrity of the person. Understanding of collective selves grew in close tandem with that of individual persons. At its most influential, collective self-determination demanded a self composed not of a dynasty or a state, nor of a disconnected, unintegrated population, but of *a* people, an organized, meaningfully integrated collectivity. This the idea of nation supplied.

The emancipation of the nation from empire and dynasty went hand in hand with the emancipation of the person from subjection to patriarchy, religion, and village custom. Subjects were rethought from the vantage point of the nation. Strengthening the nation meant, many nationalists argued, liberating the capacities of individual citizens. It is no accident that projects of linguistic reform have been nearly universal features of nationalist (and democratic) projects. Aristocracies used language partly to parcel out differential standing, forever distinguishing refined from vulgar usage. Democracies claimed rights to public participation for all the people – the nation. Equally, advocates of national self-strengthening sought the education of those same people, and often their inclusion in the political process.

Just as individuals could take on projects of self-reform, self-strengthening, and moral improvement, so could nations. An ancient concept, "nation" was as much transformed in the modern era as the idea of person. In their transformed and never quite fixed meanings, each term was also constitutive of modernity. Though represented sometimes as opposites, the two ideas were intimate partners. They were joined among other things by the claim to refer to integral, indivisible wholes – individuals. Likewise, their objects were presented as simultaneously natural, always already there, and in need of energetic making, of *bildung* (to echo the classic arguments of Herder and Fichte).

To be sure, movements for national independence often empowered certain elites and subordinated some citizens. Many easily shifted into projects of subjection of other populations or repression of other nations. But to understand nationalism only as a rhetoric of domination would wrongly denigrate the meaning and accomplishments of national liberation movements. These have not only fought external oppression, they have brought much wider ranges of people into the political process. They have often helped to create the nations whose independence they sought, but also to create citizens (even if post-liberation politics has often undone many of the gains).

In every democratic struggle, the solidarity of "the people" has been forged from a range of specific cultural and social sources. This is not merely a matter of finding common denominators among an externally identified population. It is a matter of cultural creativity, personal decision, and persuasion. All tradition is invented; all identities are in some degree chosen in competition with other possible ways of forging personality and social ties. How much anyone will emphasize nation, or religion, or class is not a matter of abstract rational calculation of interest but of innumerable highly situated decisions, of what becomes habit, and occasionally of commitments made at dramatic junctures. People arrive at both their daily small decisions and their rare moments of major self-defining choice by diverse trajectories and in diverse contexts. Democracy, accordingly, must develop with diverse cultures. It will differ among nations. It will also differ within them, as different people struggle to make something better of their people and for their people.

Nationalism is always Janus-faced, as Tom Nairn has stressed.[25] Not only does it look both backward and forward, it simultaneously embodies claims to distinctive cultural identities and social solidarities and to legitimate global standing and at least partial sovereignty. It mediates as few other political rhetorics can between the production of internal solidarity and the need for external recognition. It helps to voice a sense of belonging together that is shaped by shared culture and social relations and that is crucial not just to the exercise but to the pursuit of democracy. For nationalism is a rhetoric available in the active as well as the passive voice.

It is not just a matter of chance that democracy happens to come into the world shaped by different cultural traditions, social relations, and geopolitical contexts. It is of the very nature of democracy that it should exist in plural forms, created by different people as they struggle with different circumstances. The specific reach of different nations is logically arbitrary, but historically meaningful. Nations reflect not merely communities of fate, but of mutual and collective responsibility.

Conclusion

To recognize that there is a community of fate and responsibility at the level of the entire world makes sense. But liberal cosmopolitanism does not provide the proximate solidarities on the basis of which better institutions and greater democracy can be built. Nations are the most important of such solidarities (though both more local ones and trans-national ones are also important). Moreover, while cosmopolitan ethics may explain why it is good for individuals to give to global charities, they do not adequately explain the obligations those who benefit from living in rich countries have to those whose lives are limited because of the way in which capitalism and the world-system of states have organized the distribution of both wealth and the "illth" that is created by many efforts to pursue wealth.[26] This is so because the benefits derive from the embeddedness of individual lives in national histories and contexts. If for example Americans are to pay reparations to countries damaged by the slave trade or other injustices, it will be because the very possibility of life as an individual American today rests on the unjust historical background. The remedy will depend not merely on a global idea of equality or justice but on the mediating solidarity. This alone will make it a felt and actionable collective responsibility.

Approaches to liberal cosmopolitanism that do not take seriously the work nationalism does in the modern era and that do not work with a strong appreciation and understanding of solidarity and subjectivity, are as apt to be pernicious as progressive in actual politics. For nationalism is not only deeply imbricated in the social arrangements of the modern era, it is basic to movements to challenge and improve those social arrangements.

The necessity of nations in contemporary global affairs is not something in itself to be celebrated. They are starting points, institutional mechanisms, and frameworks of struggle more than indicators of ultimate values or goals. In one of the common meanings of the word, indeed, nationalism refers to a passionate attachment to one's own nation that underwrites outrageous prejudice against others. But we should not try to grasp the phenomenon only through instances of passionate excess or successful manipulation by demagogues. For nationalism is equally a discursive formation that facilitates mutual recognition among polities that mediate different histories, institutional arrangements, material conditions, cultures, and political projects in the context of intensifying globalization. Nationalism offers both a mode of access to global affairs and a mode of resistance to aspects of globalization. To wish it away is more likely to invite the dominance of neoliberal capitalism than to usher in an era of world citizenship.

Not least of all, nationalism is a reminder that democracy depends on solidarity. This may be achieved in various ways. It is never achieved outside of history and culture. Democratic action, therefore, is necessarily the action of people who join with each other in particular circumstances, recognizing and nurturing distinctive dimensions of belonging together. Nationalist ideologies sometimes encourage the illusion that belonging together is either natural or so ancient as to be prior to all contemporary choices. But liberalism conversely encourages neglect of the centrality of solidarity and especially the cultural constitution of historical specificity of persons – potential subjects of liberal politics. More helpfully, we can recognize that solidarities, including but not limited to national ones, are never simply given but have to be produced and reproduced. This means they are subject to change; this change may be pursued in collective struggle. Women and minority groups have been integrated into the political life of many modern states not simply despite nationalism (though certainly despite certain versions of nationalism), but through the transformation of nationalism. Nationalism then becomes in part the history of such struggles.

Nationalism also underpins social institutions created in the course of historical struggles, such as public schools, health care, and other dimensions of welfare states. It may underpin struggles to defend such institutions – and the very idea of the public good – against neoliberal privatization. The institutions differ from each other, and struggle is necessarily about improving them not simply protecting them. The same is true of culture and structures of social relations. These are constitutive for democracy, but they are also subject to democratic action and change. For these reasons, the cultures of democracy necessarily differ from each other. National solidarities are resources for democracy and also arenas of democratic struggle.

Conclusion

Acceleration of globalization in recent years has been greeted alternately, and sometimes simultaneously, with hope and panic. It has brought pursuit of human rights and pursuit of terrorists. Democracy has made headway in some settings, but hardly everywhere as some hoped after 1989. Humanitarian emergencies have exacted a brutal toll, though on the positive side they have also brought forward a considerable response. Migration has been one force furthering global cosmopolitanism, but it is also met with reinvigorated border controls and immigration restrictions. While it has sometimes been portrayed as movement beyond the state, the growth of new non-state global governance institutions has been uneven and in some domains halting, and if many states are indeed in crisis, states remain central political actors. The importance of the state is evident in the problems attendant on weak states in Africa, the muscle-flexing of emerging powers like India and China, and both the military and the political interventions of the US. In brief, globalization is real but not quite the uncontested and unambiguously positive transformation some enthusiasts have suggested. And while new institutions outside or beyond nation-states are important, nation-states themselves are called on to play central roles in the context of globalization. Indeed, much of the contemporary form of globalization is produced and driven by nation-states – at least certain powerful nation-states.

Globalization and the coming of postnational and transnational society are often presented as matters of necessity. Globalization appears as an inexorable force – perhaps of progress, perhaps simply of a capitalist juggernaut, but in any case irresistible. European integration, for example, is often sold to voters as a necessary response to the global integration of capital. In Asia, Latin America, and elsewhere, a similar economistic imaginary is deployed to suggest that globalization moves of itself, and governments and citizens have only the option of adapting. Even where the globalist imaginary is not overwhelmingly economistic, it commonly shares in the image of progressive modernization and necessity. Many accounts of the impact and implications of information technology exemplify this.

Alternatives to globalization, on the other hand, are generally presented in terms of inherited identities and solidarities in need of defense. Usually this means nations and cultural identities imagined on the model of nations; sometimes it means religions, civilizations, or other structures of identity presented by their advocates as received rather than created. These are denigrated by proponents of transnational society who see the national and many other local solidarities as backward or outmoded, impositions of the past on the present. A prime example is the way both nationalist economic protectionism and Islamist movements are seen as simply the regressive opposite of globalization. In each case, this obscures the often transnational organization of the resistance movements. Likewise, the social imaginary of inherited cultural tradition and social identity is prominent in ideologies of Hindutvah, essential Ethiopianness, the idea that an insult to "Turkishness" should be a crime, and widespread notions of "cultural survival."

This is doubly confusing. First, many of the supposed alternatives to globalization are in fact responses to it and efforts to shape it. Second, there is a confusion between the fact of growing global connections – the minimalist core of globalization – and the specific institutional and market forms of globalization that have predominated so far. Like modernization theory two generations ago, accounts of globalization today tend to imply a single developmental direction for change. It makes more sense, as a variety of scholars have recognized, to conceive of multiple modernities or projects outside the simplistic contrast of the traditional and the modern. So too it is important to recognize that contemporary struggles are not simply for and against globalization but struggles over its form, over who benefits and who suffers, and over what existing solidarities and values must be sacrificed to secure an attractive global order.

In many settings, the economistic/technological imaginary of modernist globalization is embraced at the same time and by the same political leaders as nationalist, religious, or other imaginaries emphasizing inherited cultural identity. The contradiction is avoided by assigning these to separate spheres. The Chinese phrase "ti-yong" has long signaled this, a condensation of "Western learning for material advancement; Eastern learning for spiritual essence." Similarly divided imaginaries inform many Asian, Middle Eastern, and other societies. Even in Canada, a recent *Financial Times* article reported, "the country wants to become a lean global competitor while maintaining traditional local values."[1]

Like many countries, Canada seeks at once to project itself internationally as a tourist destination and domestically as an object of political cathexis. Like many other countries as well, it does so with both enthusiastic representations of its rich internal diversity and an effort to articulate the claims of the whole over its parts. Nationalism provides a prominent rhetoric to both the holistic and the sectional, sometimes separatist, projects. It offers categories for understanding the demarcation of cultures, the ways in which individuals belong to larger groups, and the ways in which such groups participate in history. It also offers what Raymond Williams called "structures of feeling" that link categories of thought to emotional engagements.[2]

Feeling that one belongs to something larger and more permanent than oneself is either a wonderful or a terrible thing. It is an inspiration for heroism and the composition of sublime works of music and art. It is a motivation for morality and a solace amidst suffering. Conversely it is sometimes the source of a claustrophobic sense of being trapped or a crushing weight of responsibility. It makes some people silently quell doubts and support dangerous policies of nationalist leaders, and makes others feel an obligation to speak out. It is also the only way in which many people are able to feel that they belong in the world.

This is not true of everyone. Some of us are happy eating at Parisian cafes, basking on Bahian beaches and attending conferences in New Haven without thinking much of national identity. Some hear Wagner without thinking of Germany or view Diego Rivera as simply a great artist not a great Mexican. But if we imagine that cosmopolitan inhabitation of the globe as a series of attractively heterogeneous sites is readily available to everyone, we deeply misunderstand the actual and very hierarchical structures of globalization.

Globalization has not put an end to nationalism – not to nationalist conflicts nor to the role of nationalist categories in organizing ordinary people's sense of belonging in the world. Indeed, globalization fuels resurgence in nationalism among people who feel threatened or anxious as much as it drives efforts to transcend nationalism in new structures of political-legal organization or thinking about transnational connections. Nationalism still matters, still troubles many of us, but still organizes something considerable in who we are. Whether and how nationalism can mediate peaceful and constructive connections of individuals to the larger world is a crucial question. Nationalism's contributions to social solidarity may never outweigh its frequent violence. Yet seeking to bypass nationalism in pursuit of a rational universalism may reflect equally dangerous illusions.

Notes

Introduction

1 Hannah Arendt, *The Origins of Totalitarianism*, second edition (New York: Harcourt Brace, 1951).

2 M. Hardt and A. Negri, *Empire* (Cambridge, MA: Harvard University Press, 2001); *Multitude* (New York: Penguin, 2004). The notion of the multitude of course has much older roots, not least in Machiavelli.

3 It has become common in contemporary usage to distinguish civil society from markets as well as states. This is contrary to a classical usage that included businesses among the range of voluntary nongovernmental organizations of civil society. Firms, in this view, are created by mutual agreement among owners and lack the coercive power of states. The contemporary usage seems to respond both to the rise of a large corporate sector distinct from smaller owner-operated businesses and to an implicit distinction between (a) the impersonal steering media of power and money, and (b) the forging of voluntary agreements. Still, the older usage is a useful reminder not to ignore the difference between businesses as social institutions and markets as "steering media."

4 See David Held, *Democracy and the Global Order: From the Modern State to Cosmopolitan Governance* (Cambridge: Polity Press, 1995), and the updating and application in *Global Covenant: The Social Democratic Alternative to the Washington Consensus* (Cambridge: Polity Press, 2004). Emphasis on these layers of non-exclusive solidarity and governance is distinctive to – and a merit of – Held's approach to cosmopolitan democracy. It sets his theory apart from accounts grounded more directly in ethical universalism or notions of centralized world government.

5 The vocabulary of this paragraph is indebted to Reinhart Koselleck's *The Practice of Conceptual History* (Stanford, CA: Stanford University Press, 2002). More generally, we depend on and are ourselves constituted by categories of thought that have histories. These are themselves shaped by social institutions and practical struggles over the production and reproduction of meaning.

1 Is it time to be postnational?

1 But see Timothy Brennan, *At Home in the World: Cosmopolitanism Now* (Cambridge, MA: Harvard University Press, 1997).

2 The most important theorist specifically of cosmopolitan democracy was Held, *Democracy and the Global Order*. Held drew on the more general theory of Jürgen Habermas who himself developed a similar idea of postnational solidarity (e.g. *The Post-national Constellation* [Cambridge, MA: MIT Press, 2001]). And a wide variety of approaches shared much of the same vision if not the same specifics. Anthologies representing diverse approaches include Daniele Archibugi and David Held (eds.), *Cosmopolitan Democracy: An Agenda for a New World* Order (Cambridge, MA: Polity Press, 1995); Daniele Archibugi, David Held, and Martin Köhler (eds.), *Re-Imagining Political Community: Studies in Cosmopolitan Democracy* (Stanford, CA: Stanford University Press, 1998); Pheng Cheah and Bruce Robbins (eds.), *Cosmopolitics: Thinking and Feeling Beyond the Nation* (Minneapolis: University of Minnesota Press, 1998); Daniele Archibugi (ed.), *Debating Cosmopolitics* (London: Verso, 2003); and Steven Vertovec and Robin Cohen (eds.), *Conceiving Cosmopolitanism* (Oxford: Oxford University Press, 2002). The last two of these anthologies include my own less optimistic assessments.

3 That there are only a handful of clear successes – say, Mozambique – seems not to dim enthusiasm for humanitarian intervention. This is renewed as part of a broader social imaginary and ethical stance more than simply a utilitarian calculation. See Craig Calhoun, "A World of Emergencies: Fear, Intervention, and the Limits of Cosmopolitan Order," the 2004 Sorokin Lecture, *Canadian Review of Sociology and Anthropology* 41, no. 4 (2004): 373–95.

4 This produced a disabling coincidence of attacks on the state from the Hayekian right and the cosmopolitan left, a coincidence that greatly weakened defense of the welfare state when its dismantling began. Hostility to the state was redoubled by desire to achieve distance from any association with the Soviet model. As Brennan suggests, "attacks on the viability of the nation-state have been the contemporary form that an attack on socialism takes. For, apart from ethnic purists and right-wing nationalists, socialists are the only ones who still defend national sovereignty in the age of the global subaltern" (*At Home in the World*, p. 301).

5 Ibid., pp. 139–40.

6 As Friedrich Meinecke argued "The current view . . . sees cosmopolitanism and national feeling as two modes of thought that mutually exclude each other, that do battle with each other, and that supplant each other. Such a view cannot satisfy the historical mind that has a deeper awareness of circumstances" (*Cosmopolitanism and the National State* [Princeton, NJ: Princeton University Press, 1970]), p. 21.

7 The project of "constitutional patriotism" has been introduced as an intermediary between problematic nationalism and overambitious cosmopolitanism (initially by Adolf Sternberger, though Jürgen Habermas has made it more prominent; see discussion in Jan-Werner Müller, "On the Origins of

Constitutional Patriotism," *Contemporary Political Theory*, 5 (2006): 278–96. This leaves the larger opposition intact, simply identifying another point on an imagined continuum between its poles. Moreover, in most discussion – including most of Habermas's work – usage of "constitutional patriotism" slides towards the cosmopolitan end of the continuum. It is premised on Kantian universalism, but acknowledges that this isn't yet embodied in institutions on a pan-global scale. It is, however, Habermas's preferred category for thinking about European unification and the basis of his support for the constitution in the Spring 2005 referenda.

8 Habermas, *The Post-national Constellation*. Habermas's concern is that economic globalization has outpaced political and social solidarity. I share that concern, though I am not clear that the best solutions are "post-national."

9 Martin Köhler, "From the National to the Cosmopolitan Public Sphere," in *Re-Imagining Political Community: Studies in Cosmopolitan Democracy*, edited by Archibugi *et al.* (Stanford, CA: Stanford University Press, 1998), p. 231.

10 Ulrich Beck, "Sociology in the Second Age of Modernity," in *Conceiving Cosmopolitanism*, edited by Steven Vertovec and Robin Cohen (Oxford: Oxford University Press, 2002).

11 See, e.g. Andrew Linklater, "Citizenship and Sovereignty in the Post-Westphalian European State," in *Re-Imagining Political Community: Studies in Cosmopolitan Democracy*, edited by Archibugi *et al.* (Stanford, CA: Stanford University Press, 1998).

12 Micheline Ishay, *Internationalism and Its Betrayal* (Minneapolis: University of Minnesota Press, 1995); Meinecke, *Cosmopolitanism*; Benno Teschke, *The Myth of 1648: Class, Geopolitics and the Making of Modern International Relations* (London and New York: Verso, 2003).

13 See the excellent anthology revisiting Kant's classic cosmopolitan essay on perpetual peace: James Bohman and Matthias Lutz-Bachmann, *Perpetual Peace: Essays on Kant's Cosmopolitan Ideal* (Cambridge, MA: MIT Press, 1997). Also see Hans Joas, *War and Modernity* (Cambridge, MA: Blackwell, 2002).

14 Jürgen Habermas, *The Inclusion of the Other: Studies in Political Theory* (Cambridge, MA: MIT Press, 1998); Martha Nussbaum, *For Love of Country* (Boston, MA: Beacon, 1996). See also the essays in Archibugi, *Debating Cosmopolitics* and my own discussion of these and other variants of cosmopolitanism in "Belonging in the Cosmopolitan Imaginary," *Ethnicities* 3 (2003): 531–53.

15 Beck, "Sociology in the Second Age of Modernity," p. 77.

16 See Mabel Berezin and Martin Schain (eds.), *Europe without Borders: Re-Mapping Territory, Citizenship and Identity in a Transnational Age* (Baltimore, MD: Johns Hopkins University Press, 2003) which includes my "The Democratic Integration of Europe: Interests, Identity, and the Public Sphere," pp. 243–74.

17 Habermas, *The Inclusion of the Other*. Habermas adopts the formulation of Dolf Sternberger. See also Meinecke, *Cosmopolitanism*, and Hans Kohn, *The*

Idea of Nationalism (New York: Macmillan, 1944) on the classic traditions of German thought that try to reclaim civic nationalism from the notion that Germans are essentially ethnic nationalists. As Meinecke wrote in 1928, "the best German national feeling also includes the cosmopolitan ideal of a humanity beyond nationality and that it is 'un-German to be merely German' "(p. 21).

18 David Held, "Democracy and Globalization," in *Re-imagining Political Community*, edited by Archibugi *et al.* (Stanford, CA: Stanford University Press, 1998), p. 13. See also Hans Kohn's words from over 60 years ago: "Important periods of history are characterized by the circumference within which the sympathy of man extends. These limits are neither fixed nor permanent, and changes in them are accompanied by great crises in history" (*The Idea of Nationalism*, p. 21).

19 Will Kymlicka, *Politics in the Vernacular* (Oxford: Oxford University Press, 2001), p. 322.

20 The work of Partha Chatterjee is particularly informative on this issue. See *Nationalist Thought and the Colonial World: A Derivative Discourse?* (London: Zed Books, 1986) and *The Nation and Its Fragments: Studies in Colonial and Post-Colonial Histories* (Princeton, NJ: Princeton University Press, 1993). See also Craig Calhoun, *Nationalism* (Minneapolis: University of Minnesota Press, 1997).

21 Pierre Bourdieu, "Unifying to Better Dominate," in *Firing Back: Against the Tyranny of the Market 2*, trans. Loïc Wacquant (New York: New Press, 2002); italics in original.

22 Eric Hobsbawm, *Nations and Nationalism Since 1780: Programme, Myth, Reality* (Cambridge: Cambridge University Press, 1990) is paradigmatic, but the tendency is widespread.

23 Ibid., p. 25.

24 See Bourdieu's discussion in *The Field of Cultural Production* (New York: Columbia University Press, 1993), esp. the title essay.

25 Weber, "The Social Psychology of World Religions," in *From Max Weber*, edited by H.H. Gerth and C. Wright Mills (London: Routledge and Kegan Paul, 1948), p. 296.

26 These are themes Bourdieu addressed in several works; see notably *Algérie 60: Structures économiques et structures temporelles* (Paris: Minuit, 1977) and Pierre Bourdieu and Abdelmalek Sayad, *Le Déracinement: La Crise d'agriculture traditionelle en Algérie* (Paris: Minuit, 1964). See also the useful discussion in Laurent Addi, *Sociologie et anthropologie chez Pierre Bourdieu: Le paradigme anthropologique kabyle et ses conséquences théoriques* (Paris: Découverte, 2003).

27 See Charles Taylor, *Modern Social Imaginaries* (Duke, NC: Duke University Press, 2004).

28 Martha Nussbaum, *Upheavals of Thought: The Intelligence of Emotions* (Cambridge and New York: Cambridge University Press, 2001), p. 367.

29 Bourdieu, *The Logic of Practice* (Stanford, CA: Stanford University Press, 1990).

2 Nationalism matters

1 This argument is developed at more length, though differently, in Calhoun, *Nationalism*.

2 Elie Kedouri, *Nationalism*, fourth edition (Oxford: Blackwell, 1993; orig. 1960), p. 1.

3 Anthony Smith, *The Ethnic Origins of Nations* (Oxford: Blackwell, 1986); Benedict Anderson, *Imagined Communities*, revised edition (London: Verso, 1991; orig. 1983).

4 Patrick J. Geary, *The Myth of Nations: The Medieval Origins of Europe* (Princeton, NJ: Princeton University Press, 2002).

5 For a sample, see Don Doyle and Marco Pamplona (eds.), *Nationalism in the New World* (Athens, GA: University Press of Georgia, 2006).

6 Susan Cotts Watkins, *From Provinces into Nations: Demographic Integration in Western Europe, 1870–1960* (Princeton, NJ: Princeton University Press, 1991).

7 Eugen Weber, *Peasants into Frenchmen* (Stanford, CA: Stanford University Press, 1976).

8 This is precisely the era of the formation of what Immanuel Wallerstein described as the modern world-system, with its global economic structure mediated by a characteristic political form of competing states (*The Modern World-System*, vol. I [La Jolla, CA: Academic Press, 1974]).

9 For example: bounded territories, indivisibility, sovereignty, legitimacy rooted in the people, a high level of popular participation in political affairs, direct individual membership (rather than mediation through intermediate associations or feudal hierarchies), common culture, ideologies of shared descent, an image of the nation in historical time, and sacralization of the "homeland." No one of these, to reiterate, is definitive; but together they are the main themes in the discourse of nations and the basis of a family resemblance among nationalist claims (see Calhoun, *Nationalism*).

10 See Chapter 5.

11 The equivalence is not just a legal formality. It is also reflected in the "isomorphism" of institutional structures within nation-states – the ways in which they imitate each other in the organization of government, for example with comparably structured ministries and social service organizations. This may be even more important than the building of museums and the celebration of national folklore to gaining international recognition. See John W. Meyer and Brian Rowan, "Institutionalized Organizations: Formal Structure as Myth and Ceremony," *American Journal of Sociology*, 83 (1977): 340–63 and P.J. DiMaggio and W.W. Powell, "The Iron Cage Revisited: Institutional Isomorphism and Collective Rationality in Organizational Fields," *American Sociological Review*, 48 (1983): 147–60, both of which are reprinted along with other relevant discussions in Walter Powell and Paul DiMaggio (eds.), *The New Institutionalism in Organizational Analysis* (Chicago, IL: University of Chicago Press, 1991).

12 John Rawls, *A Theory of Justice* (Cambridge, MA: Harvard University Press, 1971).

13 John Rawls, *Political Liberalism* (New York: Columbia University Press, 1993), p. 41.

14 John Rawls, *The Law of Peoples* (Cambridge, MA: Harvard University Press, 1999).

15 Many of Habermas's most theoretically developed analyses are collected in *The Inclusion of the Other*; see also Habermas, "The European Nation-State and the Pressures of Globalization," pp. 217–34 in P. De Greiff and C. Cronin (eds.), *Global Justice and Transnational Politics* (Cambridge, MA: MIT Press, 2002). But this was a theme Habermas also pursued in a variety of less theoretical political interventions. Some of these are collected in *The Postnational Constellation*. The theme remains current for him and for Europe, however, as shown by his leadership of a transnational effort to produce a European-wide debate about the nature of the European public itself in the context of opposition to the US invasion of Iraq. A collection of these interventions is in Daniel Levy *et al.* (eds.), *Old Europe, New Europe, Core Europe: Transatlantic Relations after the Iraq War* (London and New York: Verso, 2005).

16 I have elsewhere ("Belonging in the Cosmopolitan Imaginary") argued that it is important to develop the notion of "public" as itself a form of social solidarity. It is more commonly treated as a realm of discourse based on solidarities and identities established "before" it, or disregarding all solidarities and identities. This seems inadequate; not only are identities formed in public engagements, so are solidarities as people are bound together through their public communication. This is partly, though not entirely, an opportunity for choice in the development of solidarity. See also the discussion of constitutional patriotism in my "Constitutional Patriotism and the Public Sphere" (pp. 275–312 in P. De Greiff and C. Cronin (eds.), *Global Justice and Transnational Politics* [Cambridge, MA: MIT Press, 2002]) with its contention that existing forms of European unification suffer a lack of such a public as well as their more famous "democratic deficit."

17 See discussion in Thomas McCarthy, "Reconciling Cosmopolitan Unity and National Diversity," pp. 235–74 in P. De Greiff and C. Cronin (eds.), *Global Justice and Transnational Politics* (Cambridge, MA: MIT Press, 2002), esp. pp. 260–1.

18 Calhoun, "The Class Consciousness of Frequent Travelers," *South Atlantic Quarterly*, 101, no. 4 (2003): 869–97.

19 For example, Michael Hechter, *Containing Nationalism* (New York: Oxford University Press, 2000).

20 For example, Habermas, *The Postnational Constellation*.

21 Ernest Gellner, *Nations and Nationalism* (Oxford: Blackwell, 1983).

22 Charles Tilly (ed.), *The Formation of National States in Western Europe* (Princeton, NJ: Princeton University Press, 1975); Liah Greenfeld, *Nationalism: Five Roads to Modernity* (Cambridge, MA: Harvard University Press, 1992).

23 Michael Mann, *Sources of Social Power*, vol. 1 (Cambridge: Cambridge

University Press, 1986.), pp. 1–2; *Sources of Social Power*, vol. 2 (Cambridge: Cambridge University Press, 1993).

24 Anthony Smith, *Ethnic Origin of Nations; National Identity* (London: Penguin, 1991); and *Nationalism and Modernism* (London: Routledge, 1998); John Armstrong, *Nations before Nationalism* (Chapel Hill: University of North Carolina Press, 1982); John Hutcheson, *The Dynamics of Cultural Nationalism*, revised edition (London: HarperCollins, 1994).

25 Michael Billig, *Banal Nationalism* (London: Sage, 1995); Lynette Spillman, *Nation and Commemoration* (Cambridge: Cambridge University Press, 1997).

26 See Anthony Giddens, *The Nation-State and Violence* (Berkeley: University of California Press, 1984).

27 Calhoun, *Nationalism*.

28 Gellner, *Nations and Nationalism*, p. 5.

29 Peter Alter, *Nationalism* (London: Edward Arnold, 1989); Calhoun, *Nationalism*; Walker Connor, *Ethnonationalism* (Princeton, NJ: Princeton University Press, 1994); John Hall, "Nationalisms, Classified and Explained," pp. 8–33 in *Notions of Nationalism*, edited by S. Periwal (Budapest: Central European University Press, 1995); Alexander J. Motyl, "The Modernity of Nationalism: Nations, States and Nation-States in the Contemporary World," *Journal of International Affairs* 45 (1992): 307–23; Anthony Smith, *Theories of Nationalism* (London: Duckworth, 1983).

30 Charles Tilly, *Big Structures, Large Processes, Huge Comparisons* (New York: Russell Sage, 1984); Rogers Brubaker, "Ethnicity without Groups," *Archives européènes de sociologie* 63, no. 2 (2002): 163–89; Rogers Brubaker and Frederick Cooper, "Beyond 'Identity'," *Theory and Society* 29 (2000): 1–47; Mann, *Sources of Social Power*, vol. 1.

31 Calhoun, *Nationalism*.

32 Geary, *The Myth of Nations*.

33 Kohn, *The Idea of Nationalism*.

34 Habermas, *The Inclusion of the Other*.

35 Kohn, *The Idea of Nationalism*; Alter, *Nationalism*.

36 Rogers Brubaker, *Citizenship and Nationhood in France and Germany* (Cambridge, MA: Harvard University Press, 1992). As Brubaker indicates, this difference in formal legal arrangements and ideological self-understandings masks a considerable commonality in the actual flows and treatment of immigrants – including, e.g. in welfare provisions. It is based on specific historical controversies and legislation that enacted formal arrangements more sharply distinct from each other than either actual practices or prevailing sentiments. In other words, at the level of practice and sentiment, France and Germany each combine ethnic and civic nationalism, even though in certain formal structures they represent contrasting types. Or at least they have represented such contrasting types; the distinction has become muddied in recent years as France has had difficulty assimilating immigrants and Germany has changed its nationality law.

37 Calhoun, *Nationalism*; Saskia Sassen, *Guests and Aliens* (Chicago, IL: University of Chicago Press, 1999).
38 Smith, *The Ethnic Origins of Nations*, p. 149.
39 Reinhard Bendix, *Nation-Building and Citizenship* (Berkeley: University of California Press, 1964); Tom Nairn, *Faces of Nationalism: Janus Revisited* (London and New York: Verso, 1997); John Schwarzmantel, *Socialism and the Idea of the Nation* (Hemel Hempstead: Harvester Wheatsheaf, 1991).
40 Kohn, *The Idea of Nationalism*; Hugh Seton-Watson, *Nations and States* (Boulder, CO: Westview Press, 1977).
41 Hobsbawm, *Nations and Nationalism*.
42 Charles Tilly, *The Formation of National States* and *Coercion, Capital and European States, AD 990–1990* (Oxford: Blackwell, 1990); Hall, "Nationalisms, Classified and Explained"; Mann, *Sources of Social Power*, vol. 2.
43 Gellner, *Nations and Nationalism*.
44 Carlton J.H. Hayes, *The Historical Evolution of Modern Nationalism* (New York: R.R. Smith, 1931).
45 Hechter, *Containing Nationalism*.
46 Kedourie, *Nationalism*.
47 Smith, *The Ethnic Origins of Nations*, p. 216.
48 Kedourie, *Nationalism*; Gellner, *Nations and Nationalism*; Anderson, *Imagined Communities*; Chatterjee, *Nationalist Thought and the Colonial World*.
49 Gellner, *Nations and Nationalism*, pp. 8–18, 61.
50 Connor, *Ethnonationalism*, p. 103.
51 This happened contrary to the predictions of numerous pundits, including George Orwell (*Taking to India* [London: Allen and Unwin, 1943]) and is only partly contradicted by the partition that created Pakistan.
52 Chatterjee, *The Nation and Its Fragments*.
53 Brubaker, *Nationalism Reframed* (Cambridge, MA: Harvard University Press, 1996).
54 Ernest Renan, "What Is a Nation?" pp. 8–22 in *Nation and Narration*, edited by Homi Bhabha (London: Routledge, 1990; orig. 1882), p. 11.
55 Homi Bhabha (ed.), *Nation and Narration* (London: Routledge, 1990).
56 Anderson, *Imagined Communities*.
57 Smith, *The Ethnic Origins of Nations*; Armstrong, *Nations before Nationalism*; Hutcheson, *The Dynamics of Cultural Nationalism*.
58 Gellner, *Nations and Nationalism*; Hobsbawn, *Nations and Nationalism*; Greenfeld, *Nationalism*.
59 Gellner, *Nations and Nationalism*.
60 Tilly, *Coercion, Capital, and European States*; Mann, *Sources of Social Power*, vol. 2.
61 Karl W. Deutsch, *Nationalism and Social Communication: An Inquiry into the Foundations of Nationality*, second edition (Cambridge, MA: MIT Press, 1966); Anderson, *Imagined Communities*.

62 Calhoun, *Nationalism*.
63 Smith, *The Ethnic Origins of Nations, National Identity*, and *Nationalism and Modernism*; Armstrong, *Nations before Nationalism*.
64 Joan S. Skurnowicz, *Romantic Nationalism and Liberalism: Joachim Lelewel and the Polish National Idea* (Boulder, CO: East European Monographs; New York: Distributed by Columbia University Press, 1981); Joseph F. Zacek, "Nationalism in Czechoslovakia," in *Nationalism in Eastern Europe*, edited by Peter F. Sugar and Ivo J. Lederer (Seattle: University of Washington Press, 1969).
65 Eric Hobsbawm and Terence Ranger, *The Invention of Tradition* (Cambridge: Cambridge University Press, 1983).
66 Hugh Trevor-Roper, "The Invention of Tradition: The Highland Tradition of Scotland," pp. 15–42 in *The Invention of Tradition*, edited by E. Hobsbawm and T. Ranger (Cambridge: Cambridge University Press, 1983).
67 Benedict Anderson, "Introduction," in *Mapping the Nation*, edited by Gopal Balakrishnan (London: Verso, 1996), p. 6.
68 Clifford Geertz, *Old Societies and New States: The Quest for Modernity in Asia and Africa* (New York: Free Press of Glencoe; London: Collier-Macmillan, 1963).
69 The distinction is made by Max Weber, *Economy and Society* (Berkeley: University of California Press, 1922; this edition 1978), p. 4. See also discussion in Bourdieu, *Algérie 60* and Craig Calhoun, *The Roots of Radicalism* (Chicago, IL: University of Chicago Press, forthcoming).
70 Hans-Georg Gadamer, *Truth and Method* (New York: Seabury, 1975).
71 See Shmuel Eisenstadt, *Modernization, Protest and Change* (Englewood Cliffs, NJ: Prentice-Hall, 1966) and *Building States and Nations* (Beverly Hills: Sage, 1973); Geertz, *Old Societies and New States*; Ernest Gellner, *Thought and Change* (London: Weidenfeld and Nicholson, 1964).
72 George Steiner, "Aspects of Counter-revolution," pp. 129–55 in G. Best (ed.), *The Permanent Revolution*. Chicago, IL: University of Chicago Press, 1988.
73 Greenfeld, *Nationalism*; Anderson, *Imagined Communities*; Alter, *Nationalism*; John Breuilly, *Nationalism and the State*, revised edition (Chicago, IL: University of Chicago Press, 1993; orig. 1982); Kedourie, *Nationalism*.
74 Calhoun, *Nationalism*.
75 Deutsch, *Nationalism and Social Communication*.
76 Tilly, *Coercion, Capital, and European States*.
77 Hayes, *Historical Evolution*; Anderson, *Imagined Communities*.
78 Breuilly, *Nationalism and the State*.
79 Charles Taylor, "Modern Social Imaginaries," *Public Culture* 14, no. 1 (2002): 91–123.
80 William Sewell, Jr. "Political Events as Structural Transformations: Inventing Revolution at the Bastille," *Theory and Society* 25 (1996): 841–81.

3 Nationalism and ethnicity

1 Walker Connor, *The National Question in Marxist-Leninist Theory and Strategy* (Princeton, NJ: Princeton University Press, 1984); Ivo Banac, *The National Question in Yugoslavia: Origin, History, Politics* (Ithaca, NY: Cornell University Press, 1984).

2 See Schwarzmantel, *Socialism and the Idea of the Nation*; Tom Nairn, "The Modern Janus," *New Left Review* 94 (1975): 3–30 and *The Break-up of Britain: Crises and Neo-Nationalism* (London: New Left Books, 1977); Régis Debray, "Marxism and the National Question," *New Left Review* 105 (1977): 20–41.

3 Brubaker, *Citizenship and Nationhood*; Nigel Harris, *National Liberation* (London: Penguin, 1990); James Mayall, *Nationalism and International Society* (New York: Cambridge University Press, 1990); Gérard Noiriel, "Le question national comme objet de l'histoire sociale," *Génèses* 4 (1991): 72–94.

4 There are innumerable other dimensions to the broad literature on nationalism and ethnicity which are not covered here. The best general reviews are Anthony Smith, "Nationalism," *Current Sociology* 21 (1973): 7–128, and *The Ethnic Revival in the Modern World* (Cambridge: Cambridge University Press, 1981). See also G. Carter Bentley, *Ethnicity and Nationality: A Bibliographic Guide* (Seattle: University of Washington Press, 1981); Karl W. Deutsch, *Nationalism and National Development: An Interdisciplinary Bibliography* (Cambridge, MA: MIT Press, 1970); Ernst B. Haas, "What Is Nationalism and Why Should We Study It?" *International Organization* 40, no. 3 (1986): 707–44; and Noiriel, "Le question national."

5 Kohn, *The Idea of Nationalism*; Liah Greenfeld, "The Emergence of Nationalism in England and France," *Research in Political Sociology* 5 (1991): 333–70 and *Nationalism*.

6 Anderson, *Imagined Communities*.

7 Alter, *Nationalism*; Geoffrey Best (ed.), *The Permanent Revolution: The French Revolution and Its Legacy, 1789–1989* (Chicago, IL: University of Chicago Press, 1988).

8 Kedourie, *Nationalism*; Breuilly, *Nationalism and the State*.

9 Geoffrey Best, *Honour Among Men and Nations: Transformations of an Idea* (Toronto: University of Toronto Press, 1982), p. 29.

10 Gellner, *Nations and Nationalism*, p. 1.

11 Kedourie, *Nationalism*, p. 9.

12 Isaiah Berlin, *Vico and Herder: Two Studies in the History of Ideas* (London: Hogarth, 1976), p. 181; Conor Cruise O'Brien, "Nationalism and the French Revolution," pp. 17–48 in *The Permanent Revolution: The French Revolution and Its Legacy, 1789–1989*, edited by Geoffrey Best (Chicago, IL: University of Chicago Press, 1988), p. 18.

13 Mayall, *Nationalism*, pp. 44–5; Hans Kohn, *The Age of Nationalism* (New York: Harper & Row, 1968; orig. 1962), pp. 133–5.

14 Daniel Chirot (ed.), *The Crisis of Leninism and the Decline of the Left: The Revolutions of 1989* (Seattle: University of Washington Press, 1991); Charles

Tilly and Lee Walker (eds.), Special Issue on Ethnic Conflict in the Soviet Union, *Theory and Society* 20, no. 6 (1991): 725–899.

15 Katherine Verdery, *National Ideology under Socialism: Identity and Cultural Politics in Ceausescu's Romania* (Berkeley: University of California Press, 1991); Connor, *The National Question.*

16 Anthony H. Birch, *Nationalism and National Integration* (London: Unwin Hyman, 1989), ch. 8; Rudy Fenwick, "Social Change and Ethnic Nationalism: An Historical Analysis of the Separatist Movement in Quebec," *Comparative Studies in Society and History* 23 (1981): 193–216; Jocelyn Létourneau, "La saga du Québec moderne en images," *Génèses* 4 (1991): 44–71; J.I. Little, *Nationalism, Capitalism and Colonization in Nineteenth-Century Quebec: The Upper St. Francis District* (Kingston, Ontario: McGill/Queen's University Press, 1989); Charles Taylor, *The Politics of Recognition* (Princeton, NJ: Princeton University Press, 1992).

17 Basil Davidson, *Black Man's Burden: Africa and the Curse of the Nation-State* (New York: Times Books, 1992); I.M. Lewis (ed.), *Nationalism and Self-Determination in the Horn of Africa* (London: Ithaca, 1983); John Markakis, *National and Class Conflict in the Horn of Africa* (London: Zed Books, 1987); Ali A. Mazrui and Michael Tidy, *Nationalism and New States in Africa from about 1935 to the Present* (Nairobi: Heinemann, 1984); Georges Nzongola-Ntalaja, "The National Question and the Crisis of Instability in Africa," pp. 55–86 in *Africa: Perspectives on Peace and Development*, edited by E. Hansen (Atlantic Highlands, NJ: Zed Books, 1987); Bereket H. Selassie, *Conflict and Intervention in the Horn of Africa* (London: Gordon & Breech, 1980).

18 Rashid Khalidi *et al.* (eds.), *The Origins of Arab Nationalism* (New York: Columbia University Press, 1991); Tawfic E. Farah (ed.), *Pan-Arabism and Arab Nationalism: The Continuing Debate* (Boulder, CO: Westview Press, 1987); Bassam Tibi, *Arab Nationalism: A Critical Enquiry*, second edition, edited and translated by Marion Farouk-Sluglett and Peter Sluglett (New York: St Martin's Press, 1990).

19 Marilyn Shevin Coetzee, *The German Army League: Popular Nationalism in Wilhelmine Germany* (New York: Oxford University Press, 1990); Geoff Eley, *Reshaping the German Right: Radical Nationalism and Political Change after Bismarck* (Oxford: Oxford University Press, 1980) and "Nations, Publics and Political Cultures: Placing Habermas in the Nineteenth Century," pp. 289–339 in *Habermas and the Public Sphere*, edited by Craig Calhoun (Cambridge, MA: MIT Press, 1992); Meinecke, *Cosmopolitanism*; George L. Mosse, *Nationalization of the Masses: Political Symbolism and Mass Movements in Germany from the Napoleonic Wars through the Third Reich* (New York: H. Fertig, 1975); James J. Sheehan, *German Liberalism in the Nineteenth Century* (Chicago, IL: University of Chicago Press, 1978).

20 Edward A. Tiryakian and Ronald Rogowski (eds.), *New Nationalisms of the Developed West: Toward Explanation* (London: Allen & Unwin, 1985); Smith, *The Ethnic Revival.*

21 James M. Blaut, *The National Question: Decolonizing the Theory of Nationalism* (Atlantic Highlands, NJ: Zed Books, 1987); Chatterjee, *Nationalist Thought.*

22 Tse-Tsung Chow, *The May 4th Movement: Intellectual Revolution in Modern China* (Cambridge, MA: Harvard University Press, 1960); Jonathan D. Spence, *The Gate of Heavenly Peace: The Chinese and their Revolution, 1895–1980* (Baltimore, MD: Penguin, 1981); Vera Schwarcz, *The Chinese Enlightenment: Intellectuals and the Legacy of the May Fourth Movement of 1919* (Berkeley: University of California Press, 1986); Kenneth M.Wells, *New God. New Nation: Protestants and Self-Reconstruction Nationalism in Korea, 1896–1937* (Honolulu: University of Hawaii Press, 1991); James W. White *et al.* (eds.), *The Ambivalence of Nationalism: Modern Japan Between East and West* (Lanham, MD: University Press of America, 1990).

23 Hobsbawm, *Nations and Nationalism*, p. 14.

24 Kohn, *The Age of Nationalism*; Meinecke, *Cosmopolitanism*; Anne M. Cohler, *Rousseau and Nationalism* (New York: Basic Books, 1970).

25 Tilly, *Big Structures*, p. 11.

26 Louis Joseph Halle, *Men and Nations* (Princeton, NJ: Princeton University Press, 1962), p. 25.

27 Giddens, *The Nation-State*; Anderson, *Imagined Communities.*

28 Raphael Samuel (ed.), *Patriotism: The Making and Unmaking of British National Identity*, 3 vols. (London: Routledge, 1989).

29 Mann, *Sources of Social Power*, vol. 1.

30 Bhabha, *Nation and Narration.*

31 Alter, *Nationalism*; Breuilly, *Nationalism*; Walker Connor, "A nation is a nation, is a state, is an ethnic group, is a . . .," *Ethnic Racial Studies* 1 (1978): 377–400; Aira Kemiläinen, *Nationalism: Problems Concerning the Word, the Concept, and Classification* (Jyväskylä: Jyväskylän Yliopistoyhdistys, 1964); Smith, "Nationalism" and *Theories of Nationalism.*

32 Diana Fuss, *Essentially Speaking: Feminism, Nature and Difference* (Oxford: Blackwell, 1989), pp. 2–6.

33 Anderson, *Imagined Communities.*

34 Chatterjee, *Nationalist Thought.*

35 Seton-Watson, *Nations and States*; Breuilly, *Nationalism*; Mayall, *Nationalism.*

36 J.L. Talmon, *The Origins of Totalitarian Democracy* (London: Secker & Warburg, 1952) and *Political Messianism, the Romantic Phase* (London: Secker & Warburg, 1960); Bendix, *Nation-Building.*

37 Alter, *Nationalism*; Jeffrey Herf, *Reactionary Modernism: Technology, Culture, and Politics in Weimar and the Third Reich* (New York: Cambridge University Press, 1984).

38 Armstrong, *Nations before Nationalism*; E.D. Marcu, *Sixteenth Century Nationalism* (Pleasantville, NY: Abaris, 1976); Smith, *The Ethnic Origins of Nations.*

39 Tilly, *Coercion, Capital and European States*, p. 2.

40 Charles Tilly, "Futures of European States," Paper presented at the Annual Meeting of the American Sociological Association, Pittsburgh, 1992.

41 Tilly, *Coercion, Capital and European States*, p. 3.

42 Ibid. p. 116; see also Watkins, *From Provinces into Nations*, on intrastate homogenization of fertility patterns.

43 Tilly, *The Formation of National States*; Perry Anderson, *Lineages of the Absolutist State* (London: New Left Books, 1974); Giddens, *The Nation-State and Violence*; Stein Rokkan, "Dimensions of State Formation and Nation-Building: A Possible Paradigm for Research on Variations within Europe," in *The Formation of National States in Western Europe*, edited by Charles Tilly (Princeton, NJ: Princeton University Press, 1975); Gianfranco Poggi, *The State: Its Nature, Development and Prospects* (Stanford, CA: Stanford University Press, 1992).

44 Immanuel Wallerstein, *The Modern World-System*, vols. 1–3 (San Diego, CA: Academic Press, 1974–88); Etienne Balibar and Immanuel Wallerstein, *Race, Nation, Class* (London: Verso, 1991); Michael Hechter, *Internal Colonialism: The Celtic Fringe in British National Development, 1536–1966* (Berkeley: University of California Press, 1975); Nairn, *The Break-up of Britain*; Peter Worsley, *The Three Worlds: Culture and World Development*, revised edition (Chicago, IL: University of Chicago Press, 1986).

45 E.g. Gellner, *Thought and Change*; Bendix, *Nation-Building*; David Apter, *The Politics of Modernization* (Chicago, IL: University of Chicago Press, 1965); Eisenstadt, *Modernization* and *Building States*; Neil J. Smelser, *Essays in Sociological Explanation* (Englewood Cliffs, NJ: Prentice-Hall, 1968).

46 Talmon, *The Origins of Totalitarian Democracy*; Talcott Parsons, *Structure and Process in Modern Societies* (Glencoe, IL: Free Press, 1960).

47 Wallerstein, *The Modern World-System*, vols. 1–3.

48 Hechter, *Internal Colonialism*.

49 Smith, *Theories of Nationalism*.

50 But see Michael Hechter, "Nationalism as Group Solidarity," *Ethnic Racial Studies* 10, no. 4 (1987): 415–26 and Michael Hechter and Celso Furtado, Jr., "The Emergence of Nationalist Politics in the USSR: A Comparison of Estonia and the Ukraine," pp. 169–204 in *Thinking Theoretically about Soviet Nationalities: Theory, History, and Comparison in the Study of the USSR*, edited by Alexander J. Motyl (New York: Columbia University Press, 1992) for revised arguments.

51 Giddens, *The Nation-State*, p. 116.

52 Gellner, *Nations and Nationalism*.

53 Ibid., p. 49.

54 Ibid., p. 55.

55 Miroslav Hroch, *Social Preconditions of National Revival in Europe* (Cambridge: Cambridge University Press, 1985).

56 Christian Topalov, "Patriotismes et citoyennetés," *Génèses* 3 (1991): 162–76; p. 176.

57 Poggi, *The State*; Jean Cohen and Andrew Arato, *Civil Society and Political*

Theory (Cambridge, MA: MIT Press, 1992); Adam B. Seligman, *The Idea of Civil Society* (New York: Free Press, 1992); John Keane, *Democracy and Civil Society* (London: Verso, 1988); Craig Calhoun, "Civil Society and the Public Sphere," *Public Culture 5*, no. 2 (1993): 267–80.

58 Kohn, *The Idea of Nationalism* and *The Age of Nationalism*; Hayes, *The Historical Evolution* and Carlton J.H. Hayes, *Essays on Nationalism* (New York: Russell & Russell, 1966; orig. 1926); Meinecke, *Cosmopolitanism*; Kedouri, *Nationalism* and Elie Kedourie, *Nationalism in Asia and Africa* (New York: New American Library, 1974).

59 Kohn, *The Idea of Nationalism*, ch. 4.

60 Anderson, *Imagined Communities*, p. 138.

61 Geertz, *Old Societies*; Gellner, *Thought and Change*; Hayes, *Essays on Nationalism*.

62 Apter, *The Politics of Modernization*.

63 Emile Durkheim, *The Division of Labor in Society* (New York: Free Press, 1893).

64 Ernst B. Haas, *Beyond the Nation-State: Functionalism and International Organization* (Stanford, CA: Stanford University Press, 1964), p. 465.

65 Haas, "What Is Nationalism."

66 Best, *The Permanent Revolution*.

67 On this classic French/German contrast in styles of nationalism, see Alter, *Nationalism*; Hayes, *The Historical Evolution* and *Essays on Nationalism*; Kedouri, *Nationalism*; and Kohn, *The Age of Nationalism*.

68 Renan, "What Is a Nation?"

69 Brubaker, *Citizenship and Nationhood*; Gérard Noiriel, *The French Melting Pot* (Minneapolis: University of Minnesota Press, 1998; orig. *Le Creuset Français* [Paris: Seuil, 1988]) and *La Tyrannie du National* (Paris: Calmann-Lévy, 1991).

70 Anderson, *Imagined Communities*.

71 See Meinecke, *Cosmopolitanism*, on Germany; Skurnowicz, *Romantic Nationalism*, on Poland; and Zacek, "Nationalism in Czechoslovakia," on Czechoslovakia.

72 Craig Calhoun, "The Radicalism of Tradition: Community Strength or Venerable Disguise and Borrowed Language?" *American Journal of Sociology* 88, no. 5 (1983): 886–914.

73 Edward Shils, *Tradition* (Chicago, IL: University of Chicago Press, 1981).

74 Pierre Bourdieu, *Outline of a Theory of Practice* (Cambridge: Cambridge University Press, 1976) and *The Logic of Practice*.

75 Gadamer, *Truth and Method* and *Philosophical Hermeneutics* (Berkeley: University of California Press, 1977).

76 Weber, *Economy and Society*; see discussion in Chapter 1, pp. 22–3 above.

77 Hobsbawm and Ranger, *The Invention of Tradition*; Hobsbawm, *Nations and Nationalism*.

78 Eisenstadt, *Modernization* and *Building States*; Geertz, *Old Societies*; Gellner, *Nations and Nationalism*.

79 Meyer Fortes, *The Web of Kinship among the Tallensi of Northern Ghana*

(Oxford: Oxford University Press, 1945) and *The Dynamics of Clanship among the Tallensi of Northern Ghana* (Oxford: Oxford University Press, 1949); Craig Calhoun, "The Authority of Ancestors: A Sociological Reconsideration of Fortes's Tallensi In Response to Fortes's Critics,"*Journal of the Royal Anthropological Institute*, New Ser. 15, no. 2 (1980): 304–19.

80 Edmund Ronald Leach, *Political Systems of Highland Burma* (Boston, MA: Beacon, 1954); Fredrik Barth (ed.), *Ethnic Boundaries* (Oslo: Norwegian University Press, 1969).

81 Donald L. Horowitz, *Ethnic Groups in Conflict* (Berkeley: University of California Press, 1985); James G. Kellas, *The Politics of Nationalism and Ethnicity* (London: Macmillan, 1991).

82 Jawaharlal Nehru, *The Discovery of India* (Oxford: Oxford University Press, 1949).

83 Sandria B. Freitag, *Collective Action and Community: Public Arenas and the Emergence of Communalism in North India* (Berkeley: University of California Press, 1989); Chatterjee, *Nationalist Thought* and *The Nation and Its Fragments*.

84 Gellner, *Nations and Nationalism*.

85 Anderson, *Imagined Communities*.

86 Deutsch, *Nationalism and Social Communication* and *Nationalism and Its Alternatives* (New York: Knopf, 1969); Craig Calhoun, "The Infrastructure of Modernity: Indirect Relationships, Information Technology, and Social Integration," pp. 205–36 in *Social Change and Modernity*, edited by Hans Haferkamp and Neil J. Smelser (Berkeley: University of California Press, 1992).

87 Johann Gottlieb Fichte, *Addresses to the German Nation* (New York: Harper & Row, 1968; orig. 1807); Meinecke, *Cosmopolitanism*, p. 92.

88 Seymour Martin Lipset, *The First New Nation* (New York: Doubleday, 1960).

89 Nehru, *The Discovery of India*; M.K. Gandhi, "Hind Swaraj," in *The Moral and Political Writings of Mahatma Gandhi*, edited by R. Iyer, vol. 1: 199–288 (Oxford: Clarendon, 1996; orig. 1939) and *Political and National Life and Affairs* (Ahmedabad: Navajivan, 1967); Chatterjee, *Nationalist Thought* and *The Nation and Its Fragments*.

90 Renan, "What Is a Nation?" p. 11.

91 Michael Sutton, *Nationalism, Positivism and Catholicism: The Politics of Charles Maurras and French Catholics 1890–1914* (Cambridge: Cambridge University Press, 1982).

92 Tzvetan Todorov, *Nous et les autres* (Paris: Editions de Seuil, 1990); Noiriel, *Le Creuset Français*.

93 Greenfeld, "The Emergence of Nationalism" and *Nationalism*.

94 Greenfeld, *Nationalism*, p. 183.

95 Savarkar, V.D. *Samagra Savarkar Wangmaya: Writings of Swatantrya Veer V. D. Savarkar*, vol. IV: *Hindu Rashtra Darshan*. Poona: Maharashtra Prantik Hindusabha, 1964 (orig. 1937), p. 264.

96 Chatterjee, *The Nation and Its Fragments*.

97 Kedouri, *Nationalism*, pp. 62–73.

98 Anderson, *Imagined Communities*, p. 196.

99 Ibid.

100 Weber, *Peasants into Frenchmen*.

101 Kohn, *The Idea of Nationalism*; Seton-Watson, *Nations and States*.

102 Hayes, *Essays on Nationalism* and *Nationalism: A Religion* (New York: Macmillan, 1960).

103 Kedourie, *Nationalism*.

104 Gellner, *Nations and Nationalism*.

105 Hobsbawm, *Nations and Nationalism* and Hobsbawm and Ranger, *The Invention of Tradition*.

106 Smith, *Theories of Nationalism, The Ethnic Origins of Nations*, and *National Identity*.

107 Smith, *The Ethnic Origins of Nations*, p. 16.

108 Ibid., p. 109.

109 Ibid., p. 134.

110 Ibid., p. 144.

111 Ibid., p. 166.

112 Ibid., pp. 212–13.

113 Ibid., pp. 218, 221.

114 Ibid., p. 216.

115 Ibid., p. 166.

116 Paul R. Brass, *Ethnicity and Nationalism: Theory and Comparison* (New Delhi and Newbury Park, CA: Sage, 1991), p. 8.

117 Gellner, *Nations and Nationalism*, p. 45.

118 Fortes, *The Web of Kinship* and *The Dynamics of Clanship*; Calhoun, "The Authority of Ancestors."

119 Charles Taylor, *The Sources of the Self* (Cambridge, MA: Harvard University Press, 1989).

120 Schwarcz, *The Chinese Enlightenment*, p. 112.

121 Louis Dumont, *Essays on Individualism* (Chicago, IL: University of Chicago Press, 1982).

122 Anderson, *Imagined Communities*, p. 168.

123 Bruce Kapferer, *Legends of People, Myths of State: Violence, Intolerance, and Political Culture in Sri Lanka and Australia* (Washington, DC: Smithsonian Institution, 1988), ch. 7; Chatterjee, *The Nation and Its Fragments*.

124 Peter P. Ekeh, "Social Anthropology and Two Contrasting Uses of Tribalism in Africa," *Comparative Studies in Society and History* 32, no. 4 (1990): 660–700.

125 Weber, *Economy and Society*, p. 389.

126 Barth, *Ethnic Boundaries*.

127 George L. Mosse, *Nationalism and Sexuality* (Madison: University of Wisconsin Press, 1985).

128 Andrew Parker *et al.* (eds.), *Nationalisms and Sexualities* (New York: Routledge, 1992).

129 Eley, "Nations, Publics and Political Cultures."

130 The contemporary discourse of multiculturalism suggests that ethnic groups are to be seen in much the same relationship of formal equivalence (Taylor, *The Politics of Recognition*).

131 Quoted in Meinecke, *Cosmopolitanism*, p. 89.

132 Kohn, *The Idea of Nationalism*; Andrej Walicki, *Philosophy and Romantic Nationalism: The Case of Poland* (New York: Oxford University Press, 1982); Skurnowicz, *Romantic Nationalism*; and Meinecke, *Cosmopolitanism*.

133 Liah Greenfeld, "The Formation of the Russian National Identity: The Role of Status Insecurity and *Ressentiment*," *Comparative Studies in Society and History* 32, no. 3 (1990): 549–91, and *Nationalism*.

134 Roman Szporluk, *Communism and Nationalism: Karl Marx versus Friedrich List* (New York: Oxford University Press, 1988), p. 115.

135 Anderson, *Imagined Communities*, p. 26.

136 See also William Bloom, *Personal Identity, National Identity and International Relations* (Cambridge: Cambridge University Press, 1990).

137 Anderson, *Imagined Communities*, p. 5.

138 Ibid., pp. 6–7.

139 Ibid., p. 44.

140 Gellner, *Nations and Nationalism*, p. 18.

141 Anderson, *Imagined Communities*, pp. 24–36.

142 Ibid., p. 37.

143 Ibid., p. 188.

144 Craig Calhoun, "Imagined Communities and Indirect Relationships: Large-Scale Social Integration and the Transformation of Everyday Life," pp. 95–120 in *Social Theory for a Changing Society*, edited by Pierre Bourdieu and James S. Coleman (Boulder, CO: Westview; New York: Russell Sage Foundation, 1991) and "The Infrastructure of Modernity."

145 Deutsch, *Nationalism and Social Communication* and *Nationalism and Its Alternatives*.

146 Anderson, *Imagined Communities*, pp. 170–8.

147 Ibid., pp. 178–85; Charles S. Maier, *The Unmasterable Past: History, Holocaust, and German National Identity* (Cambridge, MA: Harvard University Press, 1987).

4   Nationalism and civil society

1 This chapter shows the marks of the time when it was written more sharply than most of the others in this book. It seemed to me to make more sense to leave the marks because they convey some useful information (no doubt about my limits as well as about the period). Accordingly, I have not amended the text written in 1992 and published in 1993.

2 This has been one of the themes of postmodernism as well as of more conventional political economy. See the sympathetic but critical survey in David Harvey, *The Postmodern Condition* (Oxford: Blackwell, 1990).

3 Of course the related end to the political-military rivalry between the capitalist world-system and communist countries is also significant. It is possible, but remains to be seen, that global integration is sufficient to prevent the emergence of a new state-capitalist military block that, like the Axis of fifty years ago, seeks to carve an alternative world-system to that built around capital accumulation through multilateral trade.

4 See the contrasting reviews and theorizations in Seligman, *The Idea of Civil Society*; Cohen and Arato, *Civil Society*.

5 Charles Taylor, "Modes of Civil Society," *Public Culture* 3, no. 1 (1991): 95–118.

6 This point is also made in a very different way by Cohen and Arato in *Civil Society*. Cohen and Arato want to get away from a simple opposition of state to all other social organization (the sort of usage that resulted in a discourse of "society *versus* the state" in Eastern Europe). They place an important stress on the role of social movements in democratic process and on "resources of solidarity" that enable individuals to join together in collective action to limit the power of state or economy (see ch. 9 esp. p. 472). Yet, drawing primarily on readings of Hegel and Habermas, they neglect both the Scottish moralists and the French tradition, treating social organization primarily in terms of notions of system integration developed by Talcott Parsons and Niklas Luhmann. Rather than calling attention to the reified and therefore anti-democratic nature of the description of social life as impersonally steered "system," they simply accept as given that much social life is so organized. Crucially, they accept without challenge the idea that power is a steering medium in the same sense as money. They also accept the Parsons-Luhmann understanding of economic life as simply a self-regulating functional system steered impersonally by money. They thus either neglect or reject the Marxian notion of the way in which capitalism structures not only the economy but the categories of economic understanding (a) so that money *appears* as the primary element in the economic system, (b) so that the centrality of capital accumulation is obscured, and (c) so that the system appears as necessary rather than transcendable. Such a view is elaborated in Moishe Postone, *Time, Labor, and Social Domination: A Reinterpretation of Marx's Critical Theory* (New York: Cambridge University Press, 1993). Their sociological theory thus marginalizes the role of direct social relations – the kinds of structures studied, for example, under the rubric of social networks, and the basis of the communities, intermediate associations, and mediating institutions vital to democratic life – and thereby underestimates the capacities of actors to create and modify social institutions.

7 See Habermas, *The Structural Transformation of the Public Sphere* (Cambridge, MA: MIT Press, 1989) and the various qualifications, extensions, and refinements suggested by the essays in Calhoun, *Habermas and the Public Sphere* (Cambridge, MA: MIT Press, 1992).

8 This is a theme associated especially with Alexis de Tocqueville, *Democracy in America* (New York: Schocken, 1840–4) but also important to Durkheim, e.g. in the preface to the second edition of *The Division of Labor in Society*

(New York: Free Press, 1933) and a range of other thinkers since Montesquieu. See also Calhoun, "Democracy, Autocracy and Intermediate Associations in Organizations: Flexibility or Unrestrained Change?" *Sociology* 4, no. 3 (1980): 345–61.

9 Even if one could point to completely self-contained island cultures some-where in the South Pacific (and my reading of the anthropological evidence is that one cannot), these would not be nations in anything like the modern sense of the term, for that implies the definition of one by contraposition to others (as, indeed, do a variety of other forms of identity from lineage seg-ment to clan to locality). Key to nationalist discourse is its rejection of any notion that identity is essentially fluid and shifting from one situation to another. National identity is commonly claimed to trump all others.

10 See especially Brubaker, *Citizenship and Nationhood in France and Germany* and Noiriel, *Le Creuset Français*.

11 Perhaps the greatest single weakness of Habermas's *Structural Transform-ation of the Public Sphere* is Habermas's treatment of identity formation as essentially private an prior to participation in the idealized public sphere of rational critical discourse. A "politics of identity," therefore, could only appear as a degenerate intrusion into the public sphere, due first to growing democratic inclusiveness and second to public relations manipulation. One result is that nationalism, a prototypical form of the politics of identity, and one broached crucially in the public sphere, did not figure significantly in Habermas's account.

12 It is common that a bit of each sort of claim is made. In France, histories trace French character back to the Gauls as well as anchoring national iden-tity crucially in the Revolution and the distinctive notion of citizenship it brought forward. In China, national identity (a notion deriving in part from contact with the West) is at once seen as something extraordinarily ancient (and this with better claim than most of the world's other peoples) and as something given special purpose by the unification under the Qin dynasty.

13 Anthony Smith, esp. in *The Ethnic Origins of Nations* is the most articulate modern voice for the importance of ethnicity to nationalism, but see also the review and critique in Calhoun, "Nationalism and Ethnicity," *Annual Review of Sociology* 19 (1993): 211–39.

14 Renan, "What is a Nation?" p. 11.

15 Anderson, *Imagined Communities*.

16 National identity, thus, in its main Western ideological form, is precisely the opposite of the reckoning of identity and loyalty outward from the family. Where the segmentary lineage system suggests "I against my brothers, I and my brothers against my cousins, I, my brothers and my cousins against the world," nationalism suggests that membership in the category of the whole nation is prior to, more basic than, any such web of relationships. This suggests also a different notion of moral commitment from previous modes of understanding existence. The prototypical discourse of nationalism car-ries the form even into non-Western settings where kinship and communal bonds may figure more prominently or be claimed specifically against

Western individualism (see Chatterjee, *Nationalist Thought and the Colonial World* and *The Nation and Its Fragments*.

17 Kohn, *The Idea of Nationalism*, Walicki, *Philosophy and Romantic Nationalism*; Skurnowicz, *Romantic Nationalism and Liberalism*; Meinecke, *Cosmopolitanism and the National State*.

18 Fichte, quoted in Meinecke, *Cosmopolitanism and the National State*, p. 89.

19 Bloom, *Personal Identity, National Identity and International Relations*.

20 Nils Kjoer to Ibsen on the celebration of his seventieth birthday (1898), quoted p. 7 in "Henryk Ibsen – Our Contemporary," *The 1991 Ibsen Stage Festival in Norway*, edited by Margrethe Aaby (Oslo: National Theater, 1991).

21 See Mosse, *Nationalism and Sexuality*.

22 See, among many general treatments, Giddens, *The Nation-State and Violence*; Tilly, *Coercion, Capital and European States AD 990–1990*; Mann, *The Sources of Social Power*, vol. 2.

23 Weber, *Peasants into Frenchmen*.

24 Watkins, *From Provinces into Nations*.

25 See Calhoun, "Imagined Communities and Indirect Relationships."

26 A relatively benign though potentially problematic aspect of nationalism in Eastern Europe and the former USSR is the intentional deintegration of markets and division of labor. Rather than enhancing their cross-border relations, most formerly communist countries seem bent on developing their own individual relations with the West, and their own autonomous development plans. Economic integration seems to be experienced as a lack of national freedom, but this both forfeits comparative advantages in economic exchange and makes future conflicts more likely.

27 Jeff Weintraub, "The Theory and Politics of the Public/Private Distinction," paper presented to the American Political Science Association, 1990, p. 16; see Weintraub and K. Kumar (eds.), *Public and Private in Thought and Practice* (Chicago, IL University of Chicago Press, 1997).

28 Gellner, *Nations and Nationalism*, p. 6.

29 As Hobsbawm writes, "we cannot assume that for most people national identification – when it exists – excludes or is always or ever superior to, the remainder of the set of identifications which constitute the social being" (*Nations and Nationalism since 1780*, p. 11). But part of nationalist ideology is precisely the notion that national identity does "trump" other identities.

30 This point is made with some force by Eric Hobsbawm in *Nations and Nationalism since 1780* and Ernest Gellner in *Nations and Nationalism*. Both authors stress that this is not accidental, for "a world of nations cannot exist, only a world where some potentially national groups, in claiming this status, exclude others from making similar claims, which, as it happens, not many of them do" (Hobsbawm, p. 78).

31 Anderson's notion of "modular" nationalism may overstate the case to the point of denying creativity and indigenous roots to later nationalist discourses. See Chatterjee, *Nationalist Thought and the Colonial World*.

32 Resentments seem especially central to some nationalisms of Central and

Eastern Europe. Some domestic religious traditions, like Russian and other "Eastern" Orthodoxies, seem to encourage xenophobia beyond any influence of historical wrongs or current international threats. See Greenfeld, "The Formation of the Russian National Identity."

33 Albert Nenarokov and Alexander Proskurin, *How the Soviet Union Solved the Nationalities Question* (Moscow: Novosti Press Agency Publishing House, 1983).

34 See Gail Kligman, *The Wedding of the Dead* (Chicago, IL: University of Chicago Press, 1984); Verdery, *National Ideology Under Socialism*.

35 Communism has always been linked to nationalism in China, though the label "nationalism" was appropriated by its competitor the Guomindang. In general, a kind of modernizing nationalism has often been part of communism's appeal, and it is no accident that communism has flourished especially in settings where people have felt cheated of their due stature by the capitalist world-system (not in the advanced centers of capitalism as Marx predicted). As the case of largely ethnically homogenous China illustrates, nationalist aspirations are not limited to the constitution of states or the alteration of their boundaries, but include pursuit of a range of goals including regeneration, liberation, modernization, and power.

36 Banac, *The National Question in Yugoslavia* Connor, *The National Question in Marxist-Leninist Theory and Strategy*.

37 It was, of course, this same nationalism and this same weakness of other cultural and movement forms which rendered the Transcaucasus unable to sustain its federation after 1917, and unable to mount significant resistance to the Red Army's imposition of Soviet rule.

38 This is congruent with the suggestion of N. Abercrombie, *et al.*, *The Dominant Ideology Thesis* (London: Allen and Unwin, 1984) that dominant ideologies are more effective in establishing cohesion among elites than in enabling elites to "delude" or persuade the "masses."

39 On the connection to war, see Bryan Turner, *Citizenship and Capitalism: The Debate over Reformism* (London: Allen and Unwin, 1986).

40 Similarly, it is analytically untenable to try to treat "nationalism" and "patriotism" (or other labels amounting to "good" and "bad" nationalism) as though they were fundamentally different ideological species. Artistic inspiration, needed identity, will to power, and politics of repression can be and often are bound inseparably together. The differences among nationalisms come as much from the nature of international contexts as from differences in internal form or content.

41 Practices are incommensurable when they are not only different but impossible to combine within the same framework of understanding and action – as for example one cannot play American football and soccer at the same time. While some differences can be resolved by translation, incommensurabilities cannot. Where they exist in important and competitive practices (like Chinese vs. Western medicine) they remain sources of tension unless overall frameworks of practice are transformed. See Charles Taylor, *Philosophy and the Human Sciences* (Cambridge: Cambridge University

Press, 1985); Calhoun, "Culture, History and the Problem of Specificity in Social Theory," pp. 244–88 in S. Seidman and D. Wagner (eds.), *Postmodernism and General Social Theory* (New York: Blackwell, 1991).

42 Charles Taylor has argued that identity and moral commitment are intimately intertwined, so that it is almost redundant to say "identities or values." See *Sources of the Self*.

43 Hannah Arendt, *The Human Condition* (Chicago, IL: University of Chicago Press, 1958), p. 39.

44 Adam Michnik, "Poland and the Jews," *New York Review of Books*, May 30, 1991, pp. 11–12, quote from p. 11.

45 This is, of course, a core theme to Habermas's work from *The Structural Transformation of the Public Sphere* to the present. One may accept the centrality of the question without accepting quite the extreme of abstraction from issues of personal identity which is characteristic of Habermas's work.

46 See Craig Calhoun, "Populist Politics, Communications Media, and Large Scale Social Integration," *Sociological Theory* 6, no. 2 (1988): 219–41.

5   Nationalism, political community, and the representation of society

1 See Calhoun, *Nationalism*, for a fuller argument that nationalism is, among other things, what Michel Foucault (*The Archaeology of Knowledge* and *Power/Knowledge*; see also Brennan, *At Home in the World*) called a "discursive formation," a way of speaking that shapes our consciousness, but also is problematic enough that it keeps generating more issues and questions, keeps propelling us into further talk, keeps producing debates over how to think about it.

2 Tilly, *Big Structures*. See also the similar challenge from Mann, *Sources of Social Power*, vol. 1, pp. 1–2.

3 Craig Calhoun, "Nationalism and the Public Sphere," pp. 75–102 in *Public and Private in Thought and Practice*, edited by Jeff Weintraub and Krishan Kumar (Chicago, IL: University of Chicago Press, 1997).

4 See Margaret Somers, "What's Political or Cultural about Political Culture and the Public Sphere?" *Sociological Theory* 13 (1995): 113–44, and "Narrating and Naturalizing Civil Society and Citizenship Theory" *Sociological Theory* 13 (1995): 229–74 for a critical historical review of the "Anglo-American discourse of citizenship," touching on this theme but focusing on issues of the internal constitution of putative whole political communities.

5 See, for example, Amitai Etzioni, *The New Golden Rule: Community and Morality in a Democratic Society* (New York: Basic Books, 1996).

6 Habermas is among the noteworthy exceptions. See *Theory of Communicative Action* (Boston, MA: Beacon Press, 1984) and *Between Facts and Norms* (Cambridge, MA: MIT Press, 1996). For a treatment of movements and civil society in a Habermasian vein, see Cohen and Arato, *Civil Society*.

7 Martin Albrow, *The Global Age: State and Society Beyond Modernity* (Stanford, CA: Stanford University Press, 1997).

8 See, for examples of the two different lines of critique, Iris Marion Young,

Justice and the Politics of Difference (Princeton, NJ: Princeton University Press, 1990); Seyla Benhabib (ed.), *Democracy and Difference* (Princeton, NJ: Princeton University Press, 1996); Patrice Diquinsio and Iris Marion Young (eds.), *Feminist Ethics and Social Policy* (Bloomington: Indiana University Press, 1997); Jean Bethke Elshtain, *Democracy on Trial* (New York: Basic Books, 1997); Etzioni, *The New Golden Rule* and Amitai Etzioni (ed.), *New Communitarian Thinking* (Charlottesville: The University Press of Virginia, 1995); Michael Sandel, *Liberalism and the Limits of Justice*, second edition (Cambridge: Cambridge University Press, 1996); Philip Selznick, *The Moral Commonwealth: Social Theory and the Promise of Community* (Berkeley: University of California Press, 1992).

9 At the same time, the Republican notion of willed community and the Jacobin notion of the nation in action are extreme meeting points for ideas of nation and citizen. They challenge the view that the nation is always somehow prior to citizenship, a basis for it, and remind us that nations are in part creatures of would-be citizens acting against kings and states (see Calhoun, "Nationalism and the Public Sphere"). However, both tend to privilege a self-same whole over heterogeneous constituent and cross-cutting groupings.

10 Compare especially Will Kymlicka, *Multicultural Citizenship: A Liberal Theory of Minority Rights* (Oxford: Clarendon Press; New York: Oxford University Press, 1995) and "Human Rights and Ethnocultural Justice," *Review of Constitutional Studies* 4, no. 2 (1998): 213–38; also Amy Gutmann (ed.), *Multiculturalism: Examining the Politics of Recognition*, revised edition. (Princeton, NJ: Princeton University Press, 1995); Benhabib, *Democracy and Difference*.

11 Note the difference between legally empowering the members of such a group and seeking to legislate changes from outside. The same issue arises in relations across state boundaries – e.g. with regard to international efforts to promote human rights including the rights of women.

12 Edward Dolnick, "Deafness as Culture," *Atlantic Monthly* 272, no. 3 (1993): 37–53.

13 Similar issues emerge with the attempt to ground citizenship (or political community) in a single notion of substantive common good. See Craig Calhoun, "The Public Good as a Social and Cultural Project," in *Private Action and the Public Good*, edited by Walter W. Powell and Elisabeth S. Clemens (New Haven, CT: Yale University Press, 1998). This leads many to suggest a purely procedural alternative. Habermas offers one famous version of this; see *Between Facts and Norms*. Chantal Mouffe, more attentive to issues of identity, offers another. As she writes: "persons . . . might be engaged in many different purposive enterprises and with differing conceptions of the public good, but . . . accept submission to the rules prescribed by the *res publica* in seeking their satisfactions and in performing their actions" ("Democratic Citizenship and the Political Community," in *Dimensions of Radical Democracy* edited by Chantal Mouffe [London: Verso, 1992], p. 235). Whatever the other merits of procedural solutions, they push to the background rather than resolving the question of what counts as a political

community and more basically what modes of social belonging are constitutive.

14 One of the key – but I think mistaken – arguments of Jürgen Habermas's classic *Structural Transformation of the Public Sphere* is that the capacity for rational-critical discussion of differing opinions is based on suppression of group differences – notably class differences, but also by implication differences of cultural identities. See counter-arguments by Oscar Negt and Alexander Kluge, *The Public Sphere and Experience* (Minneapolis: University of Minnesota Press, 1994); by Nancy Fraser, "What's Critical about Critical Theory," in *Unruly Practices* (Minneapolis: University of Minnesota Press, 1989); by various authors in Calhoun (ed.), *Habermas and the Public Sphere*; and Calhoun, "Civil Society and the Public Sphere."

15 Think of Harold Garfinkel's famous breaching experiments and *Studies in Ethnomethodology* (Englewood Cliffs, NJ: Prentice-Hall, 1967). Garfinkel not only had students and other research subjects breach norms to see what would happen, but implicitly or explicitly tried to get people to make radically explicit their tacit understandings of the rules by which they conducted their lives. Among other things, this made everyday life impossible. See also Goran Palme's evocation of what would happen to family life if we tried to use the "rational-critical" methods of bureaucratic organizations to allocate tasks (*The Flight from Work* [New York: Free Press, 1982]).

16 Etzioni clearly recognizes that community has elements of both networks and categories. He writes, thus, that "community is defined by two characteristics: first, a web of affect-laden relationships among a group of individuals, relationships that often criss-cross and reinforce one another (rather than merely one-on-one or chainlike individual relationships), and second, a measure of commitment to a set of shared values, norms, and meanings, and a shared history and identity – in short, to a particular culture" (*The New Golden Rule*, p. 127). This is a definition that makes plausible sense on the scale of villages, but the two dimensions apply very differently to large populations and states.

17 See Manthia Diawara (ed.), "The Black Public Sphere," special issue of *Public Culture* 7, no. 1 (1994); Paul Gilroy, *The Black Atlantic: Modernity and Double Consciousness* (Cambridge, MA: Harvard University Press, 1993).

18 See Meinecke, *Cosmopolitanism*; Ishay, *Internationalism*.

19 W.E.B. Du Bois, *The Souls of Black Folk* (New York: Bantam, 1989; orig. 1903).

20 Most social and political theory has rooted the idea of tradition in reflections on feudal Europe – paradigmatically Weber's. More fully kinship-based, stateless, and non-literate societies actually offer a much better model; see Calhoun, *Nationalism*, ch. 2.

21 Gilroy, *The Black Atlantic*, p. 96.

22 Renan, "What is a Nation," p. 11.

23 Gilroy, *The Black Atlantic*, p. 1.

24 See Craig Calhoun, *Critical Social Theory: Culture, History, and the Challenge of Difference* (Cambridge, MA: Blackwell, 1995), esp. ch. 8.

25 See Jürgen Habermas, "Citizenship and National Identity: Some Reflections on the Future of Europe," *Praxis International* 12, no. 1 (1992): 1–19 and "Struggles for Recognition in the Democratic Constitutional State," in *Multiculturalism: Examining the Politics of Recognition*, revised edition, edited by Amy Gutmann (Princeton, NJ: Princeton University Press, 1994).

26 Talk of being "at home" should evoke Heidegger, and talk of "public space" will I hope recall Arendt – and the juxtaposition will suggest some of the crucial differences between their linked philosophies.

6 Inventing the opposition of ethnic and civic nationalism

1 Kohn had used versions of this distinction earlier; it did not appear *ex nihilo* in 1944. And of course the general ideas that made it possible were older. But the specific contrast, implicitly evaluative and linked to geographical East and West and ideas of late historical development, was put in play largely by Kohn. It is instructive, for example, that Louis Wirth's article on "Types of Nationalism" (*American Journal of Sociology* 41, no. 6 [1936]: 723–37) makes no mention of this contrast. His types are hegemony nationalism, particularistic nationalism, marginal nationalism, and the nationalism of minorities. Or again, in perhaps the single most influential American study before Kohn's, Carlton Hayes's *The Historical Evolution of Modern Nationalism* employed the typology: humanitarian nationalism, Jacobin nationalism, traditional nationalism, liberal nationalism, and integral nationalism. See also Louis L. Snyder, *The Meaning of Nationalism* (New Brunswick, NJ: Rutgers University Press, 1954), p. 121 on the "Kohn Dichotomy."

2 Kohn, *The Idea of Nationalism*, p. 204.

3 Ibid., p. 215.

4 Kohn covered the time period projected for the second volume in *The Age of Nationalism*, but in a more "popular" mode and not with the attention to intellectual history of *The Idea of Nationalism*.

5 Perhaps the most important recent restatement of this conception of liberal nationalism is Yael Tamir, *Liberal Nationalism* (Princeton, NJ: Princeton University Press, 1993).

6 Kohn, *The Idea of Nationalism*, p. 576.

7 Ibid., p. 36.

8 See his discussion in Hans Kohn, *A History of Nationalism in the East* (New York: Harcourt Brace, 1929).

9 Kohn wrote several semi-popular works for that purpose, like *Force or Reason* (Cambridge, MA: Harvard University Press, 1937), *Revolutions and Dictatorships* (Cambridge, MA: Harvard University Press, 1939), *Not By Arms Alone: Essays on Our Time* (Cambridge, MA: Harvard University Press, 1940), and *World Order in Historical Perspective* (Cambridge, MA: Harvard University Press, 1942). The first traced the "cult of force" and "dethronement of reason" to the bewilderment of the masses after World

War I. The second compared instances of revolution and dictatorship culminating in an account of why fascism was especially dangerous, why appeasement wouldn't work, and why inspirational renewal of democracy was crucial to fight it. In the third, he focused on the fascist exaltation of war, tracing a lineage from Sparta to the Third Reich, argued that a democratic revolution would be needed to overcome fascism, and held that Austria had created a "better German civilization" which should have evolved into a federal union. And in the last he addressed the ways in which struggle against fascism could be a step towards world unification, supporting the United Nations as part of a general progress towards world order. It was crucial, he argued, that fascism had managed to range against itself every force in the world that affirmed the universality of values including liberalism, communism, the papacy and the British Empire, Protestants and Jews. As one reviewer remarked, the book was an excellent statement of the liberal progressive view, but its weaknesses were those of all who based their arguments on the philosophical ideals of the eighteenth and nineteenth centuries. Such authors "adore Jefferson and Condorcet but do not appear to know Burke or Montesquieu. They overestimate the importance of abstract ideals in history and minimize the tenacious strength of the concrete" (Ross Hoffman, "Review of *World Order in Historical Perspective*," *Journal of Modern History* 15, no. 2 [1943]: 155–6).

10 See Hayes, *The Historical Evolution*. Eric Hobsbawm quotes A. Kemiläinen describing Kohn and Hayes as "the twin founding fathers" of the academic study of nationalism, praises Kemiläinen, but indicates that he would not put either Kohn or Hayes on his reading list (*Nations and Nationalism*, p. 3). Kohn was not opposed to Hayes's account of nationalism as a replacement for religion, though he had other emphases and intellectual agendas. He had a very inclusive style as an historian, which meant among other things that he was loath to make a single variable determinative.

11 Frederick Hertz, "The Nature of Nationalism," *Social Forces* 19, no. 3 (1941): 409–15.

12 There is no consistent label for the Zionism of Ahad Ha'am (the pen name of Asher Ginsberg, which translates as "one of the people"), a near-contemporary as well as an opponent of Herzl. It combined a strong emphasis on ethics, spiritual strivings, and cultural renewal – themes some later distinguished. Ha'am was also an important advocate for Hebrew and considered a master of Hebrew style – part of his program of cultural identity and, it is worth noting, at once an innovation and an advocacy for distinctive tradition. For a brief account of Ha'am, see Shlomo Avineri, *The Making of Modern Zionism: The Intellectual Origins of the Jewish State* (New York: Basic Books, 1981). Martin Buber was among the most important intellectuals joining Ha'am in this movement.

13 Herzl somewhat vacillated among civic, ethnic, and racial definitions of Jews, though his nationalism was always political rather than cultural or spiritual. When he met Israel Zangwill for the first time, he described him as a Jew "of the long-nosed negroid type"; see Desmond Stewart, *Theodore*

Herzl (New York: Doubleday, 1974). Zionism was of course in large part a product of nineteenth-century European thought – racial theories as well as socialism, Romanticism, and nationalism. Part of Kohn's project is to emphasize that it was also a product of eighteenth-century Enlightenment rationalism and universalism – and that they in turn drew on Jewish sources for inspiration.

14 Each offers, in part, philosophical reworkings and developments of themes from Hassidic thought.

15 On Zangwill, and his eventual break with Zionism, see Hani A. Faris, "Israel Zangwill's Challenge to Zionism," *Journal of Palestine Studies* 4, no. 3 (1975): 74–90.

16 Kohn, *The Idea of Nationalism*, p. 45.

17 Ibid., p. 44.

18 Cited in Ken Wolf, "Hans Kohn's Liberal Nationalism," *Journal of the History of Ideas* 37, no. 4 (1976): 651–72; p. 654.

19 Zangwill's play, *The Melting Pot*, appeared in 1908. But of course the phrase had much older roots. Emerson, for example, referred in 1845 to racial and cultural mixture through the metaphor of "the smelting pot"; there were still earlier anticipations in Crèvecoeur and other colonial commentators. And Zangwill was not only a playwright, but the author of books like *The Principle of Nationalities* (London: Watts & Co., 1917). The "melting" metaphor was also used to discuss the question of how autonomous and distinct the separate states should be, as in Winterbotham's (1795) observation that: "some from jealousy of liberty were afraid of giving too much power to their rulers; others, from an honest ambition to aggrandize their country, were for paving the way to national greatness by melting down the separate states into a national mass." The passage (quoted by Kohn, *The Idea of Nationalism*, on p. 288) reminds us helpfully of the parallel between debates over the integration of immigrants and those over the incorporation of disparate regions, provinces, and states into a larger common nation-state. And it is worth noting that the hero of Zangwill's play is a Jewish immigrant who falls in love with and wins the heart of a Christian – Jewish particularism was not ethnic insularity for Zangwill. Interestingly, the hero and his love interest are both Russian, she a noblewoman, he the child of parents slaughtered in a pogrom. Old World antipathies are overcome in the New World, but Old World cultural commonalties apparently still count.

20 See Faris, "Israel Zangwill's Challenge."

21 Cited in Wolf, "Hans Kohn's Liberal Nationalism," p. 653.

22 Ibid.

23 Online at: http://www.passia.org/publications/research_studies/peace/chapter2.html

24 Lest the present generation feel uniquely deficient in this regard, note the words of a reviewer in 1944: "Even an adept linguist may sometimes feel staggered by all the quotations offered without translation in Latin and Greek, French and German, Italian and Spanish, Dutch and Polish. But we must assume the blame ourselves, not put it on the learned author" (Halvdan

Koht, "Review of *The Idea of Nationalism*," *American Historical Review* 50, no. 1 [1944]: 93–6).

25 Kohn, *The Idea of Nationalism*, p. 27.

26 Ibid. Kohn does not consider how much or how little this extended to women.

27 Kohn, *The Idea of Nationalism*, p. 28.

28 Wolf, "Hans Kohn's Liberal Nationalism," p. 654.

29 Kohn, *The Idea of Nationalism*, p. 34.

30 Ibid., pp. 56–7.

31 Ibid., p. 57.

32 See F.E. Peters, *The Harvest of Hellenism* (New York: Simon and Schuster, 1970).

33 Kohn, *The Idea of Nationalism*, p. 59.

34 Ibid., p. 60.

35 See, for example, Hobsbawm and Ranger, *The Invention of Tradition*, though both editors might bridle at being called liberals.

36 Wolf, "Hans Kohn's Liberal Nationalism," pp. 655–6.

37 There are many who would emphasize these phases more. See, for example, Geary, *The Myth of Nations*, and for a more general claim to long-term ethnic continuity with less break between medieval and modern, see Smith, *The Ethnic Origins of Nations*.

38 Kohn, *The Idea of Nationalism*, p. 65.

39 Ibid., p. 70. It is interesting that Kohn claims mainly the Roman Empire for the story of nationalism when so many of the eighteenth-century thinkers he admires saw in it the corruption of the purer ideals of the Republic. In his cultural Zionism as well, Kohn retained a liberal imperialist attitude. In the same essay in which he spoke of the moral responsibility Jewish nationalism must take on itself he wrote: "let us not be fooled by national chauvinism, or we will be slaves of yesterday, not the imperialists of tomorrow" (cited in Wolf, "Hans Kohn's Liberal Nationalism," p. 654).

40 Kohn, *The Idea of Nationalism*, p. 69.

41 Ibid., p. 75.

42 Here it is worth noting that the East clearly means the world of Orthodox Christianity. Indeed, as Kohn notes, in medieval Islam "universalism remained a reality much longer than in Western Christianity" (ibid., p. 79).

43 Ibid., p. 78.

44 Ibid., p. 79. Only later will Kohn note that there were significant challenges to what he here describes as simply the political thought of the age – challenges that become important to some later thinkers like Gierke.

45 Ibid., p. 92.

46 Ibid., p. 104.

47 Here Kohn takes up a theme central to later "state-centered" theories of nationalism. See Gellner, *Nations and Nationalism*; Mann, *Sources of Social Power*, esp. vol. 1; and specifically on absolutism, exploring Europe's East–West and other contrasts, Anderson, *Lineages*.

48 Kohn, *The Idea of Nationalism*, p. 125; see also, p. 178.

49 Ibid., p. 166. "This religious nationalism," Kohn argued, "was experienced by the English people as a revival of Old Testament nationalism" (p. 168). "English nationalism was born in the great decisive hour of its history by repeating the experience of the chosen people and of the Covenant" (p. 176). Certainly Old Testament themes were important, as in the birth of American nationalism a little later, but perhaps not quite so unambiguously dominant as Kohn suggests.

50 Kohn quotes Milton: "If men within themselves would be governed by reason, and not generally give up their understanding to a double tyranny, of Custom from without, and blind affection within, they would discern better, what it is to favor and uphold the Tyrant of a Nation" (ibid., pp. 170–1).

51 Ibid., p. 178. Not unrelatedly, the birth of English nationalism coincided with the rise of the middle classes (p. 179) and Locke's two principles are basic: that individuals are primary and government a moral trust (p. 182).

52 Ibid., p. 183.

53 Ibid., p. 188.

54 Kohn quotes with approval the German nationalist Karl von Moser, the first to speak of a *Nationalgeist* (translating Montesquieu's *esprit de nation*): "In every political constitution there must be one great, one general idea, the punctum saliens, which represents the vitalizing power of the national mind" (ibid., p. 375). The approval is for the fact that "Moser made it clear that his national spirit was a political idea, much more akin to the concepts of the West . . . than to the later German *Volksgeist*."

55 Ibid., p. 16.

56 I would prefer to speak of the "discourse" of nationalism since, as Kohn acknowledges, rather than a single idea of nationalism developing, a range of ideas interrelate in shifting patterns; see Calhoun, *Nationalism*. Anderson (*Imagined Communities*) has influentially argued this point, portraying nationalism as one way of imagining large-scale community among strangers, facilitated by various communicative, administrative, and other innovations, and with a variety of more specific contents that vary among cases. To define nations, nationalities, of nationalism by their contents has proved all but impossible. As Kohn himself writes, "Nationalities come into existence only when certain objective bonds delimit a social group. A nationality generally has several of these attributes; very few have all of them. The most usual of them are common descent, language, territory, political entity, customs and traditions, and religion. A short discussion will suffice to show that none of them is essential to the existence or definition of nationality" (*The Idea of Nationalism*, pp. 13–14).

57 Kohn, *American Nationalism*, p. 309. Kohn developed his treatment of US nationalism at greater length but with mostly similar argument in *American Nationalism: An Interpretative Essay* (New York: Macmillan, 1957). His enthusiasm for the idea of nationalism as a step on the road to human self-perfection is revealed in an error of the sort that non-specialists dread making when working with historical sources. He quotes John Adams's famous letter to Thomas Jefferson affirming that "our pure, virtuous, public-spirited,

federative republic will last forever, govern the globe and introduce the per-fection of man" (p. 13). Unfortunately, Kohn doesn't notice that Adams was being sarcastic (at least one reviewer did; see Marvin Meyers, "Review of Hans Kohn, *American Nationalism: An Interpretative Essay*," *Political Science Quarterly* 72, no. 4 [1957]: 628–30).

58 Ibid., p. 308.

59 Ibid., p. 292.

60 Ibid., p. 301.

61 Quoted on p. 313.

62 Ibid., p. 271.

63 More than a few recent historians have placed greater emphasis on the specif-ically English, or at least British, claims of the colonists; see Gordon Wood, *The Radicalism of the American Revolution* (New York: Random House, 1991). Wood does not dispute the pivotal significance of the revolution for making Americans – an important theme for Kohn (see below). But he would insist that until the break with Britain came, most colonial leaders insisted on their Englishness and saw their rights mainly in terms of English historical liberties (and the claims to historical liberties are in fact more English than British). Kohn acknowledges this up to a point, but associates worries over English liberties more with Loyalists who saw the Revolution as illiberal (Kohn, *American Nationalism*, pp. 281–4).

64 Kohn, *American Nationalism*, p. 275.

65 Ibid., p. 289.

66 Ibid., quoted on pp. 275–6.

67 Ibid., p. 276.

68 See Hannah Arendt, *On Revolution* (New York: Penguin, 1963).

69 One has to wonder at the assurance with which Kohn writes of France in the second half of the eighteenth century that "This new intimate connection between national welfare and the life of the individual became a great and beneficial force of intellectual awakening and moral fervor in a spiritual climate in which its possible excesses were strictly controlled by a rational conception of men's freedom and a universal conception of their equality" (*American Nationalism*, p. 263).

70 See Michel Foucault, *Discipline and Punish* (New York: Pantheon, 1977). Compare also Taylor's account in *Sources of the Self* of the religious roots of the rise of this sort of self-fashioning moral individualism, largely but not only within Protestantism. Of course, as Taylor suggests, much of the orien-tation becomes pervasive in modernity and loses any link to its specifically religious origins.

71 Kohn, *The Idea of Nationalism*, p. 225; see Deutsch, *Nationalism and Social Communication*.

72 Kohn, *The Idea of Nationalism*, p. 201. See Deutsch, *Nationalism and Social Communication*.

73 Kohn, *The Idea of Nationalism*, p. 226.

74 Talcott Parsons, *The Structure of Social Action* (Glencoe, IL: Free Press, 1936).

75 Kohn, *The Idea of Nationalism*, p. 226.
76 The difficulty of achieving this integration became the occasion for an ever
    more individualistic liberalism and then a "communitarian" reaction stress-
    ing the impossibility of life outside cultural and social relations. This was
    central to debate in political theory (and *Political Theory*) from the 1980s
    through the 1990s.
77 Kohn, *The Idea of Nationalism*, p. 249.
78 Ibid., p. 246.
79 Ibid., p. 249.
80 Ibid., pp. 253–4.
81 Ibid., p. 257.
82 Kant, much influenced by Rousseau, embraces a similar idea with a similar
    lack of recognition of this sociological significance of scale. See "Perpetual
    Peace: A Philosophical Sketch," pp. 93–130 in H. Reiss (ed.), *Kant's Political
    Writings* (Cambridge: Cambridge University Press, 1970).
83 Ibid., pp. 8–9.
84 See Habermas, *The Inclusion of the Other*; also my discussion in
    "Constitutional Patriotism."
85 Kohn, *The Idea of Nationalism*, p. 251.
86 Ibid., p. 259.
87 Kohn's reading is at least as tendentious and glosses over themes like Rous-
    seau's recurrent if not consistent anticosmopolitanism. In his advice to
    Poland, for example, he makes the sort of connection to the ancient world
    that Kohn also emphasizes, but to an unKohnian, antiassimilationist end.
    Rosseau praises Moses as a great nation-builder, but points out that "all the
    fraternal bonds with which he drew together the members of his republic
    were as many barriers keeping them separate from their neighbors and pre-
    venting them from mingling with them"; "Considerations on the Govern-
    ment of Poland," in *Jean Jacques Rousseau: Political Writings*, translated
    and edited by Fredrick Watkins (Madison, WI: University of Wisconsin
    Press, 1986).
88 For many others, it will appear largely as a matter of historical "lateness," as
    late-developing nations cohere around more ethnic, traditionalist national-
    isms and are either more aggressive or more defensive or both; see, e.g.
    Alter's appropriation of the civic/ethnic contrast in *Nationalism*. Kohn cer-
    tainly sees something of this, but he is at pains to emphasize that ethnic
    nationalism diverges also on more intellectual grounds, not least in the pur-
    suit of indigenous originality. It is a different branch in an initially shared
    intellectual and political lineage, not simply more intense or the product of
    different circumstances.
89 Kohn, *The Idea of Nationalism*, p. 3.
90 See (among many and in addition to all the general histories) Lynn Hunt, *The
    Family Romance of the French Revolution* (Berkeley: University of Califor-
    nia Press, 1993) and William H. Sewell, Jr., "Le Citoyen, La Citoyenne:
    Activity, Passivity and the French Revolutionary Concept of Citizenship,"
    pp. 105–25 in *The French Revolution and the Creation of Modern Political*

Culture, vol. 2, edited by Colin Lucas (Oxford: Pergamon Press, 1988). Other essays in the Lucas collection are also relevant as are several essays by Sewell hopefully forthcoming in book form. See also his *A Rhetoric of Bourgeois Revolution: The Abbé Sieyes and What Is the Third Estate?* (Durham, NC: Duke University Press, 1994), though in it Sewell focuses on economic and class distinctions and makes little of Sieyes's nationalism, though in *What Is the Third Estate?* he wrote "the nation exists before all, it is the origin of all."

91 See discussion in R.R. Palmer, "The National Idea in France before the Revolution," *Journal of the History of Ideas* 1, no. 1 (1940): 95–111. Palmer notes that those who took the lead in the Revolution "spoke of the 'nation' even more often than of 'nature,' and with at least equal fervor" (p. 96). They and their late eighteenth-century forebears also brought back the word "patrie" from obscurity. The *philosophes* embraced patriotism and the Revolutionaries identified it with citizenship. This informed a later usage that treats patriotism as a sort of benign and appropriate love of country by contrast to more aggressive nationalism. But patriotism was for the *philosophes* if anything a more militant term than nationalism. And for the most part the patriotism/nationalism distinction turns out to be little more than an alternative phrasing for civic vs. ethnic nationalism.

92 As Gellner remarks, "Nationalism . . . above all is not what it seems to itself" (*Nations and Nationalism*, p. 56).

93 Nussbaum is notable, not least because she draws significantly on the Stoics, whom Kohn also likes; see especially *For Love of Country*.

94 I have discussed the implications of such accounts in "Belonging."

95 And indeed, the egalitarianism of the Revolution can easily be overstated. This is a key theme of Sewell, *A Rhetoric of Bourgeois Revolution*.

96 Quoted from Juan Cole, "Three Episodes in the Rhetoric of Liberal Imperialism: French Egypt, British Egypt, American Iraq," in *Lessons of Empire*, edited by Craig Calhoun *et al.* (New York: New Press, 2006).

97 Kohn, *The Idea of Nationalism*, p. 4.

98 To what extent this vaunted contrast of French imperialism to British "indirect rule" and indeed to many other models of empire was mere ideology and form and to what extent it deeply shaped the practice of government is debated; see Frederick Cooper and Ann Laura Stoler (eds.), *Tensions of Empire: Colonial Cultures in a Bourgeois World* (Berkeley: University of California Press, 1997). This collection is useful more generally as an introduction to a new generation of research that tries to address metropoles and colonies as part of the same analytic field.

99 Kohn was ambivalent about imperialism, thinking it both an understandable project of newly united European nations and an oppression that "inflamed" the nationalism of conquered peoples (see *Nationalism and Imperialism in the Hither East* [New York: Harcourt, Brace, 1932], p. 49). He also thought that imperialism performed "a service of historic importance" by spreading Western values and Enlightenment, but that where it succeeded it "destroyed its own basis" (see *Force or Reason*, p. 94).

100 Kohn, *The Idea of Nationalism*, pp. 572–3.
101 Kohn offers his version of at least part of this story in several articles presumably intended as sketches for the unwritten second volume: "The Paradox of Fichte's Nationalism," *Journal of the History of Ideas* 10, no. 3 (1949): 319–43; "Napoleon and the Age of Nationalism," *Journal of Modern History* 22, no. 1 (1950): 21–37; "The Eve of German Nationalism," *Journal of the History of Ideas* 12, no. 2 (1951): 6–84; and a book of lectures, *Prelude to Nation-States: The French and German Experience, 1789–1815* (Princeton, NJ: Van Nostrand, 1967).
102 Kohn, *The Idea of Nationalism*, p. 330.
103 Ibid., p. 331.
104 Habermas, *The Inclusion of the Other*, p. 115.
105 Ibid., p. 117.
106 Though most Chinese find it as hard as Japanese to imagine an openly assimilative nation, thinking about civic dimensions of nationalism is pressed on them by the distribution of Chinese people across multiple states – in some cases developing distinct national traditions and legal orders. The Chinese case in the era of Sun Yat-sen also reveals the extent to which a racial nationalism could be advanced in tandem with republican political ideology and forward-looking projects of cultural reform; see Frank Dikötter, *The Discourse of Race in Modern China* (Stanford, CA: Stanford University Press, 1992). Sun's vision of saving Chineseness by transforming it was not in every respect different from some of the versions of the Zionist project with which it was contemporaneous.
107 Brubaker, *Citizenship and Nationhood*.
108 Kohn, *The Idea of Nationalism*, p. 428.
109 Ibid., p. 433.
110 Ibid., p. 429.
111 See Meinecke's classic treatment in *Cosmopolitanism*.
112 Kohn, *The Idea of Nationalism*, p. 380.
113 Quoted in ibid., p. 409.
114 Quoted in ibid., pp. 398–9.
115 Ibid., p. 354.
116 Ibid., p. 362.
117 Ibid., p. 352.
118 Quoted in ibid., p. 374.
119 Ibid., p. 455.
120 Ibid., p. 509.
121 Ibid., p. 569.
122 Ibid., p. 474.
123 The intense engagement of early German nationalists with Greek thought – certainly carried through to Nietzsche and beyond – is an embeddedness in Western civilization, not in the East to which Greek was largely consigned by Constantine's split in Christendom. Elsewhere, to his credit, Kohn is much more attentive to the idea that ethnic and civic ideas are in struggle within German nationalism – and indeed Russian and other "Eastern"

nationalisms; see *The Mind of Germany: The Education of a Nation* (New York: Scribner's, 1960) and also the discussion in Wolf, "Hans Kohn's Liberal Nationalism," p. 668. He is more attentive to the struggle within "derivative" nationalisms – as he saw all outside the Western core – than to that same struggle within English, French, or American nationalism.

124 Quoted in Kohn, *The Idea of Nationalism*, p. 435. This is of course a theme Humboldt would later take up, emphasizing both national and individual *bildung*.

125 Quoted in ibid., p. 431.

126 Herder, along with Humboldt and Hegel, is a key source for Charles Taylor's more recent philosophical challenge to atomistic, acultural individualism; see among many of his writings "The Importance of Herder," pp. 79–99 in *Philosophical Arguments* (Cambridge, MA: Harvard University Press, 1995) and "Language and Human Nature," pp. 21–47 in *Human Agency and Language*, vol. 1 (New York: Cambridge University Press, 1985).

127 Quoted in Kohn, *The Idea of Nationalism*, p. 433.

128 Habermas, "Struggles for Recognition." Habermas is reacting to Taylor's "The Politics of Recognition," in the same volume (in *Multiculturalism: Examining the Politics of Recognition*, revised edition, edited by Amy Gutmann (Princeton, NJ: Princeton University Press, 1994).

129 Kohn, *The Idea of Nationalism*, p. 441.

130 Quoted in ibid., p. 441.

131 Indeed, Kohn's vision of civic nationalism owes much to both social contract theory and the more general use of contractarian language which is one of the links between later liberalism, the seventeenth-century English Civil War, and the ancient Hebrew Bible. See David Zaret's discussion of the latter two elements in *The Heavenly Contract: Ideology and Organization in Pre-Revolutionary Puritanism* (Chicago, IL: University of Chicago Press, 1985).

132 Kohn, *The Idea of Nationalism*, p. 351.

133 Ibid., p. 396.

134 Ibid., p. 414.

135 Hayes, *The Historical Evolution*; and see n. 1 above for Hayes's typology.

136 Renan, "What Is a Nation?" p. 11.

137 Kohn, *The Idea of Nationalism*, p. 574.

138 See Chatterjee's complaint in the opening chapter of *Nationalist Thought*.

7 Nationalism and the cultures of democracy

1 Nationalism is a "discursive formation," in Foucault's sense; see *The Archaeology of Knowledge* and *Power/Knowledge*. That is, it is a way of talking that inescapably exceeds the bounds of any single usage, that endlessly generate more talk, and that embody tensions and contradictions. Nationalism is not simply a settled position, but a cluster of rhetoric and reference that enables people to articulate positions which are not settled and

to take stands in opposition to each other on basic issues in society and culture. Nationalist rhetoric provides the modern era with a constitutive framework for the identification of collective subjects, both the protagonists of historical struggles and those who experience history and by whose experience it can be judged good or bad, progress or regress or stagnation. In this, nationalism most resembles another great discursive formation, also constitutive for modernity, individualism. See Calhoun, *Nationalism*.

2 The status of this hyphen is subject to considerable controversy. It is common to speak of "nations" without distinguishing the state from the ostensibly integrated population associated with it. This is in fact hard to avoid without pedantry, and while I shall at certain points make clear that I mean one or the other, like most writers I shall not consistently make clear that the relationship between national identity or integration and state authority or structure is not stable or consistent. As a discursive formation, nationalism continually reproduces the idea that there should be a link between nation and state as well as various forms and dimensions of national identity, integration, distinction, and conflict.

3 John Rawls, *Political Liberalism*, p. 41.

4 Of course it is worth recalling that the 1648 Peace of Westphalia did not transform the world overnight into one of strongly institutionalized nation-states and international relations. It is more a myth or symbol for the project of remaking the world in these terms than a token of such achievement. See Benno Teschke, *The Myth of 1648*.

5 Allen Buchanan, "Rawls' Law of Peoples: Rules for a Vanished Westphalian World," *Ethics* 110, no. 4 (2000): 697–721.

6 Rawls, *A Theory of Justice* and *The Law of Peoples*; see also Charles R. Beitz, "Rawls' Law of Peoples," *Ethics* 110, no. 4 (2000): 669–96 and Rex Martin and David Reidy (eds.), *Rawls's Law of Peoples: A Realistic Utopia?* (Oxford: Blackwell, 2006).

7 By "encompassing" I mean to echo Louis Dumont's argument about the ways in which culture may bring together dimensions that cannot be logically integrated. National cultures often encompass different subcultures without integrating them and encompass logically contradictory values, creating nonetheless a sense in which they belong as parts of the larger whole. See Dumont, *Homo Hierarchicus* (Chicago, IL: University of Chicago Press, 1966).

8 The best and most careful of such cosmopolitan theoretical visions come from Jürgen Habermas (e.g. *Inclusion of the Other*); and David Held (e.g. *Democracy and the Global Order*). See also essays in Archibugi and Held, *Cosmopolitan Democracy*, Archibugi *et al.*, *Re-Imagining Political Community*, Archibugi, *Debating Cosmopolitics*, and Vertovec and Cohen, *Conceiving Cosmopolitanism*. These cosmopolitan visions are clearly Kantian; for elaboration of that heritage see Bohman and Lutz-Bachmann, *Perpetual Peace: Essays on Kant's Cosmopolitan Ideal*. My reference here is mainly to these more political theories of cosmopolitanism, not to the accounts of "vernacular cosmopolitanism" in which some anthropologists and

historians have urged us to look at the more concrete and often local transactions and cultural productions in which people actually forge relations with each other across lines of difference. See Pollock *et al.*, "Cosmopolitanisms," *Public Culture* 12, no. 3 (2000). In a sense, I pursue in this paper a meeting point between these two perspectives, one which I think is impossible to discern if one focuses only on transcending the nation, imagining the world mainly globally "at large" and relating this to the local and immediate rather than emphasizing the importance of the mediating institutions of which nations and states are among the most important.

9 See Craig Calhoun, *Cosmopolitanism and Belonging* (London: Routledge, forthcoming).

10 Nationalism figures prominently as an example of "categorical" identities in which each individual figures as an equivalent token of the larger type. But this does not exhaust the ways in which national culture matters to the production of solidarity. Common language and frameworks of meaning, for example, may integrate people without suggesting that they are equivalent. Common projects create alliances among otherwise dissimilar people. Communities understand their solidarity to be embeddedness in webs of relationships as well as "categorical" distinctions from other communities. Of course, culture may also figure as ideology underwriting, for better or worse, functional integration among national institutions or nationally organized markets, and direct exercise of power. See Calhoun, *Cosmopolitanism and Belonging*.

11 Martha Nussbaum can serve as an exemplar of such "extreme cosmopolitans" reasoning from the ethical equivalence of individuals. See her *For Love of Country*. See also discussion in Samuel Scheffler, *Boundaries and Allegiances: Problems of Justice and Responsibility in Liberal Thought* (Oxford: Oxford University Press, 2001) and Calhoun, "Belonging in the Cosmopolitan Imaginary."

12 See Richard Bernstein, *The Abuse of Evil* (Cambridge: Polity, 2005), ch. 2.

13 Hobsbawm and Ranger, writing in *The Invention of Tradition*, are thus right about invention but wrong about its implications.

14 To imagine a politics without agonism, a democratic citizenship merely of agreement, is a contradiction in terms, as Chantal Mouffe and others have suggested. See Mouffe, *Dimensions of Radical Democracy* and continued discussion in more recent works.

15 Arendt, *On Revolution; Between Past and Future* (New York: Viking, 1968).

16 This side of nationalism is emphasized by institutionalist theories such as the "world polity" theory of John Meyer and a range of colleagues; for an early statement that helped launch the perspective and informed discussion of "institutional isomorphism," see, Meyer and Rowan, "Institutionalized Organizations."

17 See Taylor, *Sources of the Self*, on horizons of moral judgment and the idea of self-transcendence.

18 This is increasingly contested, both by the writing of global history and by efforts to internationalize national histories. See for an example of the latter,

Thomas Bender, *A Nation among Nations* (New York: Hill and Wang, 2006) and the reflections on internationalizing American history in his edited collection, *Rethinking America in a Global Age* (Berkeley: University of California Press, 2002).

19 Ernest Gellner, *Nationalism* (New York: New York University Press, 1997), p. 34.

20 See, for example, Arjun Appadurai, "Difference and Disjuncture in the Global Cultural Economy," *Public Culture* 2, No. 2 (1990): 1–24 and the *Public Culture* special issue on "Alternative Modernities" (Dilip Gaonkar, ed.), 11, No. 1 (1999).

21 Hobsbawm and Ranger, *The Invention of Tradition*.

22 I have elaborated on this theme, and on the language of category and network, at more length in *Nationalism*, esp. ch. 3. My usage is indebted to the anthropological distinction of clan and lineage, and to the specific formulation of S.F. Nadel, *The Theory of Social Structure* (London: Cohen and West, 1965).

23 The popularity of mixed-race self-identifications in the US Census of 2000 is an example, but of course the categories to which people feel they belong are not all ethnic; they may be based on a variety of membership criteria from class and religion to sexual orientation or occupation.

24 *The Discovery of India* not only integrates the Vedas, the Gitas, the Mughals, and the Congress Party into a single national story, it does this in a style influenced by Western narrative history and in English, the language of British colonialism which India made also one of her own.

25 Tom Nairn, *Faces of Nationalism: Janus Revisited* (London: Verso, 1997).

26 The useful concept of "illth" – the negative counterparts to wealth, like environmental degradation – was introduced in 1860 by John Ruskin; see the title essay in *Unto this Last and Other Writings* (London: Penguin, 1986). It remains inadequately integrated into economic thought. "Negative externalities" addresses related problems but more narrowly from the perspective of the individual economic actor.

Conclusion

1 Scott Morrison and Ken Warn, "Liberals strive to sharpen competitive edge," *Financial Times*, June 11, 2001, "Canada Survey," pp. 1–2.

2 Raymond Williams, *The Long Revolution* (Harmondsworth: Pelican, 1965).

Bibliography

Aaby, Margrethe (ed.). *The 1991 Ibsen Stage Festival in Norway*. Oslo: National Theater, 1991.

Abercrombie, N., Bryan Turner, and Stephen Hill. *The Dominant Ideology Thesis*. London: Allen and Unwin, 1984.

Addi, Laurent. *Sociologie et anthropologie chez Pierre Bourdieu: Le paradigme anthropologique kabyle et ses conséquences théoriques*. Paris: Découverte, 2003.

Adorno, Theodore. *The Jargon of Authenticity*. Evanston, IL: Northwestern University Press, 1973.

——. *Minima Moralia*. London: Verso, 1974.

Agamben, Georgi. *State of Exception*. Chicago, IL: University of Chicago Press, 2004.

Ajami, Fouad. "The Summoning," *Foreign Affairs*, Sept./Oct. (1993): 2–10.

Albrow, Martin. *The Global Age: State and Society Beyond Modernity*. Stanford, CA: Stanford University Press, 1997.

Alter, Peter. *Nationalism*. London: Edward Arnold, 1989.

Anderson, Benedict. *Imagined Communities*, revised edition. London: Verso, 1991 (orig. 1983).

——. "Introduction," in *Mapping the Nation*, edited by Gopal Balakrishnan. London: Verso, 1996.

Anderson, Perry. *Lineages of the Absolutist State*. London: New Left Books, 1974.

Appadurai, Arjun. "Difference and Disjuncture in the Global Cultural Economy," *Public Culture* 2, no. 2 (1990): 1–24.

Apter, David. *The Politics of Modernization*. Chicago, IL: University of Chicago Press, 1965.

Archibugi, Daniele (ed.). *Debating Cosmopolitics*. London: Verso, 2003.

Archibugi, Daniele and David Held (eds.). *Cosmopolitan Democracy: An Agenda for a New World Order*. Cambridge, MA: Polity Press, 1995.

Archibugi, Daniele, David Held, and Martin Köhler (eds.). *Re-Imagining Political Community: Studies in Cosmopolitan Democracy*. Stanford, CA: Stanford University Press, 1998.

Arendt, Hannah. *The Origins of Totalitarianism*, second edition. New York: Harcourt Brace, 1951.

——. *The Human Condition*. Chicago, IL: University of Chicago Press, 1958.

——. *On Revolution*. New York: Penguin, 1963.

——. *Between Past and Future*. New York: Viking, 1968.

——. "Tradition and the Modern Age," in *Between Past and Future*. New York: Viking Penguin, 1968.

Armstrong, John. *Nations before Nationalism*. Chapel Hill: University of North Carolina Press, 1982.

Avineri, Shlomo. *The Making of Modern Zionism: The Intellectual Origins of the Jewish State*. New York: Basic Books, 1981.

Balibar, Etienne and Immanuel Wallerstein. *Race, Nation, Class*. London: Verso, 1991.

Banac, Ivo. *The National Question in Yugoslavia: Origin, History, Politics*. Ithaca, NY: Cornell University Press, 1984.

Barber, Benjamin. *Jihad vs. McWorld*. New York: Times Books, 1995.

Barnett, Michael. *Eyewitness to a Genocide: The United Nations and Rwanda*. Ithaca, NY: Cornell University Press, 2002.

Barnett, Tony and Alan Whiteside, *AIDS in the Twenty-First Century*. London: Palgrave, 2002.

Barth, Fredrik (ed.). *Ethnic Boundaries*. Oslo: Norwegian University Press, 1969.

Bauman, Zygmunt. *Modernity and the Holocaust*. Ithaca, NY: Cornell University Press, 1989.

——. *The Community Seeking Safety in an Insecure World*. London: Blackwell, 2001.

Beck, Ulrich. *The Risk Society: Towards a New Modernity*. Newbury Park, CA: Sage, 1992.

——. "Sociology in the Second Age of Modernity," in *Conceiving Cosmopolitanism*, edited by Steven Vertovec and Robin Cohen. Oxford: Oxford University Press, 2002.

——. "The Analysis of Global Inequality: From National to Cosmopolitan Perspective," in *Global Civil Society 2003*, edited by Mary Kaldor, Helmut Anheier, and Marlies Glasius. Oxford: Oxford University Press, 2003.

Beetham, David. *Max Weber and the Theory of Modern Politics*, revised edition. Cambridge: Polity Press, 1985.

Beitz, Charles. *Political Theory and International Relations*. Princeton, NJ: Princeton University Press, 1979.

——. "Rawls' Law of Peoples," *Ethics* 110, no. 4 (2000): 669–96.

Bender, Thomas (ed.). *Rethinking America in a Global Age*. Berkeley: University of California Press, 2002.

——. *A Nation among Nations: America's Place in World History*. New York: Hill and Wang, 2006.

Bendix, Reinhard. *Nation-Building and Citizenship*. Berkeley: University of California Press, 1964.

Benhabib, Seyla (ed.). *Democracy and Difference*. Princeton, NJ: Princeton University Press, 1996.

Benjamin, Walter. "Theses on the Philosophy of History," in *Illuminations*, edited by Hannah Arendt, trans. Harry Zohn. New York: Shocken, 1969.

Bentham, Jeremy. *Principles of Jurisprudence*. London: Methuen, 1982 (orig. 1789).

Bentley, G. Carter. *Ethnicity and Nationality: A Bibliographic Guide*. Seattle: University of Washington Press, 1981.

Berezin, Mabel and Martin Schain (eds.). *Europe without Borders: Re-Mapping Territory, Citizenship and Identity in a Transnational Age*. Baltimore, MD: Johns Hopkins University Press, 2003.

Berlin, Isaiah. *Vico and Herder: Two Studies in the History of Ideas*. London: Hogarth, 1976.

Bernstein, Richard. *The Abuse of Evil*. Cambridge: Polity Press, 2005.

Best, Geoffrey. *Honour Among Men and Nations: Transformations of an Idea*. Toronto: University of Toronto Press, 1982.

—— (ed.). *The Permanent Revolution: The French Revolution and Its Legacy, 1789–1989*. Chicago, IL: University of Chicago Press, 1988.

Bhabha, Homi (ed.). *Nation and Narration*. London: Routledge, 1990.

Billig, Michael. *Banal Nationalism*. London: Sage, 1995.

Birch, Anthony H. *Nationalism and National Integration*. London: Unwin Hyman, 1989.

Blaut, James M. *The National Question: Decolonizing the Theory of Nationalism*. Atlantic Highlands, NJ: Zed Books, 1987.

Bloom, William. *Personal Identity, National Identity and International Relations*. Cambridge: Cambridge University Press, 1990.

Bohman, James and Matthias Lutz-Bachmann. *Perpetual Peace: Essays on Kant's Cosmopolitan Ideal*. Cambridge, MA: MIT Press, 1997.

Bourdieu, Pierre. *Outline of a Theory of Practice*. Cambridge: Cambridge University Press, 1976.

——. *Algérie 60: Structures économiques et structures temporelles*. Paris: Minuit, 1977.

——. *The Logic of Practice*. Stanford, CA: Stanford University Press, 1990.

——. *The Field of Cultural Production*. New York: Columbia University Press, 1993.

——. *Masculine Domination*. Stanford, CA: Stanford University Press, 2001.

——. *Le bal des célibataires: Crise de la societé paysanne en Béarn*. Paris: Seuil, 2002.

——. "Unifying to Better Dominate," in *Firing Back: Against the Tyranny of the Market 2*, trans. Loïc Wacquant. New York: New Press, 2002.

Bourdieu, Pierre and Abdelmalek Sayad. *Le Déracinement: La Crise d'agriculture traditionelle en Algérie*. Paris: Minuit, 1964.

Bowen, John. *Modernizing Muslims through Discourse*. Princeton, NJ: Princeton University Press, 1993.

Brass, Paul R. *Ethnicity and Nationalism: Theory and Comparison*. New Delhi and Newbury Park, CA: Sage, 1991.

Brennan, Timothy. *At Home in the World: Cosmopolitanism Now*. Cambridge, MA: Harvard University Press, 1997.

Breuilly, John. *Nationalism and the State*, revised edition. Chicago, IL: University of Chicago Press, 1993 (orig. 1982).

Brown, Seyom. *The Illusion of Control: Force and Foreign Policy in the Twenty-First Century*. Washington, DC: Brookings Institution Press, 2003.

Brubaker, Rogers. *Citizenship and Nationhood in France and Germany*. Cambridge, MA: Harvard University Press, 1992.

——. *Nationalism Reframed*. Cambridge, MA: Harvard University Press, 1996.

——. "Ethnicity without Groups," *Archives européènes de sociologie* 63, no. 2 (2002): 163–89.

——. "Neither Individualism nor 'Groupism': A Reply to Craig Calhoun," *Ethnicities* 3 (2003): 554–7.

Brubaker, Rogers and Frederick Cooper. "Beyond 'Identity'," *Theory and Society* 29 (2000): 1–47.

Buchanan, Allen. "Rawls' Law of Peoples: Rules for a Vanished Westphalian World," *Ethics* 110, no. 4 (2000): 697–721.

Calhoun, Craig. "The Authority of Ancestors: A Sociological Reconsideration of Fortes's Tallensi In Response to Fortes's Critics," *Journal of the Royal Anthropological Institute*, New Ser. 15, no. 2 (1980): 304–19.

——. "Community: Toward a Variable Conceptualization for Comparative Research," *Social History* 5, no. 1 (1980): 105–29.

——. "Democracy, Autocracy and Intermediate Associations in Organizations: Flexibility or Unrestrained Change?" *Sociology* 4, no. 3 (1980): 345–61.

——. "The Radicalism of Tradition: Community Strength or Venerable Disguise and Borrowed Language?" *American Journal of Sociology* 88, no. 5 (1983): 886–914.

——. "Populist Politics, Communications Media, and Large Scale Social Integration," *Sociological Theory* 6, no. 2 (1988): 219–41.

——. "Culture, History and the Problem of Specificity in Social Theory," in *Postmodernism and General Social Theory*, edited by S. Seidman and D. Wagner. New York: Blackwell, 1991.

——. "Imagined Communities and Indirect Relationships: Large-Scale Social Integration and the Transformation of Everyday Life," in *Social Theory for a Changing Society*, edited by Pierre Bourdieu and James S. Coleman. Boulder, CO: Westview; New York: Russell Sage Foundation, 1991.

——. (ed.). *Habermas and the Public Sphere*. Cambridge, MA: MIT Press, 1992.

——. "The Infrastructure of Modernity: Indirect Relationships, Information Technology, and Social Integration," in *Social Change and Modernity*, edited by Hans Haferkamp and Neil J. Smelser. Berkeley: University of California Press, 1992.

——. "Civil Society and the Public Sphere," *Public Culture* 5, no. 2 (1993): 267–80.

——. *Critical Social Theory: Culture, History, and the Challenge of Difference*. Cambridge, MA: Blackwell, 1995.

——. "Postmodernism as Pseudohistory," in *Critical Social Theory: Culture,*

History, and the Challenge of Difference. Cambridge, MA: Blackwell, 1995.

——. *Nationalism*. Minneapolis: University of Minnesota Press, 1997.

——. "Nationalism and the Public Sphere," in *Public and Private in Thought and Practice*, edited by Jeff Weintraub and Krishan Kumar. Chicago, IL: University of Chicago Press, 1997.

——. "The Public Good as a Social and Cultural Project," in *Private Action and the Public Good*, edited by Walter W. Powell and Elisabeth S. Clemens. New Haven, CT: Yale University Press, 1998.

——. "Constitutional Patriotism and the Public Sphere: Interests, Identity, and Solidarity in the Integration of Europe," in *Global Justice and Transnational Politics: Essays on the Moral and Political Challenges of Globalization*, edited by Pablo De Greiff and Ciaran Cronin. Cambridge, MA: MIT Press, 2002.

——. "Imagining Solidarity: Cosmopolitanism, Constitutional Patriotism and the Public Sphere," *Public Culture* 14, no. 1 (2002): 147–72.

——. "Belonging in the Cosmopolitan Imaginary," *Ethnicities* 3, no. 4 (2003): 531–53.

——. "The Class Consciousness of Frequent Travelers: Toward a Critique of Actually Existing Cosmopolitanism," *South Atlantic Quarterly*, 101, no. 4 (2003): 869–97.

——. "The Democratic Integration of Europe: Interests, Identity, and the Public Sphere," in *Europe without Borders: Re-Mapping Territory, Citizenship and Identity in a Transnational Age*, edited by Mabel Berezin and Martin Schain. Baltimore, MD: Johns Hopkins University Press, 2003.

——. "Variability of Belonging: A Reply to Rogers Brubaker," *Ethnicities* 3 (2003): 558–68.

——. "A World of Emergencies: Fear, Intervention, and the Limits of Cosmopolitan Order," the 2004 Sorokin Lecture, *Canadian Review of Sociology and Anthropology*, 41, no. 4 (2004): 373–95.

——. *Cosmopolitanism and Belonging*. London: Routledge, forthcoming.

——. *The Roots of Radicalism*. Chicago, IL: University of Chicago Press, forthcoming.

Calhoun, Craig and Dale Whittington. "Who Really Wants Donor Coordination? Reflections on the Development of a Microcomputer-Based Development Project Directory in the Sudan," *Development Policy Review* 6, no. 3 (1988): 295–309.

Calhoun, Craig, Frederick Cooper, and Kevin Moore (eds.). *Lessons of Empire*. New York: New Press, 2006.

Carr, E.H. *Nationalism and After*. London: Macmillan, 1945.

Chatterjee, Partha. *Nationalist Thought and the Colonial World: A Derivative Discourse?* London: Zed Books, 1986 (revised edition, Minneapolis: University of Minnesota Press, 1993).

——. *The Nation and Its Fragments: Studies in Colonial and Post-Colonial Histories*. Princeton, NJ: Princeton University Press, 1993.

Cheah, Pheng and Bruce Robbins (eds.). *Cosmopolitics: Thinking and*

Feeling Beyond the Nation. Minneapolis: University of Minnesota Press, 1998.

Chirot, Daniel (ed.). *The Crisis of Leninism and the Decline of the Left: The Revolutions of 1989*. Seattle: University of Washington Press, 1991.

Chow, Tse-Tsung. *The May 4th Movement: Intellectual Revolution in Modern China*. Cambridge, MA: Harvard University Press, 1960.

Clifford, James. "Traveling Cultures," in *Cultural Studies*, edited by Lawrence Grossberg, Cary Nelson, and Paula Treichler. New York: Routledge, 1992.

Coetzee, Marilyn Shevin. *The German Army League: Popular Nationalism in Wilhelmine Germany*. New York: Oxford University Press, 1990.

Cohen, Jean and Andrew Arato. *Civil Society and Political Theory*. Cambridge, MA: MIT Press, 1992.

Cohler, Anne M. *Rousseau and Nationalism*. New York: Basic Books, 1970.

Cole, Juan. "Three Episodes in the Rhetoric of Liberal Imperialism: French Egypt, British Egypt, American Iraq," in *Lessons of Empire*, edited by Craig Calhoun, Frederick Cooper, and Kevin Moore. New York: New Press, 2006.

Collins, Randall. "A Sociological Guilt Trip," *American Journal of Sociology* 102, no. 6 (1997): 1558–64.

Connell, Robert. "Why Is Classical Theory Classical?" *American Journal of Sociology* 102, no. 6 (1997): 1511–57.

Connor, Walker. "A nation is a nation, is a state, is an ethnic group, is a . . .," *Ethnic Racial Studies* 1 (1978): 377–400.

——. *The National Question in Marxist-Leninist Theory and Strategy*. Princeton, NJ: Princeton University Press, 1984.

——. *Ethnonationalism*. Princeton, NJ: Princeton University Press, 1994.

Cooper, Frederick. "Modernizing Colonialism and the Limits of Empire," *Items and Issues* 4, no. 4 (2003): 1–3.

Cooper, Frederick and Ann Laura Stoler (eds.). *Tensions of Empire: Colonial Cultures in a Bourgeois World*. Berkeley: University of California Press, 1997.

Davidson, Basil. *Black Man's Burden: Africa and the Curse of the Nation-State*. New York: Times Books, 1992.

Debray, Régis. "Marxism and the National Question," *New Left Review* 105 (1977): 20–41.

Deutsch, Karl W. *Nationalism and Social Communication: An Inquiry into the Foundations of Nationality*, second edition. Cambridge, MA: MIT Press, 1966.

——. *Nationalism and Its Alternatives*. New York: Knopf, 1969.

——. *Nationalism and National Development: An Interdisciplinary Bibliography*. Cambridge, MA: MIT Press, 1970.

Diawara, Manthia (ed.). "The Black Public Sphere," special issue of *Public Culture* 7, no. 1 (1994).

Dikötter, Frank. *The Discourse of Race in Modern China*. Stanford, CA: Stanford University Press, 1992.

DiMaggio, Paul J. and W.W. Powell. "The Iron Cage Revisited: Institutional Isomorphism and Collective Rationality in Organizational Fields," *American Sociological Review* 48 (1983): 147–60.

Diquinsio, Patrice and Iris Marion Young (eds.). *Feminist Ethics and Social Policy*. Bloomington: Indiana University Press, 1997.

Dolnick, Edward. "Deafness as Culture," *Atlantic Monthly* 272, no. 3 (1993): 37–53.

Doyle, Don and Marco Pamplona. *Nationalism in the New World*. Athens, GA: University Press of Georgia, 2006.

Du Bois, W.E.B. *The Souls of Black Folk*. New York: Bantam, 1989 (orig. 1903).

Duffield, Mark R. *Global Governance and the New Wars*. New York: Zed Books, 2001.

Dumont, Louis. *Homo Hierarchicus*. Chicago, IL: University of Chicago Press, 1966.

——. *Essays on Individualism*. Chicago, IL: University of Chicago Press, 1982.

Durkheim, Emile. *The Division of Labor in Society*. New York: Free Press, 1893 (second edition 1933).

Eisenstadt, Shmuel. *Modernization, Protest and Change*. Englewood Cliffs, NJ: Prentice-Hall, 1966.

——. *Building States and Nations*. Beverly Hills, CA: Sage, 1973.

Ekeh, Peter P. "Social Anthropology and Two Contrasting Uses of Tribalism in Africa," *Comparative Studies in Society and History* 32, no. 4 (1990): 660–700.

Eley, Geoff. *Reshaping the German Right: Radical Nationalism and Political Change after Bismarck*. Oxford: Oxford University Press, 1980.

——. "Nations, Publics and Political Cultures: Placing Habermas in the Nineteenth Century," in *Habermas and the Public Sphere*, edited by Craig Calhoun. Cambridge, MA: MIT Press, 1992.

Elshtain, Jean Bethke. *Democracy on Trial*. New York: Basic Books, 1997.

Etzioni, Amitai (ed.). *New Communitarian Thinking*. Charlottesville: The University Press of Virginia, 1995.

——. *The New Golden Rule: Community and Morality in a Democratic Society*. New York: Basic Books, 1996.

Evans-Pritchard, E.E. *The Nuer*. Oxford: Oxford University Press, 1940.

Farah, Tawfic E. (ed.). *Pan-Arabism and Arab Nationalism: The Continuing Debate*. Boulder, CO: Westview Press, 1987.

Faris, Hani A. "Israel Zangwill's Challenge to Zionism," *Journal of Palestine Studies* 4, no. 3 (1975): 74–90.

Fenwick, Rudy "Social Change and Ethnic Nationalism: An Historical Analysis of the Separatist Movement in Quebec," *Comparative Studies in Society and History* 23 (1981): 193–216.

Ferguson, Niall. *Empire: The Rise and Fall of the British World Order and the Lessons for Global Power*. New York: Basic Books, 2003.

Fichte, Johann Gottlieb. *Addresses to the German Nation*. New York: Harper and Row, 1968 (orig. 1807).

Finnemore, Martha. *The Purpose of Intervention: Changing Beliefs of the Use of Force*. Ithaca, NY: Cornell University Press, 2003.

Fischer, Michael M.J. and Mehdi Abedi. *Debating Muslims: Cultural Dialogs in Postmodernity and Tradition*. Madison: University of Wisconsin Press, 1990.

Flint, Julie and Alex DeWaal. *Darfur: A Short History of a Long War*. London: Zed Books, 2005.

Foreman, Shepard and Stewart Patrick (eds.). *Good Intentions: Pledges of Aid for Postconflict Recovery*. Boulder, CO: Lynne Rienner, 2000.

Fortes, Meyer. *The Web of Kinship among the Tallensi of Northern Ghana*. Oxford: Oxford University Press, 1945.

——. *The Dynamics of Clanship among the Tallensi of Northern Ghana*. Oxford: Oxford University Press, 1949.

Foucault, Michel. *The Archaeology of Knowledge*. New York: Pantheon, 1969.

——. *The Order of Things: An Archaeology of the Human Sciences*. New York: Pantheon, 1971.

——. *Discipline and Punish*. New York: Pantheon, 1977.

——. *Power/Knowledge: Selected Interviews and Other Writings, 1972–1977*. New York: Pantheon, 1977.

Fraser, Nancy. "What's Critical about Critical Theory," *Unruly Practices*. Minneapolis: University of Minnesota Press, 1989.

Freitag, Sandria B. *Collective Action and Community: Public Arenas and the Emergence of Communalism in North India*. Berkeley: University of California Press, 1989.

Frisby, David. *Fragments of Modernity*. Cambridge, MA: Blackwell, 1985.

Fuss, Diana. *Essentially Speaking: Feminism, Nature and Difference*. Oxford: Blackwell, 1989.

Gadamer, Hans-Georg. *Truth and Method*. New York: Seabury, 1975.

——. *Philosophical Hermeneutics*. Berkeley: University of California Press, 1977.

Gandhi, M.K. *Political and National Life and Affairs*. Ahmedabad: Navajivan, 1967.

——. "Hind Swaraj," in *The Moral and Political Writings of Mahatma Gandhi*, edited by R. Iyer. Oxford: Clarendon, 1996 (orig. 1939).

Gaonkar, Dilip (ed.). "Alternative Modernities," special issue of *Public Culture* 11, no. 1 (1999).

Garfinkel, Harold. *Studies in Ethnomethodology*. Englewood Cliffs, NJ: Prentice-Hall, 1967.

Geary, Patrick J. *The Myth of Nations: The Medieval Origins of Europe*. Princeton, NJ: Princeton University Press, 2002.

Geertz, Clifford. *Old Societies and New States: The Quest for Modernity in Asia and Africa*. New York: Free Press of Glencoe; London: Collier-Macmillan, 1963.

Gellner, Ernest. *Thought and Change*. London: Weidenfeld and Nicholson, 1964.

——. *Nations and Nationalism*. Oxford: Blackwell, 1983.

——. *Nationalism*. New York: New York University Press, 1997.

Giddens, Anthony. *The Nation-State and Violence*. Berkeley: University of California Press, 1984.

——. *Consequences of Modernity*. Stanford, CA: Stanford University Press, 1990.

Gilroy, Paul. *The Black Atlantic: Modernity and Double Consciousness*. Cambridge, MA: Harvard University Press, 1993.

Gitlin, Todd. *The Twilight of Common Dreams*. New York: Holt, 1995.

Gole, Nilufer. *The Forbidden Modern: Civilization and Veiling*. Ann Arbor: University of Michigan Press, 1996.

——. "Studying Islam as a Contemporary Social Movement," paper presented to the conference on The Sociology of Islamic Social Movements, New York University, 19–20 February, 2000.

Gourevitch, Philip. *We Wish to Inform You that Tomorrow We Will Be Killed with our Families: Stories on Rwanda*. London: Picador, 1999.

Granovetter, Mark. "The Strength of Weak Ties," *American Journal of Sociology* 78 (1973): 1360–80.

Greenfeld, Liah. "The Formation of the Russian National Identity: The Role of Status Insecurity and *Ressentiment*," *Comparative Studies in Society and History* 32, no. 3 (1990): 549–91.

——. "The Emergence of Nationalism in England and France," *Research in Political Sociology* 5 (1991): 333–70.

——. *Nationalism: Five Roads to Modernity*. Cambridge, MA: Harvard University Press, 1992.

Gutmann, Amy (ed.). *Multiculturalism: Examining the Politics of Recognition*, revised edition. Princeton, NJ: Princeton University Press, 1995.

Haas, Ernst B. *Beyond the Nation-State: Functionalism and International Organization*. Stanford, CA: Stanford University Press, 1964.

——. "What Is Nationalism and Why Should We Study It?" *International Organization* 40, no. 3 (1986): 707–44.

Habermas, Jürgen. *Theory of Communicative Action*. Boston, MA: Beacon Press, 1984.

——. *The Structural Transformation of the Public Sphere*. Cambridge, MA: MIT Press, 1989.

——. "Citizenship and National Identity: Some Reflections on the Future of Europe," *Praxis International* 12, no. 1 (1992): 1–19.

——. "Struggles for Recognition in the Democratic Constitutional State," in *Multiculturalism: Examining the Politics of Recognition*, revised edition, edited by Amy Gutmann. Princeton, NJ: Princeton University Press, 1994.

——. *Between Facts and Norms*. Cambridge, MA: MIT Press, 1996.

——. *The Inclusion of the Other: Studies in Political Theory*. Cambridge, MA: MIT Press, 1998.

——. *The Post-national Constellation: Political Essays*. Cambridge, MA: MIT Press, 2001.

——. "The European Nation-State and the Pressures of Globalization," in *Global Justice and Transnational Politics*, edited by P. De Greiff and C. Cronin. Cambridge, MA: MIT Press, 2002.

Hall, John. "Nationalisms, Classified and Explained," in *Notions of Nationalism*, edited by S. Periwal. Budapest: Central European University Press, 1995.

Halle, Louis Joseph. *Men and Nations*. Princeton, NJ: Princeton University Press, 1962.

Hannaford, Ivan. *Race: The History of an Idea in the West*. Baltimore, MD: Johns Hopkins University Press and the Woodrow Wilson Center Press, 1996.

Hannerz, Ulf. "The World in Creolisation," *Africa* 57 (1988): 546–59.

———. *Cultural Complexity: Studies in the Social Organization of Meaning*. New York: Columbia University Press, 1992.

Hardt, M. and A. Negri. *Empire*. Cambridge, MA: Harvard University Press, 2001.

———. *Multitude*. New York: Penguin, 2004.

Harris, Nigel. *National Liberation*. London: Penguin, 1990.

Harvey, David. *The Postmodern Condition*. Oxford: Blackwell, 1990.

Hayes, Carlton J.H. *The Historical Evolution of Modern Nationalism*. New York: R.R. Smith, 1931.

———. *Nationalism: A Religion*. New York: Macmillan, 1960.

———. *Essays on Nationalism*. New York: Russell & Russell, 1966 (orig. 1926).

Hechter, Michael. *Internal Colonialism: The Celtic Fringe in British National Development, 1536–1966*. Berkeley: University of California Press, 1975.

———. "Nationalism as Group Solidarity," *Ethnic Racial Studies* 10, no. 4 (1987): 415–26.

———. *Containing Nationalism*. New York: Oxford University Press, 2000.

Hechter, Michael and Celso Furtado, Jr. "The Emergence of Nationalist Politics in the USSR: A Comparison of Estonia and the Ukraine," in *Thinking Theoretically about Soviet Nationalities: Theory, History, and Comparison in the Study of the USSR*, edited by Alexander J. Motyl. New York: Columbia University Press, 1992.

Held, David. *Democracy and the Global Order: From the Modern State to Cosmopolitan Governance*. Cambridge: Polity Press, 1995.

———. "Democracy and Globalization," in *Re-imagining Political Community: Studies in Cosmopolitan Democracy*, edited by Daniele Archibugi, David Held, and Martin Köhler. Stanford, CA: Stanford University Press, 1998.

———. *Global Covenant: The Social Democratic Alternative to the Washington Consensus*. Cambridge: Polity Press, 2004.

Helton, Arthur C. *The Price of Indifference*. Oxford: Oxford University Press, 2002.

———. "Rescuing the Refugees," *Foreign Affairs* 81, no. 2 (2002): 71–82.

Herf, Jeffrey. *Reactionary Modernism: Technology, Culture, and Politics in Weimar and the Third Reich*. New York: Cambridge University Press, 1984.

Hertz, Frederick. "The Nature of Nationalism," *Social Forces* 19, no. 3 (1941): 409–15.

Hobsbawm, Eric. *Nations and Nationalism Since 1780: Programme, Myth, Reality*. Cambridge: Cambridge University Press, 1990.

Hobsbawm, Eric and Terence Ranger. *The Invention of Tradition*. Cambridge: Cambridge University Press, 1983.

Hoffman, Ross. "Review of *World Order in Historical Perspective*," *Journal of Modern History* 15, no. 2 (1943): 155–6.

Horowitz, Donald L. *Ethnic Groups in Conflict*. Berkeley: University of California Press, 1985.

Hroch, Miroslav. *Social Preconditions of National Revival in Europe*. Cambridge: Cambridge University Press, 1985.

Hughes, H. Stuart. *Consciousness and Society*. New York: Random House, 1961.

Hunt, Lynn. *The Family Romance of the French Revolution*. Berkeley: University of California Press, 1993.

Huntington, Samuel. *The Clash of Civilizations and the Remaking of the World Order*. New York: Simon and Schuster, 1996.

Hutcheson, John. *The Dynamics of Cultural Nationalism*, revised edition London: HarperCollins, 1994.

Hutchinson, Sharon. *Nuer Dilemmas: Coping with Money, War, and the State*. Berkeley: University of California Press, 1995.

Ignatieff, Michael. *The Lesser Evil: Political Ethics in an Age of Terror*. Princeton, NJ: Princeton University Press, 2004.

International Federation of Red Cross and Red Crescent Societies. *World Disasters Report*. Bloom field, CT: Kumarian Press, 2001.

Ishay, Micheline. *Internationalism and Its Betrayal*. Minneapolis: University of Minnesota Press, 1995.

Joas, Hans. *War and Modernity*. Cambridge, MA: Blackwell, 2002.

Kalipeni, Ezekiel, Susan Craddock, Joseph R. Oppong, and Jayati Ghosh, *HIV/AIDS in Africa*. Oxford: Blackwell, 2004.

Kant, Immanuel. "Perpetual Peace: A Philosophical Sketch," in *Kant's Political Writings*, edited by H. Reiss. Cambridge: Cambridge University Press, 1970.

Kapferer, Bruce. *Legends of People, Myths of State: Violence, Intolerance, and Political Culture in Sri Lanka and Australia*. Washington, DC: Smithsonian Institution, 1988.

Keane, John. *Democracy and Civil Society*. London: Verso, 1988.

Kedouri, Elie. *Nationalism*, fourth edition. Oxford: Blackwell, 1993 (orig. 1960).

——. *Nationalism in Asia and Africa*. New York: New American Library, 1974.

Kellas, James G. *The Politics of Nationalism and Ethnicity*. London: Macmillan, 1991.

Kemiläinen, Aira. *Nationalism: Problems Concerning the Word, the Concept, and Classification*. Jyväskylä: Jyväskylän Yliopistoyhdistys, 1964.

Kennedy, David. *The Dark Sides of Virtue: Reassessing International Humanitarianism*. Princeton, NJ: Princeton University Press, 2004.

Kennedy, Paul. *The Rise and Fall of the Great Powers*. New York: Vintage Books, 1989.

Khalidi, Rashid, Lisa Anderson, Muhammad Muslih, and Reva S. Simon (eds.). *The Origins of Arab Nationalism*. New York: Columbia University Press, 1991.

Kligman, Gail. *The Wedding of the Dead*. Chicago, IL: University of Chicago Press, 1984.

Klugman, Jeni. *Social and Economic Policies to Prevent Complex Humanitarian Emergencies: Lessons from Experience*. Helsinki: United Nations University, World Institute for Development Economics Research, 1999.

Köhler, Martin. "From the National to the Cosmopolitan Public Sphere," in *Re-Imagining Political Community: Studies in Cosmopolitan Democracy*, edited by Daniele Archibugi, David Held, and Martin Köhler. Stanford, CA: Stanford University Press, 1998.

Kohn, Hans. *A History of Nationalism in the East*. New York: Harcourt Brace, 1929.

——. *Nationalism and Imperialism in the Hither East*. New York: Harcourt, Brace, 1932.

——. *Force or Reason*. Cambridge, MA: Harvard University Press, 1937.

——. *Revolutions and Dictatorships*. Cambridge, MA: Harvard University Press, 1939.

——. *Not By Arms Alone: Essays on Our Time*. Cambridge, MA: Harvard University Press, 1940.

——. *World Order in Historical Perspective*. Cambridge, MA: Harvard University Press, 1942.

——. *The Idea of Nationalism*. New York: Macmillan, 1944.

——. "The Paradox of Fichte's Nationalism," *Journal of the History of Ideas* 10, no. 3 (1949): 319–43.

——. "Napoleon and the Age of Nationalism," *Journal of Modern History* 22, no. 1 (1950): 21–37.

——. "The Eve of German Nationalism," *Journal of the History of Ideas* 12, no. 2 (1951): 6–84.

——. *American Nationalism: An Interpretative Essay*. New York: Macmillan, 1957.

——. *The Mind of Germany: The Education of a Nation*. New York: Scribner's, 1960.

——. *Prelude to Nation-States: The French and German Experience, 1789–1815*. Princeton, NJ: Van Nostrand, 1967.

——. *The Age of Nationalism*. New York: Harper and Row, 1968 (orig. 1962).

Koht, Halvdan. "Review of *The Idea of Nationalism*," *American Historical Review* 50, no. 1 (1944): 93–6.

Koselleck, Reinhart. *The Practice of Conceptual History*. Stanford, CA: Stanford University Press, 2002.

Kuperman, Alan. *The Limits of Intervention: Genocide in Rwanda*. Washington, DC: Brookings Institution Press, 2001.

Kymlicka, Will. *Multicultural Citizenship: A Liberal Theory of Minority Rights*. Oxford: Clarendon Press; New York: Oxford University Press, 1995.

——. "Human Rights and Ethnocultural Justice," *Review of Constitutional Studies* 4, No. 2 (1998): 213–38.

——. *Politics in the Vernacular*. Oxford: Oxford University Press, 2001.

Leach, Edmund Ronald. *Political Systems of Highland Burma*. Boston, MA: Beacon, 1954.

Létourneau, Jocelyn. "La saga du Québec moderne en images," *Génèses* 4 (1991): 44–71.

Levy, Daniel, Max Pensky, and John Torpey (eds.). *Old Europe, New Europe, Core Europe: Transatlantic Relations after the Iraq War*. London, New York: Verso, 2005.

Lewis, I.M. (ed.). *Nationalism and Self-Determination in the Horn of Africa*. London: Ithaca, 1983.

Linklater, Andrew. "Citizenship and Sovereignty in the Post-Westphalian European State," in *Re-Imagining Political Community: Studies in Cosmopolitan Democracy*, edited by Daniele Archibugi, David Held, and Martin Köhler. Stanford, CA: Stanford University Press, 1998.

Lipset, Seymour Martin. *The First New Nation*. New York: Doubleday, 1960.

Little, J.I. *Nationalism, Capitalism and Colonization in Nineteenth-Century Quebec: The Upper St. Francis District*. Kingston, Ontario: McGill/Queen's University Press, 1989.

Lovejoy, Arthur. *The Great Chain of Being*. Cambridge, MA: Harvard University Press, 1936.

Lyotard, Jean-François. *The Postmodern Condition: A Report on Knowledge*, trans. Geoff Bennington and Brian Massumi. Minneapolis: University of Minnesota Press, 1984.

McCarthy, Thomas "Reconciling Cosmopolitan Unity and National Diversity," in *Global Justice and Transnational Politics*, edited by P. De Greiff and C. Cronin. Cambridge, MA: MIT Press, 2002.

Maier, Charles S. *The Unmasterable Past: History, Holocaust, and German National Identity*. Cambridge, MA: Harvard University Press, 1987.

Mallaby, Sebastian. "The Reluctant Imperialist: Terrorism, Failed States, and the Case for American Empire," *Foreign Affairs* 81, no. 2 (2002): 2–7.

Mandelbaum, Maurice. *History, Man, and Reason: A Study in Nineteenth-Century Thought*. Baltimore, MD: Johns Hopkins University Press, 1971.

Mann, Michael. *The Sources of Social Power*, vol. 1, *A History of Power from the Beginning to AD 1760*. Cambridge: Cambridge University Press, 1986.

——. *The Sources of Social Power*, vol. 2, *The Rise of Classes and Nation-States, 1760–1914*. Cambridge: Cambridge University Press, 1993.

Marcu, E.D. *Sixteenth Century Nationalism*. Pleasantville, NY: Abaris, 1976.

Markakis, John. *National and Class Conflict in the Horn of Africa*. London: Zed Books, 1987.

Martin, Randolph. "Sudan's Perfect War," *Foreign Affairs* 81, no. 2 (2002): 111–27.

Martin, Rex and David Reidy (eds.). *Rawls's Law of Peoples: A Realistic Utopia?* Oxford: Blackwell, 2006.

Mayall, James. *Nationalism and International Society*. New York: Cambridge University Press, 1990.

Mazrui, Ali A. and Michael Tidy. *Nationalism and New States in Africa from about 1935 to the Present*. Nairobi: Heinemann, 1984.

Meinecke, Friedrich. *Cosmopolitanism and the National State*, trans. R.B. Kilmer. Princeton, NJ: Princeton University Press, 1970.

Melvern, Linda. *A People Betrayed: The Role of the West in Rwanda's Genocide*. New York: Zed Books, 2000.

Merton, Robert K. "The Normative Structure of Science," in *The Sociology of Science*. Chicago, IL: University of Chicago Press, 1973.

——. "The Thomas Theorem and the Matthew Effect," *Social Forces* 74, no. 2 (1995): 379–424.

Meyer, John W. and Brian Rowan. "Institutionalized Organizations: Formal Structure as Myth and Ceremony." *American Journal of Sociology*, 83 (1977): 340–63.

Meyers, Marvin. "Review of Hans Kohn, *American Nationalism: An Interpretative Essay*," *Political Science Quarterly* 72, no. 4 (1957): 628–30.

Michnik, Adam. "Poland and the Jews," *New York Review of Books*, May 30, 1991, pp. 11–12.

Mommsen, Wolfgang. *Max Weber and German Politics, 1890–1920*, revised edition. Chicago, IL: University of Chicago Press, 1984.

Moore, S.F. "Legal Liability and Evolutionary Interpretation: Some Aspects of Strict Liability, Self-Help and Collective Responsibility," in *The Allocation of Responsibility*, edited by M. Gluckman. Manchester: Manchester University Press, 1972.

Morrison, Scott and Ken Warn. "Liberals strive to sharpen competitive edge," *Financial Times*, June 11, 2001, "Canada Survey," pp. 1–2.

Moses, Wilson. *The Golden Age of Black Nationalism, 1850–1925*. New York, Oxford: Oxford University Press, 1988.

Mosse, George L. *Nationalization of the Masses: Political Symbolism and Mass Movements in Germany from the Napoleonic Wars through the Third Reich*. New York: H. Fertig, 1975.

——. *Nationalism and Sexuality: Middle-class Morality and Sexual Norms in Modern Europe*. Madison: University of Wisconsin Press, 1985.

Motyl, Alexander J. "The Modernity of Nationalism: Nations, States and Nation-States in the Contemporary World," *Journal of International Affairs* 45 (1992): 307–23.

—— (ed.). *Thinking Theoretically about Soviet Nationalities: Theory, History, and Comparison in the Study of the USSR*. New York: Columbia University Press, 1992.

Mouffe, Chantal (ed.). *Dimensions of Radical Democracy*. London: Verso, 1992.

Müller, Jan-Werner. "On the Origins of Constitutional Patriotism," *Contemporary Political Theory*, 5 (2006): 278–96.

Nadel, S.F. *The Foundations of Social Anthropology*. London: Cohen and West, 1951.

——. *The Theory of Social Structure*. London: Cohen and West, 1965.

Nairn, Tom. "The Modern Janus," *New Left Review* 94 (1975): 3–30.

——. *The Break-up of Britain: Crises and Neo-Nationalism*. London: New Left Books, 1977.

——. *Faces of Nationalism: Janus Revisited*. London: Verso, 1997.

Negt, Oscar and Alexander Kluge. *The Public Sphere and Experience*. Minneapolis: University of Minnesota Press, 1994.

Nehru, Jawaharlal. *The Discovery of India*. Oxford: Oxford University Press, 1949.

Nenarokov, Albert and Alexander Proskurin. *How the Soviet Union Solved the Nationalities Question*. Moscow: Novosti Press Agency Publishing House, 1983.

Noiriel, Gérard. "Le question national comme objet de l'histoire sociale," *Génèses* 4 (1991): 72–94.

——. *La Tyrannie du National*. Paris: Calmann-Lévy, 1991.

——. *The French Melting Pot*. Minneapolis: University of Minnesota Press, 1998 (orig. *Le Creuset Français* [Paris: Seuil, 1988]).

Nussbaum, Martha. *For Love of Country*. Boston, MA: Beacon, 1996.

——. *Cultivating Humanity*. Cambridge, MA: Harvard University Press, 1997.

——. *Upheavals of Thought: The Intelligence of Emotions*. Cambridge, New York: Cambridge University Press, 2001.

Nzongola-Ntalaja, Georges. "The National Question and the Crisis of Instability in Africa," in *Africa: Perspectives on Peace and Development*, edited by E. Hansen. Atlantic Highlands, NJ: Zed Books, 1987.

O'Brien, Conor Cruise. "Nationalism and the French Revolution," in *The Permanent Revolution: The French Revolution and Its Legacy, 1789–1989*, edited by Geoffrey Best. Chicago, IL: University of Chicago Press, 1988.

Okamura, Jonathan "The Illusion of Paradise: Privileging Multiculturalism in Hawai'i," in *Making Majorities: Constituting the Nation in Japan, Korea, China, Malaysia, Fiji, Turkey, and the United States*, edited by Dru C. Gladney. Stanford, CA: Stanford University Press, 1998.

Orwell, George (ed.). *Taking to India*. London: Allen and Unwin, 1943.

Palme, Goran. *The Flight from Work*. New York: Free Press, 1982.

Palmer, R.R. "The National Idea in France before the Revolution," *Journal of the History of Ideas* 1, no. 1 (1940): 95–111.

Parker, Andrew, Mary Russo, Doris Sommer, and Patricia Yaeger (eds.). *Nationalisms and Sexualities*. New York: Routledge, 1992.

Parsons, Talcott. *The Structure of Social Action*. Glencoe, IL: Free Press, 1936.

——. *Structure and Process in Modern Societies*. Glencoe, IL: Free Press, 1960.

Patterson, Orlando. "Ecumenical America: Global Culture and the American Cosmos," *World Policy Journal* 11, no. 2 (1994): 103–17.

Perrow, Charles. *Normal Accidents*, revised edition. Princeton, NJ: Princeton University Press, 1999.

Peters, F.E. *The Harvest of Hellenism*. New York: Simon and Schuster, 1970.

Poggi, Gianfranco. *The State: Its Nature, Development and Prospects*. Stanford, CA: Stanford University Press, 1992.

Pollock, Sheldon. "Cosmopolitan and Vernacular in History," *Public Culture* 12, no. 3 (2000): 591–626.

Pollock, Sheldon, Homi Bhabha, Carol Breckenridge, and Dipesh Chakrabharty. "Cosmopolitanisms," *Public Culture* 12, no. 3 (2000).

Postone, Moishe. *Time, Labor, and Social Domination: A Reinterpretation of Marx's Critical Theory*. New York: Cambridge University Press, 1993.

Powell, Walter and Paul DiMaggio (eds.). *The New Institutionalism in Organizational Analysis*. Chicago, IL: University of Chicago Press, 1991.

Power, Samantha. *A Problem from Hell: America in the Age of Genocide*. New York: Basic Books, 2002.

Prunier, Gerard. *Darfur: The Ambiguous Genocide*. Ithaca, NY: Cornell University Press, 2005.

Rawls, John. *A Theory of Justice*. Cambridge, MA: Harvard University Press, 1971.

——. *Political Liberalism*. New York: Columbia University Press, 1993.

——. *The Law of Peoples*. Cambridge, MA: Harvard University Press, 1999.

Relief Web. *Relief Web: United Nations Appeals*. http://www.reliefweb.int/appeals/01appeals.html (2001); accessed 26 March 2004.

——. *Relief Web: Complex Emergencies*. http://www.ReliefWeb.int/w/rwb.nsf/WCE?OpenForm (2004); accessed 26 March 2004.

Renan, Ernest. "What Is a Nation?" trans. M. Thom, in *Nation and Narration*, edited by Homi Bhabha. London: Routledge, 1990 (orig. 1882).

Rieff, David. *A Bed for the Night: Humanitarianism in Crisis*. New York: Simon and Schuster, 2003.

Robertson, Roland. *Globalization*. London: Sage, 1992.

Rokkan, Stein. "Dimensions of State Formation and Nation-Building: A Possible Paradigm for Research on Variations within Europe," in *The Formation of National States in Western Europe*, edited by Charles Tilly. Princeton, NJ: Princeton University Press, 1975.

Rousseau, Jean Jacques. "Considerations on the Government of Poland," in *Jean Jacques Rousseau: Political Writings*, translated and edited by Fredrick Watkins. Madison: University of Wisconsin Press, 1986.

Rushdie, Salman. "In Good Faith," in *Imaginary Homelands: Essays and Criticism 1981–1991*. London: Granta Books, 1991.

Ruskin, John. *Unto this Last and Other Writings*. London: Penguin, 1986.

Samuel, Raphael (ed.). *Patriotism: The Making and Unmaking of British National Identity*. 3 vols. London: Routledge, 1989.

Sandel, Michael. *Liberalism and the Limits of Justice*, second edition. Cambridge: Cambridge University Press, 1996.

Sassen, Saskia. *Guests and Aliens*. Chicago, IL: University of Chicago Press, 1999.

Savarkar, V.D. *Samagra Savarkar Wangmaya: Writings of Swatantrya Veer V.D. Savarkar*, vol. IV: *Hindu Rashtra Darshan*. Poona: Maharashtra Prantik Hindusabha, 1964 (orig. 1937).

Scheffler, Samuel. *Boundaries and Allegiances: Problems of Justice and Responsibility in Liberal Thought*. Oxford: Oxford University Press, 2001.

Schmitt, Carl. *The Concept of the Political*. Chicago, IL: University of Chicago Press, 1996.

Schwarcz, Vera. *The Chinese Enlightenment: Intellectuals and the Legacy of the May Fourth Movement of 1919*. Berkeley: University of California Press, 1986.

Schwarzmantel, John. *Socialism and the Idea of the Nation*. Hemel Hempstead: Harvester Wheatsheaf, 1991.

Selassie, Bereket H. *Conflict and Intervention in the Horn of Africa*. London: Gordon and Breech, 1980.

Seligman, Adam B. *The Idea of Civil Society*. New York: Free Press, 1992.

Selznick, Philip. *The Moral Commonwealth: Social Theory and the Promise of Community*. Berkeley: University of California Press, 1992.

Sennett, Richard. *The Uses of Disorder*. New York: Vintage, 1970.

——. *The Fall of Public Man*. New York: Knopf, 1977.

Seton-Watson, Hugh. *Nations and States*. Boulder, CO: Westview Press, 1977.

——. "Le Citoyen, La Citoyenne: Activity, Passivity and the French Revolutionary Concept of Citizenship," in *The French Revolution and the Creation of Modern Political Culture*, vol. 2, edited by Colin Lucas. Oxford: Pergamon Press, 1988.

——. *A Rhetoric of Bourgeois Revolution: The Abbé Sieyes and What Is the Third Estate?* Durham, NC: Duke University Press, 1994.

Sewell, William H., Jr. "Political Events as Structural Transformations: Inventing Revolution at the Bastille," *Theory and Society* 25 (1996): 841–81.

Sheehan, James J. *German Liberalism in the Nineteenth Century*. Chicago, IL: University of Chicago Press, 1978.

Shils, Edward. *Tradition*. Chicago, IL: University of Chicago Press, 1981.

Simmel, Georg. "The Metropolis and Mental Life," in *The Sociology of Georg Simmel*, edited and translated by K. Wolff. New York: Free Press, 1950.

Skurnowicz, Joan S. *Romantic Nationalism and Liberalism: Joachim Lelewel and the Polish National Idea*. Boulder, CO: East European Monographs; New York: Distributed by Columbia University Press, 1981.

Smelser, Neil J. *Essays in Sociological Explanation*. Englewood Cliffs, NJ: Prentice-Hall, 1968.

Smith, Anthony. "Nationalism," *Current Sociology* 21 (1973): 7–128.

——. *The Ethnic Revival in the Modern World*. Cambridge: Cambridge University Press, 1981.

——. *Theories of Nationalism*. London: Duckworth, 1983.

——. *The Ethnic Origins of Nations*. Oxford: Blackwell, 1986.

——. *National Identity*. London: Penguin, 1991.

——. *Nationalism and Modernism*. London: Routledge, 1998.

Smith, M.G. "On Segmentary Lineage Systems," in *Corporations and Society*. London: Duckworth, 1956.

Snyder, Louis L. *The Meaning of Nationalism*. New Brunswick, NJ: Rutgers University Press, 1954.

Somers, Margaret. "Narrating and Naturalizing Civil Society and Citizenship Theory" *Sociological Theory* 13 (1995): 229–74.

——. "What's Political or Cultural about Political Culture and the Public Sphere?" *Sociological Theory* 13 (1995): 113–44.

Sorokin, Pitirim. *Social and Cultural Dynamics*. Boston, MA: Porter Sergeant, 1957.

Spence, Jonathan D. *The Gate of Heavenly Peace: The Chinese and their Revolution, 1895–1980*. Baltimore, MD: Penguin, 1981.

Spillman, Lynette. *Nation and Commemoration*. Cambridge: Cambridge University Press, 1997.

Stedman, Stephen John and Fred Tanner (eds.). *Refugee Manipulation: War, Politics, and the Abuse of Human Suffering*. Washington: Brookings Institute, 2003.

Steiner, George, "Aspects of Counter-revolution," in *The Permanent Revolution*, edited by G. Best. Chicago, IL: University of Chicago Press, 1988.

Stewart, Desmond. *Theodore Herzl*. New York: Doubleday, 1974.

Sutton, Michael. *Nationalism, Positivism and Catholicism: The Politics of Charles Maurras and French Catholics 1890–1914*. Cambridge: Cambridge University Press, 1982.

Szporluk, Roman. *Communism and Nationalism: Karl Marx versus Friedrich List*. New York: Oxford University Press, 1988.

Tajfel, Henri. "Experiments in Intergroup Discrimination," *Scientific American* 223 (1970): 96–102.

Talmon, J.L. *The Origins of Totalitarian Democracy*. London: Secker & Warburg, 1952.

——. *Political Messianism, the Romantic Phase*. London: Secker & Warburg, 1960.

Tamir, Yael. *Liberal Nationalism*. Princeton, NJ: Princeton University Press, 1993.

Taylor, Charles. "Language and Human Nature," in *Human Agency and Language*, vol. 1. New York: Cambridge University Press, 1985.

——. *Philosophy and the Human Sciences*. Cambridge: Cambridge University Press, 1985.

——. *The Sources of the Self*. Cambridge, MA: Harvard University Press, 1989.

——. "Modes of Civil Society," *Public Culture* 3, no. 1 (1991): 95–118.

——. *The Politics of Recognition*. Princeton, NJ: Princeton University Press, 1992.

——. "The Politics of Recognition," in *Multiculturalism: Examining the Politics of Recognition*, revised edition, edited by Amy Gutmann. Princeton, NJ: Princeton University Press, 1994.

——. "The Importance of Herder," in *Philosophical Arguments*. Cambridge, MA: Harvard University Press, 1995.

——. "Modern Social Imaginaries," *Public Culture* 14, no. 1 (2002): 91–123.

——. *Modern Social Imaginaries*. Duke, NC: Duke University Press, 2004.

Terry, Fiona. *Condemned to Repeat? The Paradox of Humanitarian Action*. Ithaca, NY: Cornell University Press, 2002.

Teschke, Benno. *The Myth of 1648: Class, Geopolitics and the Making of Modern International Relations*. New York: Verso, 2003.

Thomas, W.I. and D.S. Thomas. *The Child in America*. New York: Knopf, 1928.

Thompson, E.P. *Customs in Common*. New York: New Press, 1993.

Tibi, Bassam. *Arab Nationalism: A Critical Enquiry*, second edition, edited and translated by Marion Farouk-Sluglett and Peter Sluglett. New York: St Martin's Press, 1990.

Tilly, Charles (ed.). *The Formation of National States in Western Europe*. Princeton, NJ: Princeton University Press, 1975.

——. *Big Structures, Large Processes, Huge Comparisons*. New York: Russell Sage, 1984.

——. *Coercion, Capital and European States, AD 990–1990*. Oxford: Blackwell, 1990.

——. "Futures of European States," paper presented at the Annual Meeting of the American Sociological Association, Pittsburgh, 1992

Tilly, Charles and Lee Walker (eds.). Special Issue on Ethnic Conflict in the Soviet Union, *Theory and Society* 20, no. 6 (1991): 725–899.

Tiryakian, Edward A. and Ronald Rogowski (eds.). *New Nationalisms of the Developed West: Toward Explanation*. London: Allen and Unwin, 1985.

de Tocqueville, Alexis. *Democracy in America*. New York: Schocken, 1840–4.

Todorov, Tzvetan. *Nous et les autres*. Paris: Seuil, 1990.

Topalov, Christian. "Patriotismes et citoyennetes," *Génèses* 3 (1991): 162–76.

Trevor-Roper, Hugh. "The Invention of Tradition: The Highland Tradition of Scotland," in *The Invention of Tradition*, edited by E. Hobsbawm and T. Ranger. Cambridge: Cambridge University Press, 1983.

Turner, Bryan. *Citizenship and Capitalism: The Debate over Reformism*. London: Allen and Unwin, 1986.

UNAIDS/WHO. *AIDS Epidemic Update: December 2004*. Geneva: UNAIDS, 2004.

UNICEF. "Humanities Principles Training: A Child Rights Protection Approach to Complex Emergencies." http://coe-dmha.org/unicef/unicef2fs.htm (1999); accessed 26 March 2004.

Van de Walle, Nicolas. *African Economies and the Politics of Permanent Crisis, 1979–1999*. New York: Cambridge University Press, 2001.

Verdery, Katherine. *National Ideology under Socialism: Identity and Cultural Politics in Ceausescu's Romania*. Berkeley: University of California Press, 1991.

Vertovec, Steven and Robin Cohen (eds.). *Conceiving Cosmopolitanism*. Oxford: Oxford University Press, 2002.

Walicki, Andrej. *Philosophy and Romantic Nationalism: The Case of Poland*. New York: Oxford University Press, 1982.

Wallerstein, Immanuel. *The Modern World-System*. Vol. I: *Capitalist Agriculture and the Origins of the European World-Economy in the Sixteenth Century*; Vol. II: *Mercantilism and the Consolidation of the European World-Economy, 1600–1750*; Vol. III: *The Second Era of Great Expansion of the Capitalist World-Economy, 1730–1840s*. San Diego, CA: Academic Press, 1974; 1984; 1988.

Watkins, Susan Cotts. *From Provinces into Nations: Demographic Integration in Western Europe, 1870–1960*. Princeton, NJ: Princeton University Press, 1991.

Weber, Eugen. *Peasants into Frenchmen*. Stanford, CA: Stanford University Press, 1976.

Weber, Max. *Economy and Society*. Berkeley: University of California Press, 1922 (this edition, 1978).

———. "The Social Psychology of World Religions," in *From Max Weber*, edited by H.H. Gerth and C. Wright Mills. London: Routledge and Kegan Paul, 1948.

Weinstein, Deena and Michael Weinstein. *Postmodern Simmel*. New York: Routledge, 1993.

Weintraub, Jeff "The Theory and Politics of the Public/Private Distinction," paper presented to the American Political Science Association, 1990.

———. Weintraub and K. Kumar (eds.). *Public and Private in Thought and Practice*. Chicago, IL: University of Chicago Press, 1997.

Wells, Kenneth M. *New God. New Nation: Protestants and Self-Reconstruction Nationalism in Korea, 1896–1937*. Honolulu: University of Hawaii Press, 1991.

Wheeler, Nicholas J. *Saving Strangers: Humanitarian Intervention in International Society*. New York: Oxford University Press, 2000.

White, James W., Michio Umegaki, and Thomas R.H. Havens (eds.). *The Ambivalence of Nationalism: Modern Japan Between East and West*. Lanham, MD: University Press of America, 1990.

Williams, Raymond. *The Long Revolution*. Harmondsworth: Pelican, 1965.

———. "The Idea of a Common Culture," in *Resources of Hope*. London: Verso, 1989.

Wirth, Louis. "Types of Nationalism," *American Journal of Sociology* 41, no. 6 (1936): 723–37.

Wolf, Ken. "Hans Kohn's Liberal Nationalism," *Journal of the History of Ideas* 37, no. 4 (1976): 651–72.

Wood, Gordon. *The Radicalism of the American Revolution*. New York: Random House, 1991.

Woodward, Peter (ed.). *Sudan after Nimeiri*. London: Routledge, 1991.

Worsley, Peter. *The Three Worlds: Culture and World Development*, revised edition. Chicago, IL: University of Chicago Press, 1986.

Young, Iris Marion. *Justice and the Politics of Difference*. Princeton, NJ: Princeton University Press, 1990.

Zacek, Joseph F. "Nationalism in Czechoslovakia," in *Nationalism in Eastern Europe*, edited by Peter F. Sugar and Ivo J. Lederer. Seattle: University of Washington Press, 1969.

Zangwill, Israel. *The Principle of Nationalities*. London: Watts & Co., 1917.

Zaret, David. *The Heavenly Contract: Ideology and Organization in Pre-Revolutionary Puritanism*. Chicago, IL: University of Chicago Press, 1985.

Index

absolutism 128–9
Adams, John 132, 201–2n57
affective attachment 110
Africa 53, 63, 157; *see also specific countries*
AIDS 6
Alexander the Great 126, 127
Algeria 15, 20, 22–3, 162
allegiances, national 153; *see also* loyalty
Alter, Peter 47, 203n88
alternative lifestyles 162
Althusius, Johannes 103
American Revolution 118, 131–2
Anderson, Benedict: colonialism 66, 74, 92; culture 28; on Gellner 46; history of nation 45, 87; imagined communities 38, 40, 55–6, 72–5; individuals 72; Latin America 47; print capitalism 63–4
anti-authoritarianism 13
anti-colonialism 123–4
anti-corporate movement 11
anti-cosmopolitanism 203n87
anti-democratic activism 78
anti-Semitism 98
Arato, Andrew 190n6
archaeology 75
Arendt, Hannah 4, 98, 132, 156, 159
Aristotle 126
Armstrong, John 46
Asian tigers 12
Asian-Americans 161
assimilationism 140
Assyrians 1
authoritarianism 95

Bacon, Francis 129
Barrès, Maurice 145
Barruel, Abbé 53

Barth, Fredrik 62, 71
Beck, Ulrich 14
belonging 27, 144–5, 157; *see also* groupings
Berber society 22
Best, Geoff 52–3
bildung 29, 164
Billig, Michael 39
Black people 110, 112
Blake, William 158–9
borders 3–4, 55, 69, 91, 147, 151
Bosnia-Herzegovina 32, 52, 54
Bourdieu, Pierre 19–20, 22–3, 25, 176n26
Brass, Paul R. 68–9
Brennan, Timothy 174n4
Breuilly, John 47
Brit Shalom movement 122
Britain: boundaries 55; colonialism 33, 34; ethnic mobilization 57; languages 40; nationalism 91; unification 25, 32
Brubaker, Rogers 40, 140, 179n36
brutality 65, 86, 145
Buber, Martin 120, 121, 122
Buchanan, Allen 151
bureaucracy 89
Burkina Faso 162
Byron, Lord George Gordon 97
Byzantium 2, 127–8

Calhoun, Craig 174n3, 194n1, 195n9, 195–6n13 201n56
Canada 170–1
capitalism: accumulation 78; democracy 77; globalization 17, 26, 101, 147; ideology 82–4; neoliberal 166; power 17–18; social relations 89–90; trade 18
categories: groupings 106; identity 51, 69, 75, 97–8, 208n10; populations 39

Catholicism 48, 59, 96
China, People's Republic of 157;
    communism 94, 193n35; national
    identity 191n12; nationalism 193n35,
    205n106; New Culture movement 70;
    student protest 99–100; United Nations
    33
Christian Democrats 96
Christianity 2, 127–8, 132
citizenship: Anglo-American 194n4;
    discourse on 105; *ethnie* 68; exclusions
    84; folk 139–40, 141; France 104, 106,
    135–6; national identity 33; nationality
    104; nation-building 61; nations 164;
    political community 24; political/legal 8;
    solidarity 106–7; state 41, 42; Western
    144
city-states 57, 125
civic nationalism: constitutional patriotism
    16, 114; and ethnic 38, 41–5, 117, 145,
    203n88; Kohn 206n131
civil liberties 7
civil rights 4
civil society 81–4; democracy 83–4;
    diversity 99; Habermas 194n6;
    international 11; markets 78–9, 173n3;
    people 103; as social realm 59;
    transitions discourse 78; voluntary
    organizations 6
class 21, 196n14, 201n51
coexistence, mutual 163
Cohen, Jean 190n6
collectivities 114–15
colonialism: Anderson 66, 74, 92;
    archaeology 75; Britain 33–4; France
    33; Iberian 40, 52–3; language 66;
    resistance 19
communalism 63
communication 47–8, 74, 89
communism: China 94, 193n35; collapse
    of 51, 53, 77, 93–4; cultural creativity
    95; Hungary 85
communitarianism 18, 106, 110
communities: fate 165; groupings 105–6;
    imagined 38, 39, 55–6, 69, 72–5;
    lifestyle 162; local 162; political 24, 81,
    104; social relationships 108; society
    105; world 126
competition 29
conflict 15, 37, 38, 62, 91; *see also* war
Connor, Walker 44
consciousness: double 112; false 43, 67
Cooper, Frederick 40, 204n98

Corsica 134
cosmopolitan city 90, 115
cosmopolitanism 24, 25–6; culture 151–2;
    democracy 11; globalization 13, 143;
    Habermas 36; Kant 207–8n8; liberal
    119–20, 165–6; nationalism 7–8, 13–14;
    particularism 136; Russia 141; Stoics
    126, 127
creativity 159, 160
Crèvecoeur, Hector Saint John de 132
crime 6
Croatia 32, 46, 91
Cromwell, Oliver 129
cultural theory 113–14
culture: communism 95; cosmopolitanism
    151–2; democracy 163–5; diversity
    159–60, 161; ethnicity 3, 62; Greek 121;
    identity 48–9; language 22, 46;
    liberalism 151; national 3, 40; national
    identity 157–8; nationalism 19–20, 28,
    38, 58; state-building 100–1; tradition
    23, 170
currency markets 6, 12
Czechoslovakia 91, 120

Dante Alighieri 128
Darfur 5, 148
deafness 108
deintegration 192n26
democracy: capitalism 77; civil society
    83–4; cosmopolitan 11; cultures of
    163–5; dictatorships 99; institutions 79,
    152, 155–6; nationalism 7, 96–101,
    149, 152; nation-state 4; people 83–4;
    self-determination 19; solidarity 166
democratization 79
demographic changes 89
Deutsch, Karl W. 74, 133
dictatorships 99, 198n9
Dictionary of Occupational Titles 161
difference 111, 114; *see also* diversity
disease 6–7, 11
diversity: civil society 99; culture 159–60,
    161; ethnic 122; imperialism 204n98;
    integration 162; loss of 159; *see also*
    difference
dot.com bust 12
double consciousness 112
Dreyfus affair 65, 98
Du Bois, W.E.B. 112
Dumont, Louis 207n7
Durkheim, Émile 37, 60, 84, 100, 107,
    161

economic development 79
education 57
Egypt 33, 137
Egyptians 1
Ekeh, Peter P. 70
elites 5, 89, 155
empire 33–4, 57, 163–4; *see also* imperialism
England 32; Civil War 47; feudalism 129; nationalism 118, 129–30, 138, 201n51; Protestant Reformation 48; Restoration 131
English language 17, 65–6, 106
Enlightenment Project 118, 119, 126, 159
entrepreneurship 79
equality 17–18, 32–3, 97, 200n26
essentialism 113
Estonia 157
Ethiopia 77, 93
ethnic cleansing 4–5, 51–2, 77
ethnic nationalism 38, 41–5, 117, 145, 203n88; *see also* ethnonationalism
ethnicity: conflict 62; culture 3, 62; diversity 122; Gellner 44; groupings 68–9, 160–1; history 59–60; identity 54, 63, 66; inclusion 2; kinship 160–1; language 66; mobilization 57–8; and nationalism 43, 45–6, 47, 58, 63, 75, 182n4; nations 43–4; solidarity 52
ethnie 67–8
ethnoculturalism 42, 132
ethnonationalism 37, 45–6, 143
Etzioni, Amitai 110, 196n16
Europe: ethnonationalism 37; integration 35–6; nationalisms 29–30, 31, 42; public life 99; states 57; unification 91; *see also specific countries*
Europe, Eastern 53, 80, 94, 100, 192n26
European Union 12, 91

false consciousness 43, 67
Ferguson, Adam 81
feudalism 89, 128–9
Fichte, Johann Gottlieb 32, 61, 64, 71, 87, 88
Financial Times 170
Finland 157
folk 139–40, 141
Foucault, Michel 103, 132, 202n70
France: Algeria 15, 20, 22–3, 162; assimilationism 140; boundaries 91; citizenship 104, 106, 135–6; colonialism 33; Dreyfus affair 65, 98; Egypt 33, 137; Enlightenment 131; Haiti 15, 33, 137; history 191n12; imperialism 136–7; Kohn 135–6; language 31, 54–5, 66; *mission civilisatrice* 88, 126; Muslims 42; nationalism 32, 42, 65, 91, 118, 136–8, 179n36; origin myths 60–1; *philosophes* 136; tolerance 98; unification 25
freedom of movement 57
free-market economies 78–9
French National Assembly 43
French Revolution: citizenship 104, 135–6; Kant 141; Kohn 132; nationalism 32, 47, 52–3, 84, 118; people power 48
Friedman, Milton 81
Fukuyama, Francis 11
fundamentalism 11

Gadamer, Hans-Georg 47, 62
Gandhi, Mahatma 65
Garfinkel, Harold 196n15
Gellner, Ernest 192n30; Anderson on 46; cultural diversity 159–60; culture 58, 63, 73; ethnicity 44; industrialization 43; nationalism 39, 69, 91
genocide 4, 61
Germany: colonialism 33; ethnic nationalism 140, 176n17; French Revolution 52–3; historical destiny 88; intellectuals 88; language 64, 73; nationalism 32, 42, 137–8, 139, 144, 179n36, 205–6n123; nationhood 140–1; origin myths 60–1; Romanticism 43, 47, 66, 67; Third Reich 30; unification 25, 91; Yugoslavia 32
Germany, East 96
Giddens, Anthony 58
Gierke, Otto von 103
Gilroy, Paul 112, 113
Ginsberg, Asher: *see* Ha'am, Ahad
globalization: borders 4; capitalism 17, 26, 101, 147; cosmopolitanism 13, 143; economic 11, 79–80, 175n8; equity 17–18; liberalism 36; modernity 11; nationalism 171; postnational society 169; protesters 5; solidarity 26, 151; transnational society 169
Goethe, Johann Wolfgang von 137–8, 144
Gorbachev, Mikhail 93
governance, global 6, 7, 169
government legitimacy 28, 30
Greeks: culture 121; nationalism 1,

118–19, 124–5, 124–6, 145;
philanthropeia 127
Greenfeld, Liah 47, 65
Grieg, Edvard Hagerup 88
group rights 107
groupings: autonomy/integration 24;
categories 106; communication 47–8;
communities 105–6; critiqued 40;
dominant 3–4; ethnic 68–9, 160–1;
identity 69; loyalty 37; publics 106;
society 38–41

Ha'am, Ahad 120, 121, 142, 198n12
Haas, Ernst B. 60
Habermas, Jürgen: civil society 194n6;
class differences 196n14; constitutional
patriotism 15–16, 114, 134, 174–5n7;
constitutional state 143;
cosmopolitanism 36; economic
globalization 175n8; identity formation
191n11; *The Inclusion of the Other*
178n15; multiculturalism 142–3;
nationalism 41–2; nation-states 35–6,
139–40; post-national constellation 14;
public sphere 81, 109
habitus 21–2, 62
Haiti 15, 33, 137
Halle, Louis Joseph 54
Hapsburg empire 32, 73, 85, 139
Hardt, Michael 5
Harvey, David 189n2
Hayes, Carlton J.H. 43, 59, 67, 119, 145,
197n1, 198n10
Hebrew nationalism: *see* Judaism
Hechter, Michael 43, 57–8
Held, David 17, 176n19
Hellenism: *see* Greeks
Henry IV, of France 136
Herder, Johann Gottfried 53, 61, 64, 140,
142, 143, 206n126
heroes 88
Hertz, Frederick 119
Herzl, Theodore 120–1, 198–9n13
heterogeneity 114–15; *see also* diversity
Hinduism 65–6
history: end of 11; ethnicity 59–60; France
191n12; global 208–9n18; language
63–6; of nation 36–7, 45, 87;
nationalism 9, 44–5, 85–6, 96–7; self-
understanding 40–1; violence 64–5
Hitler, Adolf 145
Hobbes, Thomas 90, 133
Hobsbawm, Eric 192n30; false

consciousness 43; modern nation 53–4;
national identity 46, 192n29;
nationalism 43, 62, 67; tradition 160
Holy Roman Empire 32, 33, 128
homeland, sacralization 177n9
homogeneity 162
homosexuality 162
Hroch, Miroslav 58–9
human rights 4–5, 6, 131–2, 149, 150
humanitarian interventions 4–5, 12, 169
humanitas 127
Hungarians 73
Hungary 85, 86, 91, 94

Ibsen, Henrik 88
identity: categories 51, 69, 75, 97–8,
208n10; collective 45, 80, 108, 152;
culture 48–9; difference 114; ethnic 54,
63, 66; groupings 69; individuals 100,
109; legitimacy 98; modernity 115;
nationalism 111; personal 109;
primordial 52; public sphere 115;
religion 94; self 70; solidarity 140;
women 95; *see also* national identity
identity formation 191n11
ideology: capitalism 82–4; gender-biased
71; liberalism 7, 95–6; nationalism
87–8, 153, 166; nationhood 61–2;
successor 93–6
illth/wealth 165, 209n26
illusio 25
imaginaries 8–9, 170
imperialism 136–7, 204n98, 204n99; *see
also* empire
independence 164
India 44, 63, 65–6
individualism 3, 70–2, 107, 111
individuals: Anderson 72; identity 100;
liberty 133; loyalty 112; national
identity 87; nations, compared 164;
social order 24; welfare 202n69
individuation 87–8
industrialization 43
information technology 12
institutionalist theories 208n16
institutions: democracy 79, 152, 155–6;
nation-states 154–5, 177n11; public
sphere 83; social 166–7, 173n5
integration: diversity 162; Europe 35–6;
global 1, 12, 80; minority groups
166; national 148, 154–5; nation-state
19; political 38; social 78, 80–1,
83; solidarity 152; structures of

152–7; violence 153; women 166
intellectuals 88
international criminal court 4
international humanitarian action 148
international law 32–3
international relations 31, 34, 36, 150–1
Internet 12
Ireland 34
Ireland, Northern 86
Islam 42, 77
Islamic movements 170
Israel 118–19
Italy 141

Jacobinism 195n9
Jefferson, Thomas 131, 201–2n57
Jewishness 120–1
Jews 1, 2, 86, 124–5
Judaism 118–19, 120, 124–5, 145
justice theory 35–6, 150

Kant, Immanuel 141, 144, 203n82, 207–8n8
Karadzic, Radovan 51–2
Kedourie, Elie 27–8, 39, 43, 47, 53, 59, 67
kinship 87, 160–1, 191–2n16
Kjoer, Nils 88
Köhler, Martin 14
Kohn, Hans 59, 123–4, 197–8n9 197n1; and Buber 122–3; civic nationalism 206n131; ethnic nationalism 203n88; France 132, 135–6; German nationalism 138, 205–6n123; Greeks 124; *The Idea of Nationalism* 117–18, 126–7, 143–4, 146, 197n4; imperialism 204n99; liberalism 126–7; nationalisms 41, 197n1; Rousseau 133–5; self-transcendence 142; solidarity 146; sovereignty 43, 67; US 130–1, 201–2n57; Zionism 120–4, 127, 129, 131, 133, 140, 142, 145, 199n13
Kymlicka, Will 17

language: Anderson 73; Britain 40; colonialism 66; culture 22, 46; ethnicity 66; France 31, 54–5, 66; history 63–6; India 65–6; Latin 2, 73; politics 59; print capitalism 64, 73, 74; Russia 66, 94; shared 66, 208n10; standardization 89; states 57; vernacular 66
Latin America 47
Latin language 2, 73

Le Pen, Jean-Marie 98
Leach, Edmund Ronald 62
League of Nations 53
legends, national 141; *see also* origin myths
legitimacy: government 28, 30; identity 98; nationalism 53; political 2; power 18–19; tradition 46–7
Levinas, Emmanuel 121
liberalism: cosmopolitanism 119–20, 141, 165–6; culture 151; globalization 36; as ideology 7, 95–6; international relations 34; Kohn 126–7; nationalism 130–1, 132–3; nations 149–52; patriotism 141; rhetoric 96; universalism 118, 137, 150
liberty, individuals 133
lifestyles 162
List, Friedrich 71–2
Lithuania 77
Locke, John 103, 201n51
loyalty 37, 48, 112, 144
Luhmann, Niklas 190n6
Lukacs, Georg 85
Luxembourg 33

Machiavelli, Niccolò 128
Mann, Michael 40
maps 74–5
market forces 59, 78–9, 89, 173n3
martyrs 71, 85, 88
Marx, Karl 71, 141
Marxism 20–1
Maurras, Charles 65, 145
Meinecke, Friedrich 59, 174n6
membership of society 105
messianism 121, 126, 137
Michnik, Adam 98
Middle Ages 128
migration flows 78, 91, 148
military service 57
millet system 2, 161
Milton, John 129, 201n50
minority groups 166
mobilization, ethnicity 57–8
modernity: globalization 11; identity 115; nationalism 3, 47, 52–3; nations 38; self-understanding 156–7; states 45–7, 56–9, 78, 89; Western/Eastern 117–18
modernization theory 57, 169–70
modernizers, late 42
Montesquieu, Charles-Louis de Secondat 33, 81, 82, 103
Moser, Karl von 141, 201n54

Mouffe, Chantal 195–6n13 208n11
Mozambique 174n3
multiculturalism 108, 110, 142–3
multinational corporations 78
Munch, Edvard 88
museums 75
Muslims: see Islam
Mussolini, Benito 145
Myer, John 208n16

Nagorno-Karabak 77
Nairn, Tom 165
Napoleon Bonaparte 137
natality 156, 159
national identity 97–8, 191n9; China
    191n12; citizenship 33; complexities
    84–5; culture 157–8; Eastern Europe 80;
    exclusions 71; Hayes 119; Hobsbawm
    46, 192n29; individual 87; kinship
    191–2n16; organizational function 7;
    Taylor 48
National Socialism 56, 119
nationalism: cosmopolitanism 7–8, 13–14;
    culture 19–20, 28, 38, 58, 63, 73; death
    of 77–8; definitions 1, 55, 86–7;
    democracy 7, 96–101, 149, 152; as
    discursive formation 27, 40, 53–6,
    206–7n1; ethnicity 43, 45–6, 47, 58, 63,
    75, 182n4; Europe 29–30, 31, 42;
    French Revolution 32, 47, 52–3, 84,
    118; Habermas 41–2; history 9, 44–5,
    85–6, 96–7; Hobsbawm 43, 62, 67;
    ideology 87–8, 93–6, 153, 166; liberal
    130–1, 132–3; modernity 3, 47, 52–3;
    real life 29; religion 119, 201n49;
    rhetorics 61, 96, 104; states 59, 63; see
    also civic nationalism; ethical
    nationalism
nationalist movements 92–3, 163
nationality 28, 84–93, 86, 104, 157
nation-building 37, 61
nationhood 54, 61–2, 140–1
nations 32; as category 100; citizenship
    164; as discourse 177n9; empire 33,
    163–4; ethnicity 43–4; founding 155–6;
    history of 36–7, 45, 87; integration
    154–5; liberalism 149–52; modernity
    38; people 34–5, 48; political histories
    153–4; responsibility 165; Smith 43–4;
    society 8; sovereignty 39–40; states
    54–5, 90–1, 134, 207n2; territories 40
nation-states 14–17, 56–7, 148; dangers 3,
    53; democracy 4; Habermas 35–6,

139–40; institutions 154–5, 177n11;
    integration 19; see also states
Naziism 119, 123–4, 133
Negri, Antonio 5
Nehru, Jawaharlal 63, 65–6, 163
neoliberalism 19, 166
Netherlands 31, 91
New Culture movement 70
New Forum 96
New World nationalisms 29, 30, 52–3
9/11: see terrorist attacks, 11 September
    2001
Norway 88, 157
Novosti Press Agency 93
Nussbaum, Martha 24, 208n11

origin myths 60–1
Ossian legend 141
Ottoman Empire 2, 33, 161

Paine, Tom 131
Palestine 122–3, 143
Palme, Goran 196n15
Palmer, R.R. 204n91
pan-nationalism 91
Parsons, Talcott 133, 190n6
particularism 136, 151
patriotism 141, 193n40; constitutional
    15–16, 35–6, 41–2, 114, 134, 174–5n7
peasant economies 111
people: civil society 103; democracy 83–4;
    nations 34–5, 48; politics 155; solidarity
    149, 164
Peter the Great 86
philanthropeia 127
Philippines 33–4
philosophes 136
Plato 125
Plutarch 126
Poland: Catholicism 48; EU 91; martyr-
    nation 71, 88; reconstruction 94;
    Solidarity 81, 94, 99–100; tolerance 98
polis 90
political histories 153–4
political theory 159
politics: community 24, 81, 104; language
    59; market forces 79; nationalism 93;
    people 155; religion 87; state 37
populations 3–4, 39, 147
Portugal 34, 40, 52–3
postcolonialism 56, 163
postmodernism 111, 189n2
post-nationalism 14, 169

Postone, Moishe 190n6
poststructuralism 114
power: capitalism 17–18; elites 5;
    legitimacy 18–19; of people 48; state 89,
    92; unification 20–1
print capitalism 63–4, 73, 74
privatization 79, 148
production/reproduction 21–2
protectionism 170
Protestant Reformation 2–3, 48, 59, 128
protesters 5, 99–100
public sphere: Europe 99; Habermas 81,
    109; identity 115; institutions 83;
    women 107
publics 106, 108–10, 178n16

Quebec separatism 53, 106

Ranger, Terence 46, 62, 160
Rawls, John 35, 150, 151
rebuilding, postwar 94
religion: depoliticized 59; fundamentalism
    11; identity 94; international relations
    31; Ireland, Northern 87; nationalism
    119, 201n49; politics 87
Renaissance 128
Renan, Ernest 44–5, 61, 64–5, 85–6,
    112–13, 145
reproduction 21–2, 39–40
Republicanism 195n9
responsibility 148–9, 165
revolution 147, 198n9
rhetoric 61, 96, 104
rights: civil 4; group 107; human 4–5, 6,
    131–2, 149, 150; of states 91
Risorgimento 141
Romania 94
Romanticism 16, 88, 97, 134; Germany
    43, 47, 66, 67
Rome 1–2, 28, 41, 127, 200n39
Roosevelt, Theodore 122
Rousseau, Jean-Jacques 82, 133–5, 141,
    203n82, 203n87
rule of law 4
Ruskin, John 209n26
Russia: identity 85; language 66, 94;
    nationalism 71, 93, 141; Peter the Great
    86

sacralization, homeland 177n9
San Marino 71
Savarkar 65
Schiller, Friedrich 140–1

Schlözer, August Ludwig von 140
Schwarcz, Vera 70
Scotland 34, 46, 81–2, 103
secession 91, 153
security, states 25
self 70
self-determination 17, 19, 51, 53, 78, 80,
    84, 163
self-government 163
self-improvement 126
self-transcendence 142, 144
self-understanding 40–1, 87, 156–7
separatism 53, 106, 153
Serbia 46, 51–2, 54, 77
Seton-Watson, Hugh 43, 67
sexism 97
sexuality 71
Simmel, Georg 95
Singapore 71
Slovenia 32
Smith, Adam 81
Smith, Anthony: culture 28; ethnicity 40,
    42, 45–6, 191n13; *ethnie* 67–8; on
    Hechter 57–8; modern nationalism 43;
    nations 43–4
Snyder, Louis L. 197n1
social capital 19
social order 6, 24
social relations 89–90, 108
social scientists 113–14
social theory 37–8
society: bounded 54–5; communities 105;
    discursive formation 103–4; groupings
    38–41; justice theory 35; membership
    105; nation 8
solidarity: citizenship 106–7; democracy
    166; Durkheim 107; ethnic 52;
    globalization 26, 151; identity 140;
    integration 152; kinship 87; Kohn 146;
    national 155, 167; people 149, 164;
    publics 178n16; social 1, 108
Solidarity, Poland 81, 94, 99–100
Sophists 125
sovereignty 6–7, 17, 39–40, 43, 130
Soviet Union (former) 77, 93, 95; *see also*
    Russia
Spain: colonialism 34, 40, 52–3; languages
    40; Thirty Years War 31–2, 33
Springtime of Peoples 16, 111, 163
Stalin, Joseph 94
state employees 82
state-building 51, 57, 100–1
states: borders 151; citizenship 41, 42;

cultural diversity 143; elites 5; Europe 57; expansion 18; failed 6; languages 57; maps 74–5; modernity 45–7, 56–9, 78, 89; multicultural 98–9; multinational 98–9; nationalism 59, 63; nationality 28; nations 54–5, 90–1, 134, 207n2; participation 18–19; politics 37; power 89, 92; security 25; war 30–1; *see also* nation-states
Stoics 126, 127
Stoler, Ann Laura 204n98
student protest 99–100
Sudan 5–6, 157
Sun Yat-sen 205n106
Sweden 157
Swiss Confederation 31
Switzerland 40

Taylor, Charles 48, 82, 142
territories 40
terrorist attacks, 11 September 2001 12, 13
Third World nationalism 56
Thirty Years War 14, 31–2, 33
Tilly, Charles 40, 54, 56, 57, 58, 66, 103
Timor, East 32–3
Tocqueville, Alexis de 81, 82, 98, 190–1n8
Toennies, Ferdinand 60
trade 18
trade unions 18
tradition 21–3, 25; collective 42–3; culture 23, 170; invented 21, 36, 40, 62, 154, 160; legitimacy 46–7; truth content 158; Weber 22–3
trafficking, illegal 11
Transcaucasus 94
transitions discourse 78
transnational movements 148
transnational society 169
tribalism 63, 78, 124

Uganda 122
Ukraine 91
unification 20–1, 25, 32, 91, 128–9
United Nations 33, 80
United States of America: Constitution 132; ethnoculturalism 132; Kohn 130–1; nationalism 131, 132–3, 139, 201–2n57; rights of states 91; self-

improvement 126; United Nations 33; women's identity 95; Yugoslavia 32; *see also* American Revolution
universalism: ethical 133; human rights 149; liberal 118, 137, 150; and messianism 126; particularism 136; *Sacerdotium/Imperium* 128

Vietnam 162
violence 64–5, 153
volk 139–40, 141
Voltaire 136
voluntary organizations 6

Wagner, Richard 141–2
Wahl, Jetty 123
Wales 34
war 5, 7, 30–1
Warsaw Pact 94
Washington, George 158
wealth 165, 209n26
Weber, Max 22–3, 37, 60, 62, 70–1
Weems, Mason Locke 158
Weintraub, Jeff 90
welfare state, attacked 174n4
welfare/individuals 202n69
Weltsch, Robert 122
Westphalia, Peace of 3, 14, 15, 31, 33, 150, 207n4
Williams, Raymond 171
Wilson, Woodrow 53
Wittgenstein, Ludwig 55, 86
women: equality 97, 200n26; identity 95; integration 166; national ideology 71; public sphere 107; trafficking in 11
women's movements 71
World Bank 6
World War II 119

xenophobia 91

Yugoslavia (former) 32, 52, 77, 84, 91

Zangwill, Israel 120–1, 132, 198–9n13; *The Melting Pot* 122, 199n19
Zeno 126
Zionism: Ha'am 120, 121, 198n12; Herder 142; Kohn 120–4, 127, 129, 131, 133, 140, 142, 145, 199n13